PSYCHOTHERAPY TRAINING
AND PRACTICE

PSYCHOTHERAPY TRAINING AND PRACTICE

A Journey into the Shadow Side

Kate Wilkinson

KARNAC

First published 2008 by
Karnac Books Ltd
118 Finchley Road, London NW3 5HT

British Library Cataloguing in Publication Data

A C.I.P. for this book is available from the British Library

ISBN: 978 1 85575 524 6

All analysts and psychotherapy trainers who have either communicated personally with me, or with whom I have conducted interviews, have granted permission for the use of their communications. In the case of the psychotherapy trainers, the material has been used in the form of quotations, where permission has been given for this, and as information only if it was requested that direct quotation be witheld.

Edited, designed and produced by The Studio Publishing Services Ltd
www.publishingservicesuk.co.uk
e-mail: studio@publishingservicesuk.co.uk

Printed in Great Britain

www.karnacbooks.com

CONTENTS

ACKNOWLEDGEMENTS

First and foremost, I would like to express my deep gratitude to Professor Paul Barber, my supervisor and my colleague, for his consistent encouragement and support, for his belief in me, for his mischievous sense of humour, which lightened my own darkness at times of struggling with my thesis and, subsequently, this book

My heartfelt thanks to Ken Evans, for his invitation, in many ways, to my spiritual journey, and for his kindness in welcoming me to his temenos in France, providing peace and solitude to "soothe" my learning process.

I am eternally grateful to Josephine Evetts-Secker for her wisdom and skill, and for her containment and understanding of my personal experience of this study. Thank you.

To all the trainers and trainees who have welcomed me into their training environments over the years and have trusted me with personal processes, thank you for what I have learned from you in my journeying.

I am in loving appreciation of my family, my four children, their partners, and their children, who tolerated my preoccupation and immersion into this project. My wish for each of you is that you make your own shadows welcome in your lives.

ABOUT THE AUTHOR

Prior to coming into the psychotherapy profession, Kate Wilkinson had fifteen years experience in the National Health Service. This was primarily as a psychiatric nurse in acute in-patient settings that housed "seclusion" rooms for potentially aggressive patients. Kate's interest in human aggression led her to work in forensic psychiatry, with people who had offended against society to the extreme of arson, rape, and manslaughter. The appalling learning that had an impact on Kate was that the most significant difference between staff and patients was the degree to which feelings and thoughts were acted out behaviourally. The potential to destroy is inherent in being human and as such, is in each one of us.

This experience enhanced Kate's sensitivity to human aggression, not least as it showed itself in the five in-depth counselling and psychotherapy trainings she undertook , prior to co-founding a training institute herself. Kate has challenged her colleague trainers and institute leaders to explore the place of shadow phenomena in the caring profession of psychotherapy. This book invites the reader to explore their own shadow experience.

Contemplating the journey

"Chaos stems from action without thought; action considered
gives birth to creativity"

Recently, I completed a Doctoral study, which brought together for
me the range of dilemmas and tensions that I have encountered
over a thirty-year period of both working with the mentally ill and
training as a psychotherapist and becoming a psychotherapy
trainer. I undertook a qualitative research study on the topic of
"shadow", which I believe to be very pertinent to integrative psychotherapy. This involved reflecting critically on methodological
issues, reviewing a relevant body of literature, conducting and
analysing in-depth interviews with senior psychotherapy trainers,
and exploring pertinent ethical concerns. I know that this issue is of
paramount importance, not only to integrative psychotherapists,
but to all psychotherapists and also to all who engage in the wide
range of helping professions across the board. The shadow aspects
of being human lurk wherever one human being engages in a relationship with another human being, to promote emotional awareness and healing.

By this I mean shadow as understood to be the dangerous and
destructive elements of human relationships.

My hope in writing this book is not to provide the reader with
any answers, but rather to encourage for each person who opens its

covers a process of introspection and self-inquiry that promotes the integrative process of becoming a whole human being.

I am interested in how human shadow phenomenon shows itself, and its impact upon integrative psychotherapy training institutes, not forgetting how this must, of course, both reflect and incorporate aspects of the wider field of all organizations and life itself. I use the term "shadow" to denote my understanding of what I believe to be a complex, in-depth, aggressive/destructive, primarily unconscious process of human relatedness. Psychotherapy is based on love of fellow humankind, and love brings with it all the things that it is not. I hope to portray how hurtful behaviour emerges and is evidenced, what factors contribute to the emergence of this experience, and what is therapeutically advisable to provide containment, rather than defensive avoidance, of the relational causation of people hurting each other.

I use in my writing information from interviews with senior psychotherapy trainers, from both university and private company settings, in England and abroad, to give a wider cultural component to the experiences explored. I chose data-gathering methodologies that invite the unconscious into conscious experience. I review the existing literature to empirically provide extensive background knowledge of the relevant material, and I conduct in-depth interviews to raise awareness of the concepts, phenomenological experience, and wealth of information that each senior trainer carries.

The theoretical review explores the extensive intra-personal, interpersonal and group/collective dynamic landscape of human experience pertinent to this understanding of the human shadow. Phenomenological enquiry invites unique, in-depth experiences, provides new insights (in one sense, this information, because it is unique, is bound to provide new experience), and together these address the complexities and diversities inherent in the emergence and containment of shadow experience in integrative psychotherapy training.

This book takes the reader through a process of qualitative research.

In Chapter One, we survey the crossing: what has brought about the interest in this topic? Chapter Two takes in provisions: this portrayal of what we need to know in order to embark on such a journey offers the theoretical understandings that act as a baseline for my thinking, primarily from a stance of the semantic landscape. Chapter Three charts the waters and offers a general impression of how this journey will take place: an explanation of my understanding of the qualitative research methods of phenomenological inquiry and heuristic process. Chapter Four, in navigating a route, uses the grounded theory perspective of data gathered to give a more objective, external process of understanding. Chapter Five weathers the storm and makes welcome, via dream analysis, the deeper, more tacit knowledge that emerges from unconscious process. Chapter Six explores life at sea: the actual experience of trainers who have had years of living alongside shadow phenomena. And, in Chapter Seven, a creative synthesis summarizes the outcomes of the both the original study, which serves almost as a scaffold for the current process of creating this manuscript, and the heuristic journey that guides my current writing. The journey ends and begins in Chapter Eight, as outcomes and implications of this work are thought through.

Throughout the book, consideration is given to the possibility that shadow phenomena are just as much a part of the caring environment as are the experiences of healing and growth through the therapeutic relationship to which psychotherapy training organizations aspire. Interspersed throughout the book, are suggestions for personal exploration and it is hoped that reading this book will both stimulate practitioners to a process of self-reflection and questioning, in relation to this theme and also support practitioner researchers in their own heuristic journey.

Look for your other half—
Who walks always next to you
And tends to be who you aren't.

(Machado, 1983, in Bly, 1990, p. 51)

CHAPTER ONE

Surveying the crossing

"I want to know if you can see beauty, even when it's not pretty, every day, and if you can source your own life from its presence"

(Oriah Mountain Dreamer, 1999, p. 70)

Rationale for these explorations

Personal experience

Having worked as a general nurse in acute psychiatry, and in search of a deeper understanding of the human pain I witnessed, I began Registered Mental Nurse Training. My Christian upbringing led me to look for the loving aspects of human nature and to want to seek to abolish what I then understood as "harmful and bad" behaviours. I had much to learn about human destructiveness.

Work in a large mental institution was a rude awakening for me, introducing me to the real, unsanitized world; a very different place to that which I had previously allowed myself to see through my "Christian rose-coloured glasses". Experiences of bullying,

1

physical and emotional neglect, depersonalization, and annihilation were just as evident as the caring, sometimes "blind" caring, as opposed to a considered and realistically thought out approach, which was also part of the psychiatric system. My interest in understanding human aggression and destruction led me to work in a Regional Forensic Unit, with ill people who had offended against society to the extreme of committing rape, arson, manslaughter and murder. The appalling learning that struck me was that the most significant difference between staff and patients was simply the degree to which feelings and thoughts were acted out behaviourally. The potential to destroy is inherent in being human, and as such is within each and every one of us. I believe that our prisons house people who are as much themselves victims as their victims.

Searching for understanding of human shadow took me to psychotherapy training. My interview for psychodynamic training brought disappointment. I was advised to undertake a year's analysis and reapply the following year; they considered me out of touch with my own dangerousness! I later learned the truth of this. Since that time, I have undergone five long-term counselling and psychotherapy trainings in four different northern institutes, plus very many seminars and workshops around the world. Human destructiveness, which I have witnessed on this journey, has been primarily at the level of emotional and verbal, often at a deep and profoundly painful level, yet with some physical experience.

The physical ramifications of destructive impulses were primarily turned against the self. Despite much wide and varied experience in psychotherapy and psychiatric settings, I was ill-prepared for the impact of the shadow experience I was to encounter myself as a psychotherapy trainer and Director of a training institute.

These shadow experiences include repeated aggression from the environment, such as

- seventy letters of complaint from neighbours to the local Borough Council, resisting the Council's readiness to allow permission to practise from our premises. This resulted in a sense of insecurity and unsettledness, a concern for the future existence of the institute, and feelings of anxiety for those who used the institute; trainers, trainees, and clients alike;

- neighbourhood meetings being held in nearby hotel to address the strategies for the proposed removal of the institute from this area;
- my arrival at work on many occasions to find that eggs had been thrown at the front door and windows of our premises;
- my arrival at work to find faeces piled on the top doorstep of our premises;
- a close neighbour approaching people entering our premises with shouts of "We don't want your sort here!" and incidents of verbal abuse to staff, trainees, and clients;
- a close neighbour watching from a window and recording in detail the timing of arrival and leaving of people entering the premises, along with a note of car registration numbers;
- the invasion of my personal space by the environment, with unordered pizzas being delivered to, and taxis arriving at, my home in the early hours of the morning;
- twenty- and thirty-page letters of scrawled, disturbing, psychotic thinking arriving regularly at the institute from an unknown source. While this may be one way of a psychotic client "containing" his/her own madness by packing it up and sending it off to a psychotherapy institute, the shadow element is evident in the imposition of this material on whoever opened and read it, without any prior agreement that this might happen;
- similarly, and probably of the same process, books arriving, of deep philosophical thinking, all extensively and confusingly annotated to say that the world is about to end.

I felt pursued and haunted by these experiences.

Police intervention and discussion with neighbours stopped most of these behaviours from outside the institute. From within the institute,

- books were removed from a reference library and were never returned despite supportive requests;
- people legitimately staying over at the institute heard others on the premises during the night, sometimes in a drunken state;
- small items were stolen occasionally from the institute;
- the Psychotherapy Training Institute's telephone bill increased by £300 when someone used the computer (in the locked office)

during the night to access internet porn (only practitioners seeing clients at the institute had keys).

Since embarking on consideration of this theme, several colleagues who are Directors of other institutes have told me of their own similar experiences. I am interested that it has taken, for me, an open, almost interrogative stance for such sharing to be forthcoming. In a talking profession, this theme is not talked about!

Within training groups, members scapegoated, rejected, and verbally attacked each other, and experienced facilitation was needed to contain these dynamics. I learned of trainers and of qualified and trainee therapists being dismissed professionally from other member organizations for severe breach of boundaries with trainees, for offences ranging from sexual contact to financial exploitation.

My reasons for exploring this theme are partly to raise my own awareness, thus enhancing my skill as a psychotherapist and trainer, and partly a wish to raise awareness generally in the field of what is needed in integrative psychotherapy training organizations in the way of a holding environment in order to address and contain what currently remains experienced and yet insufficiently addressed. I would hope, also, that the novice psychotherapy researcher might find the process of research methodology described here useful in gleaning understanding for research projects of their own.

Information from the field

It is increasingly acknowledged in the therapy professions that it is the relationship between client and therapist that heals old wounds and promotes personal growth (primarily for the client and also in the therapist). This human connectedness is the very core of integrative psychotherapeutic work, and therapist personality plays an important part here. The British Association for Counselling and Psychotherapy (BACP) now values the importance of therapists undertaking their own therapy—forty hours of personal work—to become able to practise openly and effectively. Integrative psychotherapy trainings believe that personal therapy throughout the duration of four years' training is necessary in order to ensure a certain level of self-reflection in the therapist, enhancing the qualities necessary in a therapist to prevent and optimally minimize any potentially abusive behaviour towards clients. The BACP (2002) lists these personal qualities necessary for professional competency as follows: empathy, sincerity in relationships, integrity, resilience, showing respect, acknowledging one's own strengths and weaknesses, employing skills competently, being fair, possessing wisdom, and courage.

While I honour this without hesitation, I wonder where the less welcome human qualities might be in a therapist. What is being insufficiently addressed here? Only one of the ten qualities listed above pays reference to human weaknesses. It is *never* professional practice to collaborate with abuse of our clients, and in order to ensure that this does not happen, I believe that we need to recognize more fully what it is in ourselves that could so easily result in that happening. Our Codes of Ethics indicate *some* unacceptable behaviours of the therapist, although no ethical code could cover all the possibilities. However, what is not explicitly acknowledged by the BACP, or by many training organizations, is that as human beings we have destructive impulses, resentments, hatred, violent and toxic thoughts, self-gratifications met through the manipulation of others, of our clients. To only implicitly or subtly address these powerful human dynamics, under the heading of "weaknesses", may contribute to a splitting process whereby professionals see themselves as "good" with potential for "bad" to become projected on to our clients and colleagues.

Walker (2002) gives one example of this dynamic, describing how clinical evangelism can result in the anger of a client being interpreted as resistance, when the therapist had made a poor, rather attacking intervention and client anger was justified. She notes also that psychotherapy trainers can turn against trainees in a way that invalidates and disempowers the trainee;

> All trainings need to be careful not to fall into the potential traps that can paradoxically be created by the very strengths and essence of the model that they are teaching. [Walker, 2002, p. 43]

To teach only the loving acceptance of another actually promotes a splitting process and denies the search for wholeness that incorporates all of human qualities. To teach only the loving acceptance of another actually promotes a splitting process and denies the search for wholeness that incorporates all of human qualities. It is beneficial in the training milieu to provide a space for airing our apprehensions and fears. These fears are better explored than avoided.

It is unwise to place too much emphasis on the positive aspects of the therapist's personality, as this may result in therapists developing an inflated idea of who they are. And in such inflation, vulnerability is defensively defended. In working holistically, we cannot deny our negative attributes so blatantly, or tilt the balance of qualities towards the positive without some consequences resulting, which themselves could be dangerous. Guggenbuhl-Craig tells how, if we fail to accept our own shadow and to model the painful expression and working through of this to our clients, then "all the patient learns from us is how to fool himself and the world" (Guggenbuhl-Craig, 1971, p. 25).

I believe that we actually do some of our best work from our most vulnerable places, where we are at our most open.

Most clients seek support as a result of painful experience. In examining our own pain, both received and what we may inflict, we inform our clients that, however wonderful life may be at times, pain must also be faced, and we enhance a relationship whereby this becomes possible. Fox supports this view in stating that "if we fail to let pain be pain . . . then pain will haunt us in nightmarish ways" (Fox, 1991, p. 142).

We would not unquestioningly amputate a broken leg, but rather encourage the healing of this. We cannot hope to heal emotionally if we were to deny (amputate) some of our life experience. And this philosophy supports the holistic practice of integrative psychotherapy. In addition, while we may defensively choose not to address our shadow, nevertheless it will inevitably have an impact upon our work. "When two people meet, the totality of their psyches encounter each other—even if much of what happens is neither stated nor directly expressed" (Guggenbuhl-Craig, 1971, p. 41).

Self-deception on the part of the therapist, with denial of shadow, cannot fail to influence the therapeutic process. Addressing our shadow, bringing the unsanitized world into the arena, promotes the healthy pathway to wholeness, in that choices can be taken over the behaviours that we employ in response to destructive, as well as caring, urges, drives, and emotions.

As Bly states,

> The savage mode does great damage to soul, earth, and humankind; we can say that though the savage man is wounded he prefers not to examine it. The Wild Man is crucial throughout. The Wild Man who has examined his wound resembles a Zen priest, a shaman, or a woodsman more than a savage. [Bly, 1990, p. x]

And Bly refers to Yeats to support this belief;

> A woman can be proud and stiff,
> When on love intent:
> But love has pitched his mansion in
> The place of excrement;
> For nothing can be sole or whole
> That has not been rent
>
> (Yeats, 1983, p. 218)

I support those of my clients who fear the loss of their joy in life if they were to become open to shadow by referring to a local country estate, which boasts a lake supporting many different species of waterlily. This is a magnificent and splendid sight and each of these lilies has its roots firmly embedded in the mud.

Without a willingness to experience animal forces of human nature, which incorporate the terror, murderousness, and destructive shadow inherent in life itself, psychotherapeutic growth becomes superficial and avoidant. In integrative psychotherapy, Clarkson (1995) believes that those animal forces, shadow phenomena somatically experienced, are part of the healing process. She tells of her client's phenomenology:

> It is not at all unusual for people to come into spiritual paths while their psyches are still so much in need of earthly help. One client, Lilly, who was regularly and frequently physically and sexually abused by both her parents and their friends, found a millenialist [sic] religion which helped her to forgive them through the spirit for what they had done to her. It was only the incessant, recalcitrant paralysis of her back which eventually seemed to force her to face some denied dimensions of herself. Her body carried scars internally as well as externally and what was needed was the

re-establishment of her healthy animal reflexes such as pain, surprise, anger and fear. These she had sublimated before and desensitized her body to its animal life. However, in her own words, "It was only after I had claimed my body and its rage, the terror in my cells and the murder of my natural childhood, that my forgiveness of my parents became true and meaningful instead of a spiritualised defence". [*ibid.*, p. 197]

I honour the words of Martin Luther King on violence:

> The ultimate weakness of violence is that it is a descending spiral, begetting the very thing it seeks to destroy. Instead of diminishing evil, it multiplies it. Through violence you may murder the liar, but you cannot murder the lie, nor establish the truth. Through violence you may murder the hater, but you do not murder hate. In fact, violence merely increases hate. So it goes. Returning violence for violence multiplies violence, adding deeper darkness to a night already devoid of stars. Darkness cannot drive out darkness: only light can do that. Hate cannot drive out hate: only love can do that. [King, 1963]

However, we can only love if we can hate. What we resist in our own personalities merely becomes a projection, perhaps somatically turned against our self, or escaping our awareness in small or larger doses that are toxic to others. We cannot truly reach a place of wholeness without incorporating the whole spectrum of human experience. The stance of loving recognition of our clients can only be achieved through acknowledging the less loving aspects of humankind, primarily in ourselves. In order not to reach the negative experience described by King, we need to phenomenologically experience our own violence in order to choose a healthy expression of its existence. I have experienced a trainer telling a trainee that he is not willing to be persecuted by the trainee, and then withdrawing from contact with that trainee. Without the willingness to support the trainee to experience and explore the more difficult to tolerate emotions, however can the trainee's negative persecutory energy be transformed? I wonder, on reflection, whose persecutory tendencies the trainer was paradoxically both avoiding and enacting. In contemplating the journey, it has already begun.

Reflective activity

1. Write a list of words describing all you aspire to as a psycho-therapist: your positive attributes, beliefs and values about yourself, your character, and your behaviour.
2. Now, alongside these words, write down their opposite qualities.
3. Slowly, with awareness, read out aloud your second list, owning theses qualities as your own, beginning with "I am—".
4. Allow yourself to notice what this experience was like for you. What did you feel? What did you think? What did you experience in your body? What images came up for you?
5. Spend some time reflecting upon:
   whom you dislike;
   what qualities you despise in others.
   what it is like for you to own these qualities in yourself.
6. Consider the situations where, and how, these shadow qualities in *others* may have shown themselves in your relationships. What was your part in that? Consider the situations where, and how, these shadow qualities in *yourself* may have shown themselves in your relationships.

That which we are most keen to disown, is that which is most likely our own.

. . . ignorance is no guarantee of security, and in fact only makes our insecurity still worse—it is probably better, despite our fear, to know where the danger lies. To ask the right question is already half the solution to a problem. [Jung, (1932) 1959, par. 23]

CHAPTER TWO

Taking in provisions

"We have to change our patterns of reacting to experience. For our problems do not lie in what we experience, but in the attitude we have towards it"

(Rimpoche, quoted in Gallman, 1991, p. 5)

Whegin embarking on a task that involves the potential experiencing of deep and painful, perhaps disturbing, emotions, it is supportive to have some theoretical information by which we can make sense of that experience. To understand why we feel as we feel and why we have the somatizations that we have brings a degree of relief. This chapter explores some well-known and pertinent theoretical perspectives which have a bearing on shadow experiences.

In the original study, my purpose was to immerse myself in literature pertaining to the theme of shadow, so that I might face the interview material with an educated ear. I began with what was familiar to me and continued with whatever literature seemed pertinent, according to the material emerging in the process of reading, of interviews, and in my own critical reflexive experience. For example, the quality of my dreaming became markedly changed since beginning the study, inviting exploration in the psychological literature pertaining to shadow aspects of dream process. This chapter portrays some of that material.

The literature I began with was an overview of the work of Jung's concepts of archetype and shadow (1952), as discussed and elucidated by Stevens (1982) and Guggenbuhl-Graig (1971) discussing power dynamics among helping professionals. This was new theoretical material for me and made real the processes I have witnessed in organizational dynamics over the years.

I was already familiar with the work of Bowlby (1979) and Winnicott (1971). To rediscover this, in the light of shadow experience, illuminated destructive behaviours directed towards the infant and also those displayed (defensively or instinctually, or both) by the infant, as did Klein's (1988) writing on motiveless malignancy. I found myself drawn to the work of Perls, Hefferline, and Goodman (1951), showing the place for healthy aggression in our environment, and to Miller (1987), who evidences soul destroying aggression, "poisonous pedagogy", in child-rearing practices.

This led to my wish to understand the effects of the external environment and the transferential situation on psychotherapy practices supporting integration; the work of Erskine and Moursund (1998), Yontef (1993), and Clarkson (1995) addresses this influence. Kepner suggests that

> The field conditions of the present, must outweigh those of the past before disconnected memories can emerge from the background and be held in the foreground long enough to be considered and explored. [Kepner, 1995, p. 33]

Throughout the literature review, I introduce examples of client work to relate theory to practice. For myself, it is the drawing on my own personal and clinical experience in relation to theory which prepares me empathically to enter the world of others as witness to their own processes. This is a deeper level of attunement and contact than that which cognitive understanding alone can provide. As Moustakas (1990) suggests, when we limit the tacit in research, we limit the possibilities of knowing. It is hoped that in reading this material, readers may become aware of their own experiences in relation to theories presented. To truly be with another person in their phenomenological experience, we need a holistic self-awareness that both incorporates and surpasses intellectual understanding.

And so, as I reintroduce the theories in this chapter, it becomes a co-creation of consideration of existing literature, themes already in my awareness alongside my own heuristic reflections, and new discoveries made in the process of writing.

The assumptions I begin with are:

1. that the human "self" is created and recreated in the life-long process of relationships;
2. that the process of relating includes destructive and aggressive, as well as loving impulses, feelings, thoughts, somatic and spiritual experiences, and behaviours;
3. that some of these impulses, feelings, thoughts, somatic and spiritual experiences, and behaviours may be primarily out of awareness;
4. that integration which supports wholeness, as the overall aim of integrative psychotherapy, requires bringing into awareness some of the above;
5. that a prerequisite for integration is a containing/holding environment;
6. that the process of relating occurs at, and is influenced by, intrapersonal, interpersonal and collective levels of experiencing;
7. that, given that psychotherapists are first human beings, all of the above dynamics are evident in psychotherapy training organizations, and all organizations.

The nature of polarities

In considering the philosophical underpinnings of psychotherapy, I am struck by the nature of polarities in human experience. Both Erskine (1991), in his concept of juxtaposition, and Whittaker (1985) in her focal conflict model, tell of human good or bad experience, which potentially faces each of us with the element of choice in our lives. Healthy choosing means not identifying with only one polarity and abandoning the other, which usually is our shadow side.

That is, not splitting (Klein, 1988, p. 324), but staying with the creative tension between the two or more different aspects of self. In psychotherapy training institutes, shadow is abandoned at a personal level (for example, in retroflecting one's own socially unacceptable traits and becoming prone to physical illness), at an interpersonal level (for example, in accusing others of being aggressive so that we do not have to face our own aggression), at a group level (for example, becoming grandiose and believing that our orientation of training is better than another orientation), or at an institutional level (for example, assuming that one institute must offer a better training than another, simply because the training fees are higher).

Bly tells us that

Rejoicing in the opposites means pushing the opposites apart with our imaginations so as to create space, and then enjoying the fantastic music coming from each side. One gets a sense of the power of that by sitting between a satir and a tabla when both are giving off music. [Bly, 1990, p. 175]

Whichever psychological or sociological perspective we support, the outcome remains the same: that, as human beings, we filter our perceptions of internal and external experience, resulting in some experience becoming out of our awareness. Society encourages that what we relegate below the level of awareness be shadow phenomena.

Guggenbuhl-Craig tells us that

By shadow, Jung means the reverse side of personal and collective ideals. In this sense, the shadow is always somewhat destructive, operating negatively upon the positive ideals taken up by the collective or the individual. [Guggenbuhl-Craig, 1971 p. 31]

Jung (1932 [1959]) refers to the human predisposition to behave in a certain way, as the archetype to specific experiences. Archetypes of the collective unconscious are actualized and individual complexes formed, in accordance with the individual's relationships with the outside world. For example, a normal mother complex develops from the mother archetype when "the personal mother is good enough", that is, her behaviour fits adequately with the child's archetypal perceptions of how a mother should be, and "when she is continuously present, or contiguous throughout the course of childhood" (Stevens, 1982, p. 65).

Hence, both collective and individual are relevant in integration. We have three spectrums already evident:

- the predisposition to specific behaviours (archetype), including shadow behaviours;
- how this disposition is activated and becomes individualized within specific and differing environments (complex) and hence how shadow might become actualized, acted upon;
- the impact of environmental conditions upon shadow behaviours (the degree of containment).

The individualization of the collective poses tensions, polarities, and choice. It is supported in much psychological and sociological study that everything in human experience is relational, has polarities, and extremes of intensity. Each entity has an opposite. Emotions, thoughts, and behaviours are open to differing qualities, differing depths or superficialities, differing lightness or emphases. Polarities are taught in fairy stories; for example, the good fairy/ wicked witch; the rich King/poor woodcutter; the handsome prince/ugly toad. Indeed, it is in the telling of these stories, a practice that occurs in cultures all over the world, that the integration of the splitting processes occurs. In these symbolic images, containment of the anxiety inherent in feeling split, i.e., "in bits", emerges healthily. At a very early age, we are already learning to tolerate the awareness of opposites.

We all know the contentment of being fed and the discomfort of feeling hunger; the lightness of a sunny summer's day as opposed to the greyness of a rainy winter evening. Part of emotional maturity is the ability to tolerate, rather than split off, that which we cannot change.

Gestalt philosophy (Perls, Hefferline, & Goodman, 1951) posits that our choices are based on life experiences that are in our awareness. Sociological theorists show how choices are influenced by society's norms, cultural beliefs and values, and our own considered responses to these factors. In this way, we can take some responsibility for how we relate to others, for defining our own ways of being in relationships, and for striving towards a way of living that supports the common good of society, or the aspects of society to which we choose to belong. Fromm (1974) shows how man lives with disequilibrium, which lies dormant until societal change brings it into our awareness. Perls and colleagues (1951) posit that the key component in choice *is* the experience of awareness, and, given that environmental (inner and outer) stimulation needs filtering to become tolerable to the individual (that is, there is limit to our awareness), then we can suppose that as some material is acknowledged, some is denied. In striving to live for the common good of humanity, then what becomes denied is primarily that which is believed to be against society's benefit, that which is not ideal. Psychotherapeutic theory understands these consciously or unconsciously denied experiences to constitute the shadow side of human nature.

When studying human nature we can do so from several viewpoints. Ethology teaches us that people are programmed to have innate processes of selection of environmental stimuli, prioritizing awareness of those that are most relevant to our survival as a species. Kepler's (1619) concept of innate inner ideas was later modified by his realization that as human beings we respond to sensations triggered by environmental stimuli (Stevens, 1982). Where, in Kepler's model, is the place for choice? In marrying the phylogenetic perspective with the ontological perspective of human development, which honours individual phenomenological experience, we are provided with a practice of inclusion of both collective and individual dynamics in the attempt to understand human nature. Hence, we might assume that all human kind (phylogeny) is capable of shadow behaviours and the extent to which these behaviours are individually actualized (ontogeny) may depend upon the relationship each individual has with collective experience of being human. This supports the integrative philosophy (Erskine, Moursund, & Trautman, 1999, p. 137) that self is formed in relationship between I and other. When Stevens tells us that "only recently have we begun to recognise that our perceptions, like many of our patterns of behaviour, have been programmed by evolutionary pressures" (Stevens, 1982, p. 55), he also continues to acknowledge the essentially subjective world in which each animal species lives. However, this does not, I think, sufficiently honour the unique phenomenological experience of each individual. One might imagine Stevens to infer a generalization of experiences. While it is innately in each of us to wish to survive at the exclusion of others, as human beings we are gregarious and need people. Even at an innate level there is conflict.

Gestalt theory (Perls, Hefferline, & Goodman, 1951) favours phenomenological experience, suggesting that our perceptions are coloured by what is figural for each of us at any given moment. This is determined by organismic self-regulation in response to (relationship with) current environmental factors. Analytic theory (Freud, 1912b), however, in the dynamic of transference, might imply that we perceive what we already know, in that we see in others what remains unaddressed in ourselves from early experiences. Hence, one aspect of our perception is projection. Whichever perspective we support, the outcome remains the same: that, as human beings, we filter our perceptions of internal and external experience, resulting in some experience becoming out of our awareness. Society, upbringing, and religion relegates shadow to below the level of awareness.

Research methodology is evolving now in the psychotherapy field, with wider application of the more qualitative approaches as opposed to quantitative methods. One could argue, of course, that, although the qualitative approach to research best fits the philosophy underpinning psychotherapeutic work, it might be useful, on the understanding that growth emerges at the interface between polarities, to employ both methodologies in psychotherapeutic research studies.

Environmental factors

In considering the individual–collective dynamic, we might wonder how destructive basic human instinct becomes activated into behaviour in a society where working for the common good is encouraged in so many environments, and in the psychotherapy profession where human growth is at the core of our *raison d'être*. Storr informs us that

> The sombre fact is that we are the cruellest and most ruthless species that has ever walked the earth; and that, although we may

recoil in horror when we read in newspaper or history book of the atrocities committed by man upon man, we know in our hearts that each one of us harbours within himself those same savage impulses which led to murder torture and to war. [Storr, 1968, p. 9]

I have a client experiencing a sense of being watched, pursued, having no space of his own in which to be private. His rage is emerging. His employer is an organization with no local premises. Hence, when he is not at work, the works vehicle stays outside his house, telephone messages are left at his home at all times of day or night, and for safety purposes work vehicles are equipped with transmitters informing head office of the whereabouts of the vehicle at all times. Organizational procedures, in the name of promoting safety, have invaded my client's personal boundaries and overtaken his individual need for privacy, and this is triggering his destructive impulses.

Some people seek an occupation of caring for others, including psychotherapists. Whether this is genuinely altruistic or a proflection of our own needs, sadly, what seems to happen is that, the larger an organization becomes, or the more senior a person becomes, the further away they find themselves from the agenda for which they originally enrolled in that organization. The organizational agenda (being cost effective, maintaining the survival of the organization) often leads away from the individual agenda of caring. In nursing, the way to progress is into teaching or management, both leading away from direct patient care. This dynamic is no less active in psychotherapy training institutes. It is a relief to me that the United Kingdom Council for Psychotherapy has recently introduced into its Continued Professional Development Policy (2004) a requirement that psychotherapists, including psychotherapy trainers, maintain a minimum level of client work.

The small, local organization for which another of my clients worked as a mobile warden has recently amalgamated with a national company. Wardens must now respond alone, rather than in pairs, to crisis calls during the night. They are afraid, angry, and at risk. Again, organizational agenda imposes upon the agendas of individuals, bringing understandable pressure; another conflict between the environmental need and the individual need, and this is precipitating anger to extreme.

Greenberg (1998) posits that aggressive feelings naturally emerge when the healthy expression of the human right to protest is denied. Unfortunately, the price we pay for striving towards a culture of caring and "love of fellow man" is that aggressive feelings often have no place to be heard, witnessed, and responded to, in any way other than through dismissal and rejection. For example, in psychiatry, if a patient protests against his treatment, his protest might easily be perceived as evidence of his illness, and the medication that he wishes not to be given will be increased! Stevens, in his reference to the "bedrock of society and culture" states that

> the very milieu that makes actualisation of the Self possible also demands that certain components of the Self remain unactualised in the unconscious, or be actively repressed there. In our own culture these "unacceptable" elements have been traditionally stigmatised as man's animal nature. Jung called them—Shadow. [Stevens, 1982, p. 221]

And, while society encourages the repression of "unacceptable" behaviours, we are drawn to, and revel in, reading about aggression in novels, watching horror movies, and police series involving violence. People write this material because society wants it. And Storr makes an interesting comment: that writers are often disappointing to meet. "This is often because their true personalities only emerge in their writings and are concealed during the ordinary interchanges of social life" Storr (1997, p. 98)

One might argue that writers are fortunate in having found an outlet for their socially "unacceptable" emotions. Perhaps the increase of horrific, violent films in today's society indicates how much more we are in need of some outlet for our basic human aggression.

I am reminded here of the 1970s, when houses were needed and inner cities flourished in the building of high-rise flats. People were expected to be pleased at opportunities to move to modern buildings, clean, well heated, and ventilated. What soon happened was that the human right to protest at the taking away of the sense of feeling grounded, the secure base of a small terraced house built on the land, the sense of ownership of space around and upon, showed itself in graffiti, destruction, violence towards property and families, in the formation of gangs and vandalism. That which is denied must show itself in some way, either healthily or not!

And we employ many defences in support of denial of our own aggression and violence. From my experience in psychiatry, I understand the most common defence to be projection. The adoption of sound moral values can lead to denial of our own less welcomed impulses and the allocation of these impulses to someone else, often the patients in our care. The patient who acts aggressively might do so because staff have consciously or unconsciously set him up to behave in that way, perhaps in their projection and perhaps in their shaming of him. This, of course, then reinforces the staff fantasy that the patient is only ever badly behaved, because that is what they see, and they then can believe that they are the ones who have the more welcome qualities of caring. The increase in staff control brings about a more angry response in the patient, which in turn brings about a greater degree of staff control, and a vicious circle is set up. Guggenbuhl-Craig depicts this dynamic in reminding us of how early Christian behaviour was to persecute those who behaved against what was then understood to constitute a society of normalcy and adjustment. "Through shock of imprisonment and torture, they had to be made to see their souls were in need of saving" (Guggenbuhl-Craig, 1971, p. 4).

Jung believes that when we strive so hard to occupy one polarity only, that of being "good", then the other polarity carries just as much energy and, paradoxically, we create what we strive to avoid. Jung repeatedly pointed out that "whenever a bright psychic content becomes lodged in consciousness, its opposite is constellated in the unconscious and tries to do harm from that vantage point" (ibid., p. 26). It is most unwise, then, for anyone in the caring professions to avoid their own potential destructiveness.

According to Guggenbuhl-Craig, in today's society religion takes the form of either patrism or matrism in its principles. The patristic culture supports both hierarchy and discipline, with individuals adapting to a preconceived set of organizational rules; for example, Catholicism might be perceived as a culture of status and control. This provides a safety net and yet, if practised to extreme, it invites protest and retaliation. Matrism, however, as in some Buddhist cultures of openness, posits a sense of equality of individuals with spontaneity and less restriction by authority, and it might be said that this again is a one-sided philosophy that, in extreme, invites confluence. Stevens (1982) would argue that these stances might follow one another in society as societies grow and change, or they might exist together. I am curious to discover how this thinking may influence psychotherapy training institutes with either male or female leaders. Is it a masculine trait to lean towards control and dominance, and a feminine trait to be so nurturing as to suffocate with boundarylessness?

It is interesting that the armed forces and the police authority, both designated to protect society, are patristically led, using controlled violence and restraint in their practices. I have a psychotherapy contract with two policing organizations, and often the client's presenting issue is fear of their own aggressive impulses becoming out of their control. Are they drawn unconsciously, I wonder, to defend against aggression in others, as a means of avoiding their own aggressive impulses? And might this also be true of psychotherapists? What might we be avoiding in ourselves in becoming a psychotherapist?

Television advertising repeatedly offers assistance and encouragement to those who might wish to sue others for malpractice. Whereas at one time it was the vulnerable public who were most at risk from professional misconduct, it seems that, under the auspices of rights of individuals, we now have the reversal of that dynamic and professionals are also at risk. Psychotherapists are increasingly very much in the public eye and are vulnerable to complaint from a client with a litigious personality. One might argue that the therapists who are most defended against their own destructiveness might well project this on to a client. The client then becomes caught in a projective identification and complains against the therapist, who has co-created this situation.

That which is becoming difficult to acquire in our culture is the experience of solitude. I am aware for myself of the irritation of mobile phones, laptop computers and Walkman radios on any train journey I take. While I am fortunate enough to live by the sea and can walk in winter months with very little contact with others, I am nevertheless increasingly aware of my own need for silence in this busy world of sensory overload. The increase in American, and now our own, society of the usefulness of sharing in therapy is seldom matched by the awareness of the benefits of solitude as a pressure release. Over the years of training that I have undertaken as a therapist, I have had only one experience where I was invited to explore my own solitude. In emphasizing the ability to be in relationship, have we overlooked the benefits of aloneness in our profession? Quite naturally, as humankind, we can create our own space by either impulsively leaving a situation or by aggressively pushing it away, behaving destructively. But, paradoxically, solitude is a self-support and not necessarily a defence, and needs experiencing in relation to other, as part of a contactful process incorporating withdrawal from, as well as reaching towards, those close to us. Solitude allows for reflection, satisfaction, and consolidation. Storr points out that

> The capacity to form attachments on equal terms is considered evidence of emotional maturity. It is the absence of this capacity which is pathological. Whether there may be other criteria of emotional maturity, like the capacity to be alone, is seldom taken into account. [Storr, 1997, p. 11]

And if our right to solitude is eroded, then protest behaviour can be expected. Do our trainings create or invite shadow in not sufficiently addressing solitude?

Whether we are influenced by family dynamics, religion, education, the psychotherapy profession itself, or all of these factors and more, much literature and experiential evidence shows that human behaviour is influenced by society in many ways. Might the interpersonal dynamics of psychotherapy training institutes be far from simple because they become microcosms of society in their own right? As I realize from the literature how extensive and broad the convolutions of understanding shadow phenomena are, I am softened to being increasingly compassionate towards those who display their aggression unhealthily.

Understanding brings compassion and is the first step in healing the splits in society and interpersonal work.

Nature vs. nurture

A question from the field, and with which doctors, scientists and philosophers have struggled for years, is that of the nature/nurture debate pertaining to humankind. How much of what we do as human beings is innate and how much is learnt? Is it so that we cannot change that which is innate or that we can unlearn what has been learned in childhood in relation to shadow?

Anna Freud taught us that the attachment to mother was displayed by the child because it was mother who provided the oral satisfaction. She wrote "When its powers of perception permits the child to form a conception of the person through whose agency it is fed, its love is transferred to the provider of the food" (A. Freud, 1946, p. 119).

Dollard and Miller (1950) supported this view, suggesting that the reciprocity of affection is learnt. However, Stevens (1982) tells us that studies at the Metera Babies Centre (1966) show differently. Although nurses were assigned to specific infants as mother substitutes, in the whole group of babies–nurses the bonds were formed between babies and nurses not specifically assigned to their care; babies chose the mother figure/nurse to whom they were able to attach, rather than the food provider. Stevens confirmed Bowlby's monotropic principle, believing that "Attachments cannot be made to order. One cannot legislate in matters of the heart" (Stevens, 1982, p. 5), and that very attachment itself is an early emotional bond, the nature of which has a formative influence on character and subsequently on the individual's capacity for aggression. While Bowlby stated in his support for individual foster care that "Bad homes are better than good institutions" (Holmes, 1993, p. 41), we must bear in mind the contextual aspect of this statement. From my experience as a psychiatric nurse I believe that a bad home with a floridly psychotic mother may be worse than most institutional care, and yet, sadly, the institutional care for the mentally ill in our country has long been stifling of the sense of self, with seclusion rooms and locked wards for the control of aggression. It is in need of change. The caring environment in itself is aggressive.

Bowlby's enlightening and revolutionary theory places enormous impact upon how we, as integrative psychotherapists, conceptualize and carry out our work (Bowlby & Robertson, 1952). It was when faced with delinquent behaviours, petty crime, from teenagers that Bowlby's correlations between lack of early attachment and adult anti-social behaviours were made. What cannot be denied is the importance of "other", early in our lives, to our

potential to form healthy relationships. Stevens states "The moment
the mother–child dyad is formed, Eros is constellated and it is out
of love that . . . selfhood and personal identity grow" (Stevens, 1982,
p. 13). Storr supports this view, stating,

> A child who from its earliest years is certain that his attachment
> figures will be available when he needs them, will develop a sense
> of security and inner confidence. In adult life, this confidence will
> make it possible for him to trust and love other human beings.
> [Storr, 1997, p. 9]

I ask myself once again, what of the destructive aspects of
human nature? If love is so important in human development, then
what of hate? Jung (1932 [1959]) would argue that our predisposition to hate is as powerful as our predisposition to love. Is it possible for an infant to have too much love? Of course, there is a need
to define love and all the maternal behaviours that this term encompasses before we can truly consider this question. I would suggest
that the mother who does not feel hate alongside love for her children learns only to idealize and risk the child perceiving that hate
outside of the mother's awareness.

Jung studied mythology, religion, legends, fairy tales, dreams,
and nightmares; a whole range of human experiences that are both
pertinent and present across cultural and societal differences. He
posits that human beings have

> given, in-built determinants to the human psyche. . . . numerous
> predispositions for perceiving, feeling, behaving and conceptualis-
> ing in specific ways. The extent to which these predispositions were
> developed or expressed depended largely upon environmental
> factors and individual life-experience. [Stevens, 1982, p. 44]

So, here, a marriage exists between the innate (nature) and the
learnt (nurture).

While Bowlby (1953) would see resistance and aggression as
part of attachment behaviour that can be observed when the child's
needs are not met, and one might then assume that a child whose
needs are met would not experience much, if any, hostility towards
others, Jung (1932 [1959]) is very clear that all aspects of human
experience are available to each of us. Stevens (1982) believes that

once an archetype has evolved as a characteristic in any species, then it does not disappear with disuse. The potential for certain behaviours is ever present. Jung believes that the intensity that we allocate to our emotions is equally given to both positive and negative feelings. If we strive to be "good", then just as much energy is given to the opposite, and this customarily resides in our "shadow". So, even in the optimum child-rearing environment, we are not released from the experience of destructive impulses.

Jung (1932 [1959]) posits that it is the specific qualities inherent in certain types of relationship that constitute the activation of the inherited archetype. The process to which Jung refers as individuation is the process by which the individual engages and relates to the collective archetype currently at work in his experience. Individuals claim their own conscious choices of how to be in life, in relation to each specific archetypal pattern and set of environmental circumstances. Individuation consists of making the unconscious conscious under optimum external conditions. If our unconscious is the place where shadow experience resides and integration requires the bringing into awareness of unconscious experience, then the shadow archetype itself deserves further exploration. I shall also consider briefly the mother and father archetypal systems, because these are triggered transferentially in psychotherapy trainings.

Archetypes

The Jungian phenomena of archetype denotes an inherited way of functioning, a pattern of behaviour potentially available to each human being, as biologically inborn in us. Jung allocates the concept of archetype to the realm of the collective unconscious, saying "I have chosen the term collective because this part of the unconscious is not individual but universal; in contrast to the personal psyche" (Jung, 1932 [1959], par. 3).

Stevens tells us that archetypes ". . . have the capacity to initiate, control and mediate the common behavioural characteristics and typical experiences of our kind, even though we are, for the most part, unaware of them" (Stevens, 1982, p. 39).

There is acknowledgement here as to the power of unconscious process and a rationale for a training culture that encourages the bringing of unconscious issues into conscious awareness.

Jung also informs us that "Just as all archetypes have a positive, favourable, bright side that points upwards, so also they have one that points downwards, partly negative and unfavourable" (Jung, 1932 [1959], par. 226).

It is important to consider both polarities of each archetypal pattern in order to avoid splitting one from the other and, through this splitting process, giving our power to that which is denied. In this way, we have more conscious choices in our behaviour. Bly celebrates this with

> To live between means not only that we recognise opposites, but rejoice that they exist. To live between, we stretch out our arms and push the opposites as far apart as we can, and then live in the resonating space between them. [Bly, 1990, p. 174]

Mother archetype

Jung (1932 [1959]) believes this archetype to be the central aspect of the archetypal feminine, not to be underestimated. For survival of both the species and the individual we initially need someone on whom to depend for emotional nurturance, feeding, and clothing, for safety and love. Bowlby believes nature allocated this role to the female. Jung describes how archetypes carry universally recurrent themes and individuation is actualized in the personalization of the collective realm. This occurs initially and primarily in the relationship between child and mother and how this relationship meets, or not, the child's and the mother's archetypal needs. This material is important professionally because very much psychotherapy theory and practice includes transferential phenomena where the clients' childhood/parental patterns are revisited theoretically and re-experienced phenomenologically.

Jung tells us that symbolically we struggle with the two aspects of mother, the good and the bad. This tension is integrated in the collective with the handing down, over generations, of stories of polarities: good fairy godmother and wicked witch, beautiful princess and ugly hag. As Jung says,

> Mother nature and earth Mother, she [maternal archetype] is goddess of fertility and dispenser of nourishment; as water or sea she represents the origins of all life as well as a symbol of the unconscious, the fount of all psychic creativity. [Stevens, 1982, p. 89]

Stevens attends here to the positive aspects of the mother archetype, and, again for all positive qualities, he believes the opposite is also true. He points out Bowlby's serious limitation in his assumption that most mothers are good enough. Bowlby would argue that damage occurs at times of the infant's separation from mother and this is very evident in his work with young offenders, evidencing a high correlation here between shadow behaviour and lack of early containment. However, it could be argued that Bowlby pays insufficient attention to the child's phenomenological experience of the nature of the attachment formed, regardless of separations. Mother can be physically available and apparently loving on the surface, but not aware of her own unconscious hostility to which the child can so easily attune. Schizoid process theory elaborates on this theme. Attachment involves much more than physical presence, and this has enormous implications for psychotherapy training, as we shall see in considering containment and integration.

Father archetype

It is this archetypal pattern that, according to Jungian philosophy, in mythology is personified as the lawgiver, the king, the voice of authority and guardian against enemies. Paternal power implies protection. However, godlike figures can also instil fear. Christian faiths teach of the "wrath of God" and mould children through fear of punishment. Archetypal patterns are portrayed in all of our literature, music, and the arts. Goya painted the god Saturn, who mythologically prevents his sons from replacing him by eating them alive. In this story, Saturn's partner, having given birth to yet another son, hides her son and presents Saturn with a rock wrapped in swaddling clothes. This causes Saturn to vomit when he eats it, and all her previous babies are returned to her.

Evidence of Jung's theory is exemplified in a case in which my adult client cannot separate from his grieving father; his father is "devouring" him with his tears and my client's strength in his therapeutic journey is in his individuation from his father's years of despair. Stevens (1982) sees the father as a symbolic bridge between family and society. My client, in having a depressed father all his life, struggles now with his sense of being welcomed by others. Jungians believe that, while mother influences primarily the world of feelings, instincts, and the unconscious, father influences the world of judgements, consciousness, and inviting the use of will. The father archetype constellates for each of us "attitudes to work, social achievement, politics and the law. . . . the world as place to be known and lived in" (Stevens, 1982, p. 105).

Both Bowlby and Jung are clear in their beliefs that pathogenic parental behaviour results in the proneness to release anger in the archetypally frustrated child. Stevens supports this, stating

> The largely unconscious resentment which this (archetypal frustration) induces tends to persist into adult life as a "chip on the shoulder": the hostility which could not be directed against the parents is displaced on to some other group (e.g. the bosses, the unions, the blacks etc., or on to someone perceived as weaker (e.g. a spouse, a child, or employee). [Stevens, 1982, p. 112]

We shall examine this dynamic further in the understanding of transference in psychotherapy trainings. One might question what happens to the resentment of a psychotherapy trainer who had the experience of being archetypally frustrated in childhood in his relationships with more vulnerable trainees. I have a colleague who fears the hostility of her current trainer, whom she sees as always dictatorial, and she also fears his vulnerability should she assert herself and address his aggressive stance in the training situation. This current impasse in which she finds herself, with the sense of being "stuck" in her professional development, is a co-creation resulting from the early unmet needs of each of them.

Shadow archetype

With maternal and paternal archetypes, we have considered that power may mean protective or punitive behaviours, with society's immediate norms influencing how the power shadow shows itself. Psychiatrists, social workers, and psychotherapists who, with good intention, intervene in family situations, are often perceived as interfering and controlling by those in their care and by the general public who have experience of those in their care. Hence, the carer tries even harder to show himself as being without malevolence, and, according to Jungian beliefs, the increased energy directed into the caring becomes matched in the shadow. In reality, carers sometimes are both interfering and controlling, especially where Mental Health Act sectioning might prove necessary. Indeed, such sectioning is much better applied for by a social worker than by a family member, because in this way there is a much greater potential to keep family dynamics healthier, despite the fact that the family dynamics may have been contributing to the client's distress in the first place. In my experience, it is the professional who knows his own shadow experience who is least likely to abuse from a pseudo-protective stance.

Without the necessary awareness, we can all find and overuse moral reasons for the practice of negative control. As Guggenbuhl-Craig realizes, "People are most cruel when they can use cruelty to enforce the 'good'" (1971, p. 8). He posits that when we adopt the role of caring, without consideration of our resentment of caring, then resentments appear in roles of the shadow, such as sadist, dominator, bully, belittler, destroyer, trickster.

Roles of the shadow

The dominance–submission archetype is discussed by Stevens as being primarily an aspect of father–child relationship. He understands patriarchal society to reinforce this, saying that men are by nature more assertive, competitive, and aggressive than women. This has been evidenced for me in psychiatry, where suicide attempts by male patients have involved profoundly greater degrees of self-harm than those by women patients. Self-mutilation is more prevalent among male patients. I have witnessed young men enucleate their own eyes, worked with male patients who have removed fingers, and one young man who amputated his penis. If people who resort to these degrees of self-harm do not come to psychotherapy for help, then why not? One might ask what is being avoided in our profession to exclude offering support to those with this level of dangerousness. Perhaps it is the case that some people with these difficulties in life do come for therapy but we do not talk about it, and again, why not? In avoiding this degree of work, are we avoiding a depth of terror and murderousness that seems uncontainable? What are we avoiding in ourselves? What is needed to offer containment to people with these very destructive processes?

Mothers can also seek to dominate their children, when their learnt currency for relationships is control. The child who is controlled may resist this dynamic while, through the processes of imitation and modelling, learning to behave in the same way. In relation to my father, I said to myself in childhood, "I shall never do this to my children", only to find myself thinking as an adult, "Goodness, I sound just like my father!" Stevens quotes Bowlby (1979, p. 141) to say, "Each of us is apt to do unto others as we have been done by. The bullying adult is the bullied child grown bigger" (Stevens, 1982, p. 132).

Luckily, in awareness, we can make significant changes.

Bowlby shows how the abandoned child will naturally respond to the experience of abandonment by crying, screaming, shouting, biting, kicking. Holmes believes

> This "bad" behaviour is the normal response to the threat to an attachment bond, and presumably has the function of trying to restore it, and, by "punishing" the care giver, of preventing further separation. [Holmes, 1993, p. 72]

In acknowledging ourselves as therapists, as care-givers/helpers, then we could easily see our clients as helpless, projecting our own needs on to them. Flemming-Crocker, in Philippson (1986, p. 74), refers to this process as "proflection", believing that the purpose this serves for the therapist is that of not having to face our own neediness and of having our own narcissistic grandiosity supported in the client's idealization of us. At this stage, Guggenbuhl-Craig (1971) would say that the helper–helpless archetype has been activated. Given the power imbalance at the commencement of a therapeutic relationship, one could recommend that this common dynamic must be worked with to prevent unconscious infantilizing of the client by the therapist, which is one way in which a therapist might abuse. To infantalize one's client leads to unhealthy client dependency and a denial by the therapist of the client's autonomy and maturational success. Hence, it is often quite unhealthy to see therapy as a re-parenting experience alone. We work with the child in the adult and must also support the adult in the adult.

Guggenbuhl-Craig believes that if we do not acknowledge such potentially unhealthy dynamics, this "does not annihilate them; it rather forces them to influence our meetings blindly" (*ibid*., p. xii) and we risk forcing the shadow into the role of destroyer. To dominate and belittle our clients in this way allows us to experience the power aspect of the polarity, which otherwise we might experience as helplessness. Again, in my experience, this is also true of the psychotherapy trainer–trainee relationship.

Stevens highlights the dynamics of a growing and changing institution, such as a training organization, when the fear of change brings an inertia and resistance and the trickster archetype emerges. He quotes Henderson (1967, p. 36), who describes the trickster as one who "knows no difference between right and wrong and accepts no discipline other than his own experimental attitude to life" (Stevens, 1982, p. 148).

Stevens believes that the trickster employs his/her strategy in an attempt to maintain the institutional dynamics as they are. The mercurial character of the trickster, who knows how to seduce, can be useful, as long as we do not use this seduction to reinforce our own grandiose self-inflation. In the real world, seduction in a partnership is healthy only when the relationship becomes "consummated". Without consummation, seduction can be painful. And so, seduction that is not in the interest also of other becomes a manipulation by the power holder. It keeps the seduced person in need and the seducer empowered. How easily a trainer, within an idealized transference, can coax a trainee into unhealthy conformity, hence halting the process of individuation for the trainee. The trainee then, even on becoming qualified, continues to seek "his own" answers from the trainer, whom he sees to be "all knowing".

As we explore the dangerousness of shadow phenomena, it is worth noting that "the experience we resist tends to persist" (Evans, 1998). Jung tells us that

> . . . ignorance is no guarantee of security, and in fact only makes our insecurity still worse. It is probably better, despite our fear, to know where the danger lies. To ask the right question is already half the solution of a problem. [Jung, 1932 [1959], par. 23]

More evidence is here to support the importance of teaching this material in psychotherapy training groups and I am encouraged by what I read. The literature discussed so far supports what my tacit understanding tells me and what emerges in my dreams.

The dream process

In the history of psychology and the human psyche, dreams have been studied from many viewpoints: Jung (1932 [1959]) studied commonalities of symbolism and process (*the collective unconscious*); Anna Freud (1936) discusses repression and projection into the unconscious of what we are unwilling to accept in waking life (*the nature of projections*); Foulkes (1966) researched the effects of differing brain rhythm patterns on our psychic experience (*brain waves*); Hadfield (1954) discusses old and modern approaches to dream interpretation (*dream interpretation*); Perls (1967) takes the viewpoint of *ownership* of our dreams (a counterapproach to traditional methods of working with dreams). What is very apparent in all reviewed literature on dream studies is the bizarre and unboundaried nature of dream experience, from early infancy, with fear, terror, and murderousness occurring in many people's dreams.

In preparing for my study of shadow, what struck me immediately was how the content of my own dreams began to change, and the growing intensity of both fear and power that I felt emotionally in relation to my dreaming. My dreaming appeared to escalate, happening every night, sometimes, I supposed, all night. When the recollection of dreams was not clear to me, the feeling of having been engaged in a working process all night stayed with me. This led me into Jungian analysis of my dreams as a means of support for myself, and exploration of this process is found later in the book.

This study involves invitation to the darker side of human experience in a profession that strives towards caring; an experience of opposites. Tensions between opposites were emerging in my dreams and in my reading: human existential issues, such as the need for structure *vs.* the need for freedom in my life, and the marrying of control *vs.* acceptance in the maintenance of democracy in my training organization. I question, in the experience of dreaming, how much control we have over our own process. How much do we need to own, to make conscious our experience, for it to be of good use? What happens if we are resistant to the process of accepting our dream life; does this mean that shadow stays out of awareness, or that dreams are not healing? Perhaps one could say that unconscious process, including dreaming, is a preparatory phase of experiencing, prior to the emergence of awareness. In this sense, dreams are not seen simply as resistance, but as part of a period of incubation within the process of becoming aware.

Kepner discusses resistance: "Since these aspects [resisted material] continue to have relevance to our functioning, despite the fact that we disown them, they are constantly seeking expression" (1987, p. 69). So, given that the dream message to the individual is striving to be heard and, in Kepner's view, is made up of material that has already been resisted at some level, again we have the tension of a meeting of opposites. As Kepner states, we may need a willingness to be open to accepting aspects of ourselves, our shadow, and a willingness to stay with the tension between the polarities of our experience, in order to consciously engage with our dream process.

> If the person who must hear the message is receptive to the communication—the important information will be conveyed. If, on the other hand, the person who must receive the message . . . in fact would like to deny the very existence of the sender, and the sender can only communicate in a relatively unknown language, then important information will be difficult to convey. [ibid.]

In our dreams, we are both the sender and the recipient of the message. Perhaps the degree to which we are open to receiving unconscious material influences the process of our "understanding", and a willingness to engage results in an increased personal clarification of the symbolic language of our dreams. The psychotherapy training group provides a milieu where self-reflection is encouraged and supported, and dreaming is part of this process. Dreams occur at an individual or at a group level. Groups are just as much prone to unconscious defence mechanisms, including projection in the form of imagery, as are individuals.

Archetypes, predispositions to particular ways of behaving, carry archetypal images, the form of representation of an archetype in consciousness. Stevens tells us that "Once activated, unlived archetypal potential begins to 'personate' in phantasies and dreams" (1982, p. 292). Hence dreamwork, I believe, is a vital part of any training group process.

The therapeutic process for one of my clients took a remarkable step forward through a dream where she imagined herself to be on a delivery table giving birth. I explored the significance of the symbolic imagery of the delivery table by requesting that my client identified with this object. Through this process of symbolic identification (*"I am held down, a great weight on top of me. I cannot escape"*), my client remembered her experience of sexual abuse at the hands of her grandfather.

We have evidence here that the language in our dream experience is representational: symbolic imagery, fantasy, and metaphor. I learned from my work with psychotic clients that they each have their own symbolic understanding of their unique phenomenology. As with any language, with time, the underlying meaning of individual symbolic patterns in dreams becomes learnt and easier to interpret and experience. It is the same with psychotic thinking.

Kalsched (1996), in considering healthy psychic self-care, explains how this is achieved at the interface between conscious and unconscious experience, part of which is served by our dream process. Perhaps Kalsched is suggesting that the dream process works of its own volition and unconsciously. He refers to how "We might imagine this self-regulatory activity as the psyche's self-care system, analogous to the body's immune system" (1996, p. 17).

If, as Stevens elucidates, shadow phenomena reside in the unconscious realm, it may be that it is useful and necessary to have a place in integrative psychotherapy training for the understanding of the dream process as a means whereby the collective archetypal territory can be personalized. Evetts-Secker (2003) describes individuation as the personal relationship to collective phenomena, believing that, without this, we are subject to denial, projections, and acting out behaviour in relation to destructive impulses. Of course, symbolic imagery is not peculiar to the dream process; dreamwork is a much employed and fruitful way—but not the only way—in which trainees are free to introduce their symbolic experience in group processing times.

The dynamics of transference and countertransference phenomena, which occur in dreams, are explored in the section titled "Transferential process".

Gestalt philosophy (Perls, Hefferline, & Goodman, 1951) would posit that, in that we are the authors of our own dreams, any destructive component therein, including symbolic representations, can only be our own.

Symbolic representation

A dictionary description of symbolism is "a sign or mark which describes something else"; a description of metaphor, "a form of words in which a thing is spoken of under the name or likeness of something else"; and of imagery, "a collection of images or pictures; descriptions in words which give lively ideas". In integrative psychotherapy schools, symbolism may be viewed as a means whereby communication is enhanced, either with the self in the raising of awareness, or with other, in the shared understanding of the individual's symbolic meaning.

Hinshelwood (1989) tells how Freud saw dreams as symbolic alternatives to words, for discharging mental energy, and that Freud notes that dreams avoid muscular action. This is not always the case. My own children moved in their sleep when dreaming and we all know how nightmares can cause physical experiences of fear, waking with tremors and perspiration. However, Klein took Freud's idea further, observing that, in play, children use muscular discharge symbolically to enact their fantasy. Klein believed "Externalisation of these phantasies in symbolic play and personifications was driven by the need to put internal states of persecution away at a distance" (Hinshelwood, 1989, p. 430). Here, symbolization is used as a defensive strategy, which, paradoxically, might in some circumstances be useful.

Segal (1978) distinguishes between symbolic *representation*, where the symbol is a substitute for the original experience, although it has characteristics other than those of the original experience (dissimilar properties) and symbolic *equation*, where material is projected into the symbol, which then attracts the same conflicts and inhibitions as the original experience (similar properties). One of my trainees used symbolic representation in temporarily removing an ornament from the training room. She had a sense of taking me home with her. A client used symbolic equation in drawing a smouldering volcano, communicating, on exploration, that she was about to erupt and had planned suicide. In our society, shadow is often expressed symbolically; I am reminded of Pan, the "good God transformed into the devil" (Stevens, 1982, p. 167) and what we understand as (Pan)ic attacks. Through symbolic representation, phobic situations can occur in varying degrees and painful emotions can become somatized.

Grove (1989) believes that a symbol is an identifiable unit within a metaphor, while a metaphor itself will encompass the entire perceptual space of the client. He continues to note that symbols are "chosen" for the qualities that link them to other symbolic qualities, and, through this process of symbol formation, qualitative change takes place in our perception; our core beliefs, values, decisions, and sense of identity might be formed and transformed at a metaphorical level. This is especially evident when working with psychotic experience. A male client of mine, suffering from a para- noid psychosis, told me that he was pregnant, saying, "and what's more, it's yours and I want to know what you're going to do about it". He was pale, perspiring, and very frightened. I suggested to him that, as we both knew, a male could not conceive (confirming reality) and so I imagined he was telling me something metaphori- cally (addressing his fantasy), that perhaps because of our relation- ship some new growth was occurring inside for him and he wanted to know that I would support him through this process, which I confirmed. He was much relieved in our mutual understanding of his metaphor, enhancing the containment necessary for him to eventually own his own projected aggression (shadow), which underlay his paranoia. At a UKCP conference, a speaker mooted that all psychotherapy trainees may need to understand their own psychotic aggression in order to be empathic with psychotic clients.

It is in human nature to identify with fantasies of destruction (archetypal imagery, the Trickster, the Destroyer) in the form of hor- ror movies, science fiction literature, and, earlier in life, in fairy sto- ries and nursery rhymes. Evetts-Secker (2003) tells how fairy stories are extreme and polarizing, working at the existential level of human experience. Narrative psychology believes that in allowing ourselves to be touched by fairy stories, we are allowing the instinctual to dwell alongside civilization, the symbolic world and the consciously understood world. This brings individuation, when, in being aware of our own aggressive impulses, we are less likely to act upon them. In my experience in forensic psychiatry it was obvious that when patients were allowed to stay awake longer for an evening, watching videos involving human aggression, they settled to sleep more easily. If sent to bed earlier, with such movies being denied them, attacks on staff the following day increased. They watched the films "as if" they were characters portrayed there, and their aggression was held, contained safely, in this imaginary process.

Meeting through stories is well explained by Mills, Crowley, and O'Ryan (2001), who agree that it is the shared phenomenological reality of symbolic communication that contains emotions. They advocate a process of six ingredients through which the healing process of fantasy in stories occurs. These are: "Metaphorical Conflict . . . Unconscious Processes and Potentials . . . Parallel Learning Situations . . . Metaphorical Crisis . . . New Identification . . . and Celebration . . ." (*ibid.*, p. 70).

I support the use of stories in psychotherapy training, to explore human destructiveness, in inviting trainees to write and share a murder story. Trainees are often shocked, sometimes physically, with pale skin and tremors, at the amount of violence they are carrying below their level of awareness. In this process, feelings from the unconscious become conscious, and, given that there are many ways of symbolically "dying" and degrees of "not having a life", it expands trainees' awareness to explore how they might restrict the "life" of another, for example, by avoiding, or critically attacking, or discounting. This exploration and thoughtful consideration is supportive of choice in behaviour. It is the working through of archetypal issues, rather than the archetype itself, which promotes change. "The archetype is not wisdom. It drives us to wisdom. How this happens is individuation. It happens in our bodies too" (Evetts-Secker, 2003).

In integrating the whole of human experience, when wholeness underpins our philosophy of work, we cannot exclude the somatic self, body process, from our enquiries.

Body process

Kalsched states

> Understanding the psyche as a half-bodily–half spiritual (or mental) entity has some important implications. One danger of

psychotherapy is that it becomes too mental (wordy) and loses the
link with the body. When this happens, psychotherapy loses the
psyche also. [1996, p. 64]

He continues by noting that the opposite is also true, that body
work can be disabling if it does not involve expression in verbal or
symbolic language. Transformative work is lost if body work does
not enhance the means whereby someone can find meaning in their
experience.

A client of mine, with a history of undisclosed childhood sexual
abuse, came into therapy with agoraphobia. Once disclosure
occurred and her secret was "out in the open", then her phobia
dissolved. Her body, in the form of phobic anxiety had been carrying the psychological process of secrecy, pertaining to shadow
activities. Introjection, messages such as "Don't tell", underpin
retroflective practices, in that the energy denied by the introject
becomes held in the body by further energy used in the denial.
Retroflection is hard work! As Philippson writes,

How do we learn to retroflect when it is against our best interests?
Originally, the energy would have been directed outward, intended
to make contact. . . . However, the response from the outside world
was . . . hostile or perhaps indifferent. . . . The conclusion (introject)
was reached something along the lines of: This behaviour/desire is
wrong, or I am bad; This behaviour/desire is punishable or I
deserve punishment; This behaviour/desire is useless or I am
worthless. [1989, p. 1]

In English culture, not only the process of introjection, but often
the introject itself depicts the withholding of somatic energy with
messages such as "stiff upper lip", "shoulders back", "grit your
teeth", and "bite your tongue!" We are encouraged to use our
bodies to "control" emotions and behave in a socially acceptable
way, which denies shadow. Toxic introjects originate from others
who are more powerful than ourselves, often when we are not yet
fully independent, and we can unconsciously take them on board,
with natural shadow impulses becoming somatized unhealthily.
Perls, Hefferline, and Goodman (1951) state

during the excitation . . . the self introjects, displaces its own potential drive or appetite with someone else's. The neurotic situation is

that in which the convention is coercive and incompatible with a lively excitation, and where in order to avoid the offence of not belonging (not to speak of further conflicts), the desire itself is inhibited and the hateful environment is both annihilated and accepted by swallowing it whole and blotting it out. [*ibid.*, p. 233]

What society forbids us to acknowledge openly, for example, aggression, we can carry somatically. Clarkson considers aggression indispensable to life and not necessarily an experience inevitably leading to destruction or damage. She describes the holding back of healthy aggression as a lack of expression of natural impulses.

The impulse to hit out remains locked in the person's body, affecting muscular patterns, abdominal tension and chemical balances in the body. Energy is used to suppress the original held-back impulses. [Clarkson, 1989, p. 54]

In retroflection, destructive damage can be turned against the self.

Sophie discovered in the process of counselling that her frequent respiratory diseases were the embodiment of the conflict between her wanting to rail and scream against her oppressive father whilst at the same time repressing this desire from fear of his reprisal, by choking herself. These primitive and undifferentiated wishes were, so to speak, clenched in her musculature. [*ibid.*, p. 116]

Kalsched (1996) tells of Lenore, who was unable to let somatic sensations into her awareness at the time when her mother abandoned her. It was when she experienced re-abandonment by her husband that her earlier memory, retained as a stomach tension, gave rise to a stomach ulcer. She had one place for encapsulated energy in her mind and another place for encapsulated energy in her body, and both were out of her awareness. In therapy, with witness to her experience, she was able to make connections between her current bodily experience and earlier emotional trauma. This is physical damage, shadow phenomena, resulting from psychological abuse.

I had a client who often sat on her left hand. We explored this experience for her to remember being caned on her left hand at school in an attempt to make her right-handed. Her body had carried the memory, which her psyche had long forgotten. This is psychical damage resulting from primarily physical abuse. Kalsched believes the role of the psyche in healthy developmental functioning is individuation, ownership, and making whole. However, in circumstances of trauma, the goal of the psyche becomes to survive, and this may entail the splitting off of emotional memory from physical experience. To extreme, this robs the person of ". . . the experience of feeling real and fully alive, a tragic condition we know as de-personalisation" (*ibid.*, p. 67).

Just as energy in childhood made unwelcome by the environment has to be withheld, so it has to be made welcome and experienced in therapy for healing to occur. The energy level of shadow is high. Given that my own personal process is to retroflect aggression somatically, I am realizing from my own phenomenology how important working with this material is in training groups in order to encourage the open expression of shadow for both trainer and trainee alike. However, the timing of the trainer's expression needs to take into consideration the developmental phase of the trainee's process.

Aggressive energy is differentiated by Perls, Hefferline and Goodman (1951) into both annihilation and destruction. In annihilation the painful object (other) is rendered non-existent:

> Primarily, annihilation is a defensive response to pain, bodily invasion, or danger. In avoidance and flight, the animal takes himself out of the painful field; in killing, he "coldly" removes the offending object from the field . . . Destroying is the demolition of a whole into fragments in order to assimilate them as parts into a new whole. [*ibid.*, p. 121]

Perls shows that annihilation results in non-contact experience, because the annihilated person is not spontaneously enjoyed. In the non-existence there can be no meeting of need, only the lack of pain in response to the need not being met. However, Perls believes that destruction has the potential for contact in that, in order for the new to be assimilated, the old is first destroyed in its original form in order to satisfy current appetite in the new way. The desire to destroy is also the desire to engage with something differently.

In this sense, Perls (1947) sees aggression as healthy, noting that it becomes unhealthy in neurotic derivations of manifestations such as sado-masochism, conquest and domination, and suicide.

Philippson (1990) sees suicide as the ultimate retroflection. Perls states, "There can be no doubt that mankind suffers from suppressed individual aggression and has become the executor and the victim of tremendous amounts of released collective aggression" (1947, p. 134).

It is in our formative years that we need environmental containment of aggression in order to make possible our own tolerance of our aggressive impulses and our choosing behaviour in respect of our aggression and potential destruction. Kepner believes biological body structure to be formed through growth and maturation. The body structure we carry as a result of life history, which may or may not include containment, Kepner terms "adaptive body structure"; that which is

> characterized as postures, stances and tensions that are:
> 1. consistently and persistently used over time.
> 2. either frozen into the musculature so that the structure is continually visible, or preprogrammed muscular responses that channel energy and movement into a stylized movement pattern.
> 3. automatic and involuntary (under most circumstances).
> 4. not easily or comfortably modified merely by trying to stand or move differently (i.e., behavioural change). [Kepner, 1987, p. 48]

He suggests a physical response to a situation of danger might be to hold the breath, hunch the shoulders, and turn aside in avoidance. These reactions, when needed repeatedly, cease to be a momentary, flexible adjustment and become a constant posture. Adaptive processes become fixed structures, which can then defensively become normalized, effectively maintaining lack of awareness of our bodily nature and the "disowned parts of our self to which these structures relate" (Kepner, 1987, p. 50).

He continues to say that, with lack of awareness of our body process, we restrict the element of choice as to how we use our body. Then aggressive responses may involve hitting out in a way that seems spontaneous and beyond our control. Kepner tells of how aggression and stubborn resistance, which is useful at times for anyone, can become readily available all the time for someone like a drill sergeant, for whom softness and more contact-orientated feelings play little part in his working life. Such a person may have a self-image of toughness that perpetuates the stiffened jaw and hardened face, or may desensitize to his physical self, presenting a toughened exterior that invites fearfulness in others while he himself feels vulnerable and easily humiliated. It would seem from this that, in integrative psychotherapy, both emotions *and* their somatizations need addressing in the holistic search for integration. As Kepner says, "bodywork which focuses on physical change and deemphasizes emotion and meaning is as one-sided and unintegrated as psychotherapy that ignores body processes" (1987, p. 53).

Containment and integration

In understanding "integration" holistically, encompassing all of the aspects of being human, a positive conception is

> the process of making whole: taking disowned, unaware aspects of the ego and making them a part of the cohesive self. Through integration, it becomes possible for people to have the courage to face each moment openly and freshly, without the protection of a preformed opinion, position, attitude or expectation. [Erskine & Moursund, 1998, p. 40]

This has the implication that without integration we are not free to engage moment by moment with our fully felt phenomenological reality. Integration then must necessarily encompass acknowledging and experiencing the shadow side of human nature and our own part played in the ownership and acting out of shadow dynamics.

Developmental studies show how integration is hindered in childhood by inadequate environmental support, and in adulthood by the structures we create in childhood to compensate for environmental deficits; it is, however, supported by the positive aspects of structure as offered in the form of good parenting. It could be, then, that in the exploration of the tension between the human need for structure and for freedom, we have the experience of containment as necessary both in childhood and in integrative psychotherapy trainings.

From my experience as a mother, psychiatric nurse, and psycho-therapist, I witness that as human beings we come into this world emotionally dependent, the quality of which changes as we indi-viduate, developing our own autonomy and responsibility reason-ably unscathed. The security of optimum environmental structure is the framework within which our own creativity, spontaneity, and freedom to choose emerges. This includes the freedom to address shadow phenomena.

Formative relationships protect and support through nurture, guidance, and limit-setting, as parents relate according to their own beliefs, cultural backgrounds, social norms, and history of being a child themselves. Family, education, religion, and the media all influence the nature and degree of structure in the life of a child. This can be positive and growth enhancing.

However, the opposite is also true. Child-rearing generally has changed in our society from a Victorian stance of control and over-structure: parental stances of "Do as I say" without explanation to support instruction, canes standing beside school blackboards to control the "unruly" child, and behaviour being powerfully shaped by the instilling of shame. This degree of structure stunts creativity and, Miller (1987) might argue, used to excess constitutes shadow.

We now have the polarity, a culture where chaos can take the place of healthy creativity due to disinterest/unavailability/fear on the part of the authority figure. This psycho–social climate of too little structure can itself trigger an overcompensation in parents, and I am recently interested in how three of my young clients who have taken drugs each have rigid, controlling parents. Perhaps the experience of drug-taking (shadow self-harm) is the only way in which they can break free from over-structured, controlling paren-tal influence and create a different experience for themselves. The same might also be true for teenagers who wish to escape the parent with no boundaries, who might suffocate and overwhelm with confluent seeking behaviours.

When the balance between structure and freedom is wrong, then emotional health is at risk, integration does not sufficiently take place and the sense of self does not fully develop. Many of the personality disorders identified in the *Diagnostic and Statistical Manual of Mental Disorders* (*DSM-IV*) (American Psychiatric Assoc-iation, 1997) give evidence of too much structure, for example, obsessive compulsive disorder, narcissistic disorder, or too little structure, for example, histrionic personality disorder, borderline disorder. The therapeutic need is the containment of both the despair and the aggression. Transactional analysis teaches that with too much or too little structure a false self is created, in the form of belief or fantasy, supported by associated emotion, somatic experience, and behaviour, to protect ourselves from our own experience of pain or fear, to extreme with a lack of sense of self. The ISA Editorial Team acknowledges this, stating that "The real self develops early in childhood and is . . . innocent in the sense that it is the impact of the environment upon the developing child which promotes a False Self" (1990, p. 73).

Winnicott believes that without sufficient environmental support the capacity to be alone with oneself and to form one's own sense of self cannot develop. Without ownership and coherence of our own feelings, impulses, and behaviours, we cannot behave in a responsible way towards others.

> It is only when alone (that is to say, alone in the presence of someone) that the infant can discover his personal life . . . In this setting, the impulse will feel real and be truly a personal experience. [Winnicott, 1969, p. 34]

Stevens also acknowledges the influence of early environment and, regarding shadow states,

> How the parents deal with anger when it arises can have profound consequences for the personality development of the child. Provided they can tolerate the expression of appropriate aggression, it tends to become integrated as an acceptable part of the child's conscious personality and his security in relationships. [1982, p. 133]

When parents cannot tolerate/contain the child's emotional expressions, then the child's aggressive energy must go somewhere. I believe that this is also true of trainees whose trainers are unable to offer containment. Stevens posits that this energy "can be turned inward as self-loathing . . . It can be displaced onto a scape-goat . . . It can be transformed into worship of the oppressor . . . It can be eroticised" (ibid., p. 134). He tells how these dynamics are played out in adult life: eroticized power may present itself as in rape of other (scapegoat), or sadistic practices where the weaker self is projected (self-loathing), or masochistic practices (where the tyrant/oppressor is worshipped).

Winnicott considers containment, stating that

> The environment is essential, and gradually becomes less essential. ... The environment, when good enough, facilitates the maturational process ...
>
> a) Good enough environmental provision really does tend to prevent psychotic or schizophrenic disorder; but b) with all the good care in the world the individual child is liable to the disturbances associated with conflict arising out of instinctual life. [1969, p. 223]

Winnicott acknowledges that tensions cannot be eradicated, but can be contained by healthy environmental circumstances. Both structure and freedom have their negative extremes, while, when in good balance, they are in creative tension but not in conflict.

Lack of containment of the discomfort of inner tension leads to secondary gestalt formation (Perls, Hefferline, & Goodman, 1951) as a survival mechanism. It is the potential to choose to dissolve these secondary *gestalten* (those to which Anna Freud [1936] refers as ego-defence mechanisms, Perls and colleagues [1951] define as blocks to contact, and Berne [1964] terms script display) that underpins integrative psychotherapy. Erskine (1991) refers to this dissolving as assimilation and harmonization of the contents of the ego states. For this to occur, he advocates a therapeutic stance in the form of enquiry, attunement, and involvement. He portrays containment as follows:

> Contact within psychotherapy is like the substructure of a building; it cannot be seen, but undergirds and supports all that is above ground. It is contact that provides the safety to drop defences, to again feel, and to remember. [*ibid.*, p. 4]

Lack of containment is epitomized as: "Often the most profound aspect of all abuse is that the child is abandoned and left alone at times of great suffering and despair" (ISA Editorial Team, 1990, p. 74).

The optimum childhood (and psychotherapy training environment) is one where emotions are psychologically contained. Bettelheim (1992) worked with child prisoners of war, acknowledging that children are remarkably resilient to trauma as long as one other person is alongside. Erskine (1996), working in war zones, tells how some children grow up reasonably sound emotionally and others experience psychosis, the difference being that the child who grows up relatively healthy has a mother who acknowledges the child's experiences. As human beings we need witness to our own phenomenology: "A child is born . . . with individual perceptions, needs and wishes which she trusts will be acknowledged and respected" (ISA Editorial Team, 1990, p. 73).

Schmukler (1998) refers to the need for containment as *primary* in the early years and *sustaining* in adulthood. The quality of need, the phenomenological experience, changes, though the experience of need for containment, in the form of recognition, remains throughout life.

Erskine (2003) describes contact as the meeting of two individuals who are present together with the totality of their phenomenological experience. In adulthood this is a relationship of equals. In childhood, when we have a meeting of adult and infant phenomenology, the adult contains the childhood experience. He notes that, when childhood experience is transferred symbolically into therapeutic relationships, containment by the therapist becomes necessary, until the relationship reaches a stage where full and vibrant contact becomes possible. Again, this transferential dynamic is evidenced in training groups and here the initial responsibility for containing falls upon the trainer.

Bowlby is one of the most influential pioneers of change in our society in relation to childhood need. His work on attachment theory pioneered the Platt Report to the Government in 1959, which opened all hospital children's wards to twenty-four hour visiting rights by parents (Bowlby & Robertson, 1952). Bowlby shows specific attachment patterns emerging when children are deprived of maternal presence, a secure base: one pattern indicates resistance, anger, and withdrawal, which may show itself either in self-harm (for example, head-banging), or as aggression towards mother.

Holmes tells how "the essence of the secure base is that it provides a springboard for curiosity and exploration" (1993, p. 70).

It becomes the emotional container for the child's healthy development. Bowlby indicated that teenagers with a childhood loss of attachment figure often developed psychopathic traits of social maladjustment and criminal tendencies. Heard and Lake (1986) believe that the need for a secure base is apparent in adulthood, in the form of "companionable interaction" and that without this we resort to defences such as the splitting off of anger, or compulsive sexualization of relationships. Lake (1987) sees the psychotherapy training group as a culture for attachment patterns, in that the individual need to belong becomes transferred, often acted out, and always in need of containment in the group process.

While Stevens recognizes the enormous prognostic significance of Bowlby's work, he criticizes Bowlby for paying insufficient attention to the quality of the mother–child bond, pointing out the dual nature of mother, acknowledging that "she who caresses also slaps, she who gives also withholds, she who grants life may also take it away" (Stevens, 1982, p. 90).

What Stevens sees as important for healthy development is not the actual behaviour of the mother, but the archetypal experiences actualized by her in the child; that is, how the child perceives the mother's actions. I support this; my own mother took me, aged three, to hospital where I was left, with only weekly visiting, for thirteen weeks. She did so out of love and for my survival. However, at three years old, this was not my perception.

Humanistic philosophy supporting integrative psychotherapy practice honours the human need to be in relationship. Rogers suggests that "given a suitable psychological climate, humankind is trustworthy, creative, self-motivated, powerful and constructive— capable of releasing undreamed of potentialities" (1980, p. 20).

In integrative psychotherapy, this "suitable climate" is the containment offered by the therapist, adopting an I–thou attitude with spontaneity, the element of surprise, the deviation from the known, and the quality of existence that makes the I–thou relationship possible. In the I–Thou moment, particular attention has been given to "the lived immediacy of the therapeutic encounter" (Spinelli, 1997, p. 2).

This I–Thou experience to which Spinelli refers is something to work towards, having first experienced a quality of relationship that is understood as transferential. It is in this transferential relationship where most misperceptions occur and where most acting out behaviours, in the form of aggression towards self and other, take place. Developmental deficits in the form of uncontained destructive impulses are re-enacted in the trainings. Ruptures may be co-created (Schmukler, 1998) in order to allow this process to emerge and the total transferential situation to be explored.

It is important here to honour Winnicott's (1965) concept of "good enough" mothering. Whether we strive for containment as parent or as trainer, the paradox of the ideal is that this creates destruction, the emergence of shadow. "The opposite of what one wants to attain is repeatedly being constellated" (Guggenbuhl-Craig, 1971, p. 26).

A good trainer will sufficiently support his or her trainees to make possible the healthy expression of what is not pleasing to the trainee. In a good trainer–trainee relationship, both positive and negative emotions are shareable. We have to disappoint our trainees in order for them to be able to work through their transferential aggressions. Containment here has been viewed primarily from the perspective of the stance of the trainer (maternal transferential object). What is also of relevance is the importance of structure as sameness of training frame: that is, time, place, duration, course requirements, as well as consistency of approach of the trainer and boundary formation. This enables childhood experience to be worked through in the transference in the training setting.

For the more senior psychotherapy trainee, as transferential processes become worked with, containment may become in part a self-reliance emerging from increased theoretical understanding and phenomenological awareness and tolerance of tensions. I believe, however, that we never fully graduate from our transferential patterns and they so easily periodically seek re-expression at times of our vulnerability, although progressively with less intensity and duration, perhaps.

Transferential process

Whichever orientation of psychotherapy we adopt, a transferential process is evident. We may choose to ignore it, work with it, or encourage it, but it cannot be absent (Clarkson, 1995). Integrative psychotherapy theory recognizes that the transference is the pivotal point for early work, deserving attention here, because shadow experience is, for the most part, unconscious, related to power imbalance, and it is transferential phenomena that are triggered by the felt sense of inequality and power differences between trainer and trainee and among fellow students.

Most literature depicting transferential understanding is in relation to therapist and client. Psychotherapy training involves experiential practice, with trainees becoming therapist and client for each other. In the therapist–client dynamic, the purpose in relationship is the growth of the client, with the therapist's growth as secondary, whereas in the training milieu a further dynamic is added because the purpose of this experience is for the learning of the "therapist", and secondarily for the "client". I think this added dynamic makes transferential understanding more complex, in that roles between trainees are interchangeable, making the holding of boundaries more difficult: that is, especially around confidentiality, between small and large group process, and between training time and social time with the same people.

Because of its complicated nature, literature pertaining to transference brings probably the most diversity of all literature to the psychotherapy profession. I share initially my own understanding gained from analytic, humanistic, behavioural, and integrative reading.

Throughout life, we consciously and unconsciously store in our memory some aspect of other individuals' appearance, approach, and character. All memories are linked by the process of associations (Lee & Herbert, 1951), which obviates itself if we spend a few minutes reflecting and noticing one memory leading to another. Sometimes, our thoughts just drift, and sometimes we make a conscious effort to remember; when recounting a story, we try to remember details that are not always readily to hand. Associations with people of our past are relatively permanent unless we make a conscious effort to override them. Hence, every time we meet a new person, we can associate some aspects of that person's personality with those of someone we have met before; we transfer associations from past relationships to present relationships, through likenesses.

We deal similarly with feelings, almost always unconsciously. Some of these associated feelings never come to consciousness;

some we are only mildly aware of, but they are always around. If we examine our feelings attached to each new individual, we can come to see these transferential experiences happening. We can then use the situations in which we find ourselves advantageously, rather than to our detriment.

Psychoanalysts view transference as a projection of our past experience on to present situations and, hence, it becomes a block to contact in gestalt terms. In this sense it is an illusion, a re-enacting of old strategies and perceptions in a current situation, in which such strategies and perceptions are out of date and defensive. The person experiencing the transference may see the other as someone from their past, (parent/teacher), when they were unable to address the original dynamics because of the power imbalance. The more powerful the transferential process, the further back it is likely to originate.

The transference aspect of relationships can present itself in all walks of life. Guggenbuhl-Craig suggests,

> As is commonly known, a patient may see in the analyst a father or brother, a lover, son or daughter, and so on. . . . Psychic structures of one's own may also be transferred onto one's partner; qualities are seen in the other which are actually problematical in oneself. [Guggenbuhl-Craig, 1971, p. 37]

I think it is the power imbalances within training relationships that are the associated situational likenesses which induce repetition of the original family situation. The environmental nature of the helper–helped and teacher–taught dynamics produces transferential situations. However, the nature and intensity of the transferential pattern is coloured by the personality of the object of the transference.

Storr (1997), referring to Saki and Kipling, gives excellent examples of the shadow side of human nature being carried transferentially. Saki's description of a schoolboy being caned and Kipling's "Stalky" stories are both seen as evidence of these authors carrying with them into adult life a sadistic streak that is probably derived from a wish for revenge on those who had tormented them in childhood. Narrative psychotherapists see fiction as metaphorically providing an acceptable outlet for the discharge of violent feelings. While Saki and Kipling had the advantage of using fantasy in story-telling to discharge feelings, it is usually the case for psychotherapy trainees that the colleague or trainer becomes the transferential object. It is a common realization, as a trainee, to suddenly become aware that one is not "seeing" the person one is interacting with, but is behaving as if one is with an older life figure, a teacher, parent, child, or lover. Glover describes this process as follows:

> An adequate conception of transference must reflect the totality of the individual's development. He displaces onto the analyst, not merely affects, but all he has ever learned or forgotten throughout his mental development. [1937, p. 125]

Waelder supports this view, stating that

> Transference may be said to be an attempt of the patient to revive and re-enact, in the analytic situation and in relation to the analyst, situations and fantasies of his childhood. Hence, transference is a regressive process . . . transference develops in consequence of the analytic situation and the analytic technique. [1956, p. 367]

Klein (1932), as a consequence of her work with children and adults, came to view all later behaviour as being very largely a repetition of relationships that she considered to be obtained in the primary year. In this understanding, no adult relationship is free of some degree of transferential phenomena.

While Greenson posits the following,

> Transference is the experiencing of feelings, drives, attitudes, fantasies and defences towards a person in the present which are inappropriate to that person, and are a repetition, a displacement of reactions originating in regard to significant persons of early child-hood. I.e. for a reaction to be transference it must have two charac-teristics
>
> 1)   It must be a repetition of the past, and
> 2)   It must be inappropriate to the present.
> [1965, p. 155]

in gestalt terms, everything is seen to be co-created, and so there must always be some truth in the illusory transferential situation. What is it in the present experience that is inviting the projection of past phenomena? Why a projection now? Why here? Why on to this person in the group and not another? A trainee who has been profoundly shamed in childhood, and who is in fear of actually having available to them in the training situation that which has been denied over the years, might transfer their rage at earlier needs being unmet on to the person who meets them now. I have seen this rage emerge as gossip to fellow professionals about perceived negative qualities of a trainer, to the point of being slanderous of someone's character and professional reputation. And, of course, we must ask, what truth is there, if any, in this trainee's experience that has been escalated out of all proportion? Why this trainer?

Whether we consider transference to be a process of ridding oneself of some old history, or a process of becoming aware of our own needs, and/or a dynamic which is co-created by two personalities, the risk of emotional harm is high, and in training situations, where painful conflict arises, the very fact that we can understand the underlying dynamics enhances compassion, reducing the risk of retraumatizing others. When we consider the whole range of emotions potentially involved in transferential phenomena, shadow emotions are highly likely to emerge, because they are the very ones that were originally denied acknowledgement and lay buried in the unconscious realm. It is human nature to seek completion and closure, when the "suitable psychological climate" (Rogers, 1980, p. 20) is offered.

Winnicott addressed the polarized emotions experienced between professional and client (trainee):

> However much he loves his patients, he cannot avoid hating them and fearing them, and the better he knows this, the less will hate and fear be the motives determining what he does to his patients. [1947, p. 195]

While a trainee may be the object of a trainer's hate, so may we, as trainers, become hated by our students. Our own hate may well need to be "kept in storage" (ibid., p. 196) until the appropriate stage in a trainee's development for this to be worked through. Trainers need to have the inner resources to tolerate such crude and primitive feelings directed towards themselves from trainees.

As I have witnessed, it is too easy for the trainer who becomes the object of an idealized transference to deny the polarity and then become resentful, narcissistically, of the trainee, who, in working through his idealization, discovers repulsion in himself towards his trainer. The trainer carrying unacknowledged hate may penalize the trainee, perhaps in the processes of assessment by unconsciously under-marking or leaving this trainee's essay until last to mark, by withholding support, by lack of invitation into experiencing, or by creating a hierarchy of favourite students and undermining this trainee. This whole phenomena is likely to be exaggerated by the sibling rivalry present in any group process. Paradoxically, treating a trainee with favouritism is also potentially a way of expressing unresolved hate, in that this is distancing him/her from peers and this distancing becomes isolating. All of these things can happen at an unconscious level. Training institutes ensure that trainees have sound clinical supervision for their work and this process is monitored. Who monitors the supervision process for the trainers?

Johnson (1991) told how the schizoid child has been hated by parents. This dynamic invites repetition transferentially in the trainer–trainee relationship. Through the process of projective identification, discussed later, the trainee induces boredom in the trainer, whereby the unaware trainer may feel resentment and hatred at "having to" put in the extra effort and energy to maintain even a minimal level of interest in this trainee's learning, or he/she may totally withdraw energy.

This transferential situation invites, symbolically, the hate that Winnicott says all mothers carry for their children. Winnicott (1947, p. 201) believes that hate is necessary, saying that a child cannot tolerate the "full extent of his own hate in a sentimental environment" and "he needs hate to hate". While I am aware that a trainer is not a trainee's therapist, and neither are trainees children, nevertheless, the power imbalance induces a powerful transference and Winnicott is honouring that hate is experienced countertransferentially. Any learning situation will invite transference, but even more so in psychotherapy training, given that this work is not so much about what we know but about who we are.

For my own hate, in choosing this theme for my writing, am I transferentially seeking to have my need for wholeness met, rather than having to live my life in the manner to which my Christian mother would have wished? Am I wanting permission and validation for my own aggression, which I know so well now phe-nomenologically, and thus the research process becomes a transfer-ential object for me, in that it allows me to explore? If I am seeking the healing of old wounds, then it is important that I acknowledge this, so as not to become too biased in my viewpoint. How much is my interest in this theme an expression from my own shadow?

Given the breadth of transferences lying unacknowledged and unexplored, the therapy training environment is actually a danger zone in that it threatens the reopening and reinflicting of old wounds, even if the intention is that these wounds be repaired and healed. Containment, which contributes to the "safe emergency" (Perls, Hefferline, & Goodman, 1951) of the therapeutic environ-ment, is paramount to the exploration of transferential material.

It is when "Such caring on the part of the therapist is non-possessive. The therapist prizes the client in a total rather than a conditional way" (Rogers, 1980, p. 116) that working with transfer-ential phenomena is possible. In prizing our trainees in a "total rather than a conditional way", we make room for hate and destructive impulses to be explored.

Integrative psychotherapy welcomes transferential issues, not, as in analysis, by the promotion of therapeutic abstinence, in which a blank screen is provided with the intention of encouraging projec-tions, but in respecting transference as a functional response. "We gain a functional view of transference if we grasp it as communica-tion and search" (Wilkinson, 1998, p. 2).

The integrative school posits that, while the underlying inten-tion of transference is to complete unfinished psychological devel-opment symbolically, the way in which it presents itself may be positive or negative. It is the acted out negative transferential feel-ings that can become dangerous. Anna Freud (1936) explains that "acting out" occurs when the transference in the therapeutic frame-work is intensified and spills over into the client's daily life. In rela-tion to training, a fellow student may be on the receiving end of a trainee's feelings towards the trainer or other group members, or, for example, anger towards a trainer may be taken home and expressed to a partner. A trainee in erotic transference with a trainer may attempt to seduce several members of the group. In "acting out", the transferential fantasy becomes made real, often in the everyday world, outside the training frame.

A transference of defence (Whittaker, 1985) occurs when some-one (a trainee) uses aggression and destructive impulses towards another in order to protect themselves from the feared danger linked with love and affection. What we most wish for is often what we most fear and, paradoxically, defend against.

Integrative psychotherapy posits that when unmet needs lie in our psyche from childhood, it is human nature to seek or create a sim-ilar situation to the original in order for the process to be completed accurately this time around. This is often referred to as incomplete *gestalten* or unfinished business. But by the same token, we cannot have what we need without becoming truly aware of what we have missed, and so having and grieving, initially, go hand in hand: the uncomfortable position of fearing what we most want. Erskine (1991) terms this process the juxtaposition. One aspect of such an ambiva-lent process is the emergence of a projective identification dynamic (Cashdan, 1988), which is part of the total transference situation in that it, too, is unconscious and of earlier times in its origin.

Cashdan (1988) describes projective identification as a three-stage process; a *projective fantasy* emerges, with a wish to rid oneself of part of the self that is perceived as bad or threatening to destroy the self from within; this becomes projected on to another. Klein (1989) believes powerful and destructive impulses are projected because the anxiety of the internal splitting process is intolerable to the projector. The felt sense of "It's not all right to be in bits" results in the bad feelings becoming projected.

> The anxiety invoked in the child by his destructive instinctual impulses makes itself felt in the ego, I think, in two directions. In the first place it implies the annihilation of his own body by his destructive impulses, which is a fear of an internal instinctual danger; but in the second place it focuses his fears on his *external* object, against whom his sadistic feelings are directed, as a source of danger. [*ibid.*, p. 127]

Cashdan shows how, continued into adulthood, the projector pressures the recipient to behave in such a way as to conform to the projective fantasy, inducing the recipient to experience the feelings associated with the fantasy, i.e., identification. The recipient then behaves in the induced way, tolerates the feeling, and may even integrate this into his/her own personality structure. The hope is that the relationship will take a new form; the projector's intention is to enhance the relationship. However, this intention is often also part of the fantasy, and so rarely comes true because the recipient feels used and manipulated. When this comes into awareness, the response is usually anger or withdrawal and confirms the projector's belief that he is bad in some way. So, Cashdan believes, although projective identification is a serious attempt to heal the projector's own pathology, because the process is a denial of the here-and-now relationship (it is the archaic field projected into the here-and-now), it is seldom successful.

The integrative view of transference, which Erskine (1991) supports, depicts how, in cases where this process is successful, though often only temporarily, the recipient is probably responding to the meta-communication, the "or else" threatened consequence of not allowing oneself to be manipulated. The mother of the recipient may have used projective identification to pressure the infant to comply with her own pathology, such as messages along the lines of "If you don't go along with me, you'll not be welcome". And so the repeated infancy pattern is there for the recipient as well as the projector. At some level, we choose partners (colleagues in training groups) whose pathology allows us to replay our own patterns in the hope of things changing this time around. In the most horrific of human experience, it is the hope of something different that keeps us going.

In a group situation, a trainee was constantly interrupting others. This was pointed out to him and he apologized, but continued to interrupt. Eventually, this continued behaviour provoked real attack from other group members and, in the face of this persecutory behaviour, the facilitator intervened and invited people to express their anger in a contact-orientated manner. When the group portrayed anger at a more acceptable level than his own internalized anger, the individual was able to own his projection. In projective identification terms, the group member found it difficult to cope with his own internal critical parent and, so as to no longer own this part of himself, he projected it on to the group and unconsciously behaved in such a way as to induce them to treat him as he had already been treated as a child, and in such a way as he had also treated others in the past and no longer wished so to do. In owning his own shadow, he could make a considered choice to allow others to have space in the group and claim his own space in a contact-orientated, non-harmful way.

The containment offered here by the facilitator was that of actually empathically feeling the feelings with all group members, being able to tolerate the anxiety of the situation, and bringing the whole process out of the unconscious realm so that it can be experienced in a new and safer way.

Table 1 describes four modes of projective identification, and the manipulative stances described therein come from shadow in personality: from that which is disowned. The fate of the projective

Table 1.   Four modes of projective identification (adapted and expanded from Cashdan, 1988, p. 77).

Projective identification	Relational stance (How the projector believes he must be for the relationship to work)	Projective fantasy (Meta-communication)	What is induced in the recipient
Dependency	Helplessness	"I can't survive"	Caretaking, omnipotence: "I must advise, support, direct you"
Power	Control Lecture, criticize, "If I'm not in control, I'll be abandoned"	"You can't survive" "I can destroy you by creating a sense of abandonment", "I'll leave if you challenge me"	Incompetence, weakness "I mustn't challenge you"
Sex	Eroticism Belief that relationships are maintained through sexuality	"I'll make you sexually whole"	Arousal. "I must be aroused, responsive, so that you will feel OK and not leave"
Ingratiation More than adaptation	Self-sacrifice Historical message of "I'm loved for what I can do"	"You owe me" "You must tell me I'm useful"	Appreciation "I must appreciate you or else . . .?"

identification lies in the recipient. If the recipient offers resistance, then the projector may feel anxiety, despair, and rage. Cashdan also suggests that the only appropriate response to this dynamic is to refuse it, and again, containment and timing of this intervention in any training environment is crucial. In my experience, the process undoubtedly escalates initially when challenged, and the rage, despair, cries of "Look what you're doing to me" to the trainer may arise. This is intensification of the attempt to manipulate or blame. The trainer may become a *displaced target* for the previous recipient. It is Cashdan's view that when one projective identification is challenged, a secondary projective identification of a different nature may emerge, and at this stage, when challenged, leave-taking is often threatened. However, when sound affectional bonds within the group have been established, leave-taking is not easy. It seems, then, that the quality of relationship to and with the group can be containing in itself.

Whereas in individual therapy there is access to one potential transference figure, in training groups transferential opportunities are immense. The following equation indicates the enormity of this: the number of members in a group squared by itself, minus the number of members and then divided by two, gives the possible transferential relationships. For example, with seven group members and a facilitator,

$8 \times 8 = 64$, $- 8 = 56$, divided by 2, $= 28$ potential transferences.

And some training groups have twenty members. One wonders how anything can ever be communicated from a conscious, choice-orientated place.

Although, as the literature informs us, people in more powerful positions experience a countertransference response in relation to transferential positions in which others see them, I have witnessed senior people in training institutes allowing a transference to emerge on to a junior colleague or trainee. This is more likely to happen when the senior person has not yet fully explored his/her own process with his/her own therapist. Guggenbuhl-Craig (1971) tells how we cannot separate the destructive impulse of therapist and client, and I believe that this is true also of trainer and trainee. He states, "As we have seen, the shadows of therapist and patient affect one another and are often linked in a close relationship" (p. 34).

As I grow older and become aware of the different phenomeno-logical experiences at different life stages, I realize that we can never fully graduate from the need for some means of exploration of our own material in relationships. Our own phenomenology is ever changing and ever needs exploration. Trainers need to dip in and out of therapy themselves, as new life circumstances and training needs arise and prescribe this.

Relational theory shows how people with differing personality traits invite differing transferential responses. Greenberg (1998) believes that someone with borderline traits will express aggression using physical expression to hurt others or themselves, whereas someone with narcissistic traits will attempt annihilation of another, cognitively accepting a defensive position of superiority, using belit-tling and shaming to express their aggression. Johnson (1994) writes of this in *Character Styles*, and, to offer further reading in more depth, Masterson (1988) writes on personality structure in *The Search for the Real Self*. Considering the myriad of intricacies in transferen-tial phenomena and the diversity of personalities in a training group, it is quite understandable that psychotherapy training groups are rife with thoughts, feelings, and potential behaviours of destruction and violence.

Again I am aware that I allocate responsibility for containment primarily to the transferential object, the person perceived to be in the more powerful position. What then of containment, as the trans-ferences become worked through? Do they ever become fully worked through? Is it ever ethical for a trainer to embark on an inti-mate relationship with a previous trainee? And when an ethical guideline is suggested, are there circumstances where this guideline might be inappropriate? No Code of Ethics can fully cover every situation, and each of us must struggle, at some time in our profes-sional career, with the tension between what is ethically advised and what our own integrity might tell us. We have even more reason here for trainers to remain open to the prospect of them-selves being in therapy.

Schizoid, borderline, and narcissistic process

In my enquiries with senior trainers, the theme of the personality traits of schizoid, borderline, and narcissistic process was repeatedly present. Aspects of these traits were mentioned in the focus group study and narcissism also appeared in literature pertaining to shadow. This level of significance marries well with my awareness from the field of these early dynamics showing themselves strikingly in training situations. It is these three developmental processes that provide the greatest understanding of the phenomenological experience of individuation in relationships and the development of self. This warrants in-depth consideration.

I shall consider the aetiology of these traits, how they become evident in training situations, and, I hope, what is needed to repair early life deficits, if indeed they are reparable? Can we really begin to change our personality, or is the goal of therapeutic work the learning to tolerate and live alongside our previous life experience in a healthier way?

This discussion is based on Greenberg (1998), which has provided insight into my own work with trainees and trainers carrying these personality styles at both a natural developmental level and when patterns have been so entrenched that they have hindered an individual's ability to relate: that is, when traits have become a personality disorder. In a letter to Martha Bernays (1885), Freud stated that his own ambition in life was to have Martha as his wife and to be able to work (e.g., "Couldn't I for once have you and work at the same time?"). Freud also referred to "Eros and Ananke" (Love and Necessity) as the foundations of society. In *Civilisation and Its Discontents* he wrote: "The communal life of human beings had, therefore, a two-fold foundation: the compulsion to work, which was created by external necessity, and the power of love . . ." (Freud, 1930a).

Because, as gestalt field theory shows, it is nature's way that what has been interrupted in early life presses for closure until needs have been met, then transferential phases *will* present themselves, chronologically, as schizoid, borderline, or narcissistic phenomena, depending both upon at which life stage needs were not met and, Stern (1985) posits, on the personality of the more powerful individual engaged in the relationship (trainer).

Schizoid process

Greenberg (1998) tells how the child with a schizoid process may have had inconsistent experience from parents, in that the parents *seem* interested and attentive, but at an unconscious level there is a reaction of disgust, especially to bodily functions. Consciously, the parents may not be aware of their reaction to the child; hence, shadow remains unaddressed.

Johnson (1994) refers to the schizoid child as the "hated" child, saying that the child is not sexed because he/she is not given an identity; the relational stance between mother and child is that of I–it (see Buber, 1923). Unconsciously cold and harsh, the rejecting parents, full of hate, resented the child's existence, so the child takes a life stance of "I don't have the right to exist". What the parents want from their child is an ideal reflection of their idealized selves, repelling live reflections of animal nature, excretion, or vomiting. Hence, a nappy might be changed with the mother, out of awareness, screwing up her face. The child, in the gaze at mother, then does not get the smiling, loving attunement he needs, but rather he sees and feels a sense of disgust about himself. The child gets to hold the parent's disgust. The spontaneous life of the baby *will* disappoint the parents, and so, unconsciously, the baby is emotionally abandoned.

Winnicott's (1969) requisite of maternal empathic ability allows the child to move into symbiosis, separation, and individuation. With this understanding, when schizoid parents, without empathic ability, turn away from the child internally, the symbiosis never occurs and the child feels the internal turning away and turns away from himself. The early need to merge is not met. This delayed process in the child's emotional development enhances symbiosis being displaced on to the environment and emotional withdrawal from others. This is not a proactive stance, and assumptions formed on this experience are of "I'm different, I'm wrong", and inner distress becomes externalized by the individual behaving differently. The strongest emotion is of intense fear: "If I am alive I will be hated. I must never be spontaneous or joyful". In infancy, the baby's experience of intense fear and rage are untenable and the parental response is to emotionally persecute, and perhaps annihilate, even more.

DSM-IV (1997) describes schizoid process in adults as follows:

A pervasive pattern of detachment from social relationships and a restricted range of expression of emotions in interpersonal settings,

beginning by early adulthood and present in a variety of contexts
as indicated by four or more of the following:

1) neither desires nor enjoys close relationships, including being
    part of a family

2) almost always chooses solitary activities

3) has little, if any, interest in having sexual experiences with
    another person

4) takes pleasure in few, if any, activities

5) lacks close friends or confidants other than first degree relatives

6) appears indifferent to the praise and criticism of others

7) shows emotional coldness, detachment, or flattened affectivity.
    [American Psychiatric Association, 301.22, 641]

I have experienced how, transferentially, the rage of the schizoid
person terrifies people, and in training groups others start to tiptoe.
The individual can only retroflect, and so, paradoxically, the organ-
ism stops living in order to say alive! The safe haven of withdrawal
becomes moved into spiritual endeavours, perhaps with an
unusual level of engagement with psychotherapy theory, as the
denial of the reality of the painful experience. The unfulfilled wish
for intimacy (reunion with parents) is automatically refused in the
training group with other group members, because the merger in
the original unhealthy symbiosis says "I hate you".

Greenberg believes that in schizoid people (trainees and trainers) we see very little affectively; we get frozen, dulling, non-spon-
taneous, machine-like learning. The individual seems detached,
flat, emotionally impassive, expressing an intrinsic lack of feeling,
interpersonal indifference (masked as profound understanding).
He/she carries a weak response to emotional gestures, offers a
weak account of sexual or emotional needs, and seems unable to
express any kind of depth of pleasure. I have noticed at UKCP Con-
ferences how people with this personality type often find themselves drawn to psychoanalytic work, which supports therapeutic
abstinence. Such abstinence comes naturally, though defensively, to
someone with a schizoid personality.

Hyper-rationality is a good defensive structure. Cognitive
processes are held in check and are used in a discriminating way to

rationalize and support the defence and, so often, a schizoid trainer might use interpretation to offer feedback to a trainee's reaction to themselves, rather than openly and holistically engaging in an alive relational stance.

When affective bonding has not occurred, people may not be sure of which feeling is their own; powers of affective discrimination are not there. In schizoid experience, then, people come too close too carelessly, too intrusively. Archetypally, the dilemma is to choose between being your slave or being your master and sado-masochism allows experimentation with the slave–master relationship.

Phenomenologically, the experience is as self in exile. The schizoid person, Greenberg notes, will not fight back—he/she does not have the words to do so in a fearful place—and the experience of shame is intense, and so the stance in confrontation is often to walk out of the group, or to remain there and withdraw internally. Often, there has been a poor social network. Stern (1985) would suspect large gaps in self-history, self-activity, self-coherence, and self-agency, resulting in the schizoid person inducing persecution in the countertransference. The attack upon the schizoid trainee, or by the schizoid trainee, may be overt and cruel or may appear in the form of avoidance and neglect. As always, when we experience fear and real terror, then aggression and rage are also in the field and can easily manifest passively. Group process becomes a terrifying arena and people can be induced to leave, or a sense of psychotic reality may emerge.

Intellectualization is a common defence in groups when members have this personality trait. The unmet need is displaced on to understanding, and to wish to make sense of one's experience is the only means of containment available to someone who has not been shown how to relate to others phenomenologically. Because, in earlier years, this person has had to work out for themselves how to be in the world and with others, then an acute sense of unconscious, tacit understanding may be available to them. They have had to learn to watch, to observe others from a distance, to determine what and who is safe in this world, and they can often intuitively attune to unconscious collective group dynamics very easily. So, making sense of group process comes much more naturally than being able to sit alongside another group member and be engaged through openness to contact in a training group.

I notice how difficult it is for me to emotionally disengage from my previous relational experience of people with this process, to remain primarily with a theoretical understanding. Such is the power of their dynamics and their relevance to unconscious process and, hence, shadow, to someone who is able to attune. For myself, as I write, containment comes at a feeling level. And this, too, is what happens in training groups; the schizoid person, through projection and perhaps a passive–aggressive component, induces others to feel for them what is intolerable to themselves.

Borderline process

Johnson (1994) refers to the borderline child as the "used" child. Greenberg (1998) suggests that the frequent scenario is that father may be absent, engaged in travel/night work, or the family home is in the suburbs, away from everyone they know. The child then becomes his/her mother's support, companion, adult friend, and relevant issues here are around separation. The deal from the mother to child is "You won't separate, you have to take care of your mother". The pay-off is that the child gets attention, or he/she does not get punished. Separation from mother means that some-one does die physically (or emotionally) and the child grows up experiencing fear, because separation is too deadly.

Mahler, Pine and Bergman (1975) portray the issues needing to be developed at this rapprochement phase as:

1. Limitation: the terrible twos! Irrespective of what parents do, the world brings frustrations, with confusion between what we want and what we need. Developmentally, here a child needs firmness, clarity of boundaries, and also space.
2. Idealization occurs as we come to terms with our lack of omnipotence and emerge with a sense of competency. The child needs to believe in an all-understanding, benign parent. The child needs connectedness and also experience that connection lessens and the parent does not disappear.
3. Splitting is occurring developmentally here between concep-tions of parent as all good or all bad. It is all around in our culture: for example, fairy stories of wicked stepmothers *vs.* fairy godmothers, television series with heroes *vs.* villains, and these stories act as containment for the child.

At two years of age, the child's mind is not fully developed. He cannot employ verbal processes to self-soothe when he feels anxiety or pain. He does not understand that while he may feel uncomfortable with mum right now, in a little while this feeling will change. When splitting occurs, the child's experience is all or nothing. When a young child's feelings are not contained by a parent he can only *do* something (act out) and then, later, containment comes with the development of language. Without containment at this stage, the child is highly mobilized, does not sit still (or does not move). There is insufficient contact for healthy introjections (safe feelings) to take place. This predisposes poor tolerance to feelings because anxiety levels are too high: "I'm anxious and I'm all right" is not what the borderline child experiences. There is great emotional instability and incongruence, with sensations excessively exaggerated and polarized. The child very quickly goes from excitement to apathy, to anger, to euphoria, when boundaries are not provided.

The older child with adequate containment can respond to language—"Come here and Mummy will kiss it better"—and by this time the child can soothe for himself. However, borderline children, (and trainees) cannot do this soothing for themselves. They may say "Don't say that", because they cannot utilize verbal support. Listening is selective, (splitting) and so people hear what confirms their reality, often only negative feedback. Greenberg considers how empathy in adulthood can trigger regression because borderline people fear it might be a manipulation, given that any attention from mother was at a cost of befriending.

Kernberg (1984) states that borderline adults, with processes ranging from mild features to a rigid pathological structure, exhibit the following:

1. A weak sense of self ("I don't know who I am"; "There's nothing there" messages to others).
2. Primitive defence mechanisms—using behaviour to self-soothe.
3. Splitting—seeing life and other people as all good or all bad.
4. Denial—avoidance of feelings.
5. Regression to primary process thinking—everything seems black and white.

6. Inability to tolerate anxiety (they suffer existential "There's something missing" experience).
7. Lack of separation of self-images (child–me) and object images (parent–you), resulting in lack of boundaries.
8. Lack of creative pleasure and satisfaction.
9. Lack of integration of good and bad.
10. Projective identification.

DSM-IV (1997) describes borderline process as follows:

A pervasive pattern of instability of interpersonal relationships, self-image and affects, and marked impulsivity beginning by early adulthood and present in a variety of contexts as indicated by five or more of the following:

1) frantic efforts to avoid real or imagined abandonment (not including suicidal or self-mutilating behaviour covered in criterion 5)

2) a pattern of unstable and intense interpersonal relationships characterized by alternating between extremes of idealization and devaluation

3) identity disturbance; markedly and persistently unstable self-image or sense of self

4) impulsivity in at least two areas that are potentially self-damaging (e.g. spending, sex, substance abuse, reckless driving, binge eating)

5) recurrent suicidal behaviour, gestures or threats, or self-mutilating behaviour.

Greenberg believes the phenomenological reality for borderline people comprises rage, hurt, and despair. In relationships, the person starts feeling the need for closeness, missing and thinking about someone. This brings about anxiety, with conscious memory of "The last time I felt like this", and the result, "He suffocated me" (this is what closeness feels like phenomenologically in this phase of the process). The person then engages in acting out behaviour, as the only way they knew how to manage their anxiety in the past. The aggressive attacks are directed towards other because the stance is that of reaching out. Environmental responses to this behaviour lead back into the repeat of old experiences and the person again facing the hurt, rage, and terror. Here, a defensive response of "Who needs them!" leads to the search for individuation.

As the person withdraws from relationship, aloneness brings something missing again, and anxiety, with the memory of "The last time I felt like this", and the result, "He left me". The person is alone and has only the self to attack, perhaps with alcoholism, bulimia, or physical self-harm, or putting oneself at risk in some other way. And so the process goes on, in cyclical form, of the person with borderline traits coming in and out of relationships, hurting self or other.

This behavioural stance, Greenberg continues, invites feedback from those around, reinforcing an underlying belief that the person is bad. A person who has no self worth lacks the ability to put value on human life and treat others with respect and due care. In training groups I have seen this acting out behaviour manifest itself as storming out of a room, directing fearful rage at other group members, developing an overuse of alcohol, and, because boundaries have never been learnt, to extreme, breaking boundaries with clients and colleagues. This level of rage and destruction is immediate, quickly escalating, loud, and potentially dangerous. Things can get broken, including ethical boundaries, and people can get hurt. Those with borderline process are often very honest, because their memory is insufficiently developed transferentially for them to be able to tell lies.

Masterson (1988) sees the underlying experience in need of containment as abandonment. He advocates confrontation of the person, with the incongruity between what they are and what they are presenting. Containment involves bringing the denied destructiveness of the person's behaviour to their attention, encouraging them to think about choices, exploring congruence and responsibility, and using "therapeutic astonishment" to heighten awareness of the issues.

Every training group I have known has carried some people who exhibit this personality trait. It is customarily the shadow behaviours that become acted out and the process is rife with contagion, which archetypally may arise from the relationship between the individual and the collective. I am aware that, as I write this material, an understanding of the process does not feel enough in itself to prevent the acting out evident in borderline process. Although it is very true that understanding in itself can bring compassion, and that thinking needs development here, borderline rage needs active and direct involvement from other in order for it to be contained.

Narcissistic process

Johnson (1994) refers to the narcissistic child as the "owned" child. Greenberg (1998) shows how parents would be either primarily exhibitionistic narcissists, believing that it is the child's duty to admire them, resulting in the child growing up to find narcissists in the world and admiring them in order to receive gifts/praise, or parents would be primarily toxic narcissists, whereby, however well the child does, parents are threatened and, hence, critical and nasty. Then the child feels humiliated and learns to hide, growing up with a fear of putting his or her ideas forward. Parental anger comes in the form of envy: if a compliment is given, it is accompanied by a devouring eye and a critical emotional annihilation. With a mother too busy looking in the mirror to be available for the child, the child has no experience of being met by a confident parent, who knows what that child's needs are. The narcissistic mother enters into competition with her child (as does the narcissistic trainer with the trainee), instead of understanding the child's behaviour. I have seen this dynamic occur between a psychotherapy trainer and a senior trainee working in the NHS, whose experience of mental health work surpasses that of the trainer. Again, this dynamic has occurred with a trainee who has more experience than the trainer of the education system. One aspect of containment in the training environment is the trainer's humility in acknowledging what he/she can learn from the trainee.

Mahler (1975) refers to the practising sub-phase of individuation. Early autonomy desires are checked out with mother, with "If I crawl away what happens?" The child watches the parent's movements, body experience and flickers, and internalizes the parental anxiety of a threatened parent. The script decision becomes, "The world's a dangerous place". When mother feels anxiety if the child moves, then the approval for venturing out is denied. The child feels shame; being seen means being humiliated. The "real", spontaneous self, who wants to explore, becomes hidden and a false self "What do you want from me for you to be all right?" is portrayed. Separation is dangerous, and if it is enforced, say, in hospitalization, the child's (and parents'!) panic escalates. Spontaneity then becomes retroflected with further cognitive adjustment of "I'll abdicate myself, so mum lives through me". "I'm safe if I hold on" brings excessive loyalty.

Greenberg (1998) posits three aspects to narcissistic process. The *closet narcissist* is phobic about the spotlight, as a result of shaming as a child, and so does all the work for the others (the trainee who washes up after each workshop), often refuses promotion at work, or is silent in group process. Being seen is excruciatingly painful. He/she wants to please, desperately hoping that someone will mind-read them and know what they want (they cannot say it); the closet narcissist clings to the extrovert and, at the same time, attempts unconsciously to repair an injury by destroying others (projection) to become omnipotent. The narcissistic child is the servant of the parent, perhaps by becoming the god the parents project. The grandiosity of "I'm wonderful" is defensive of "I'm worthless", and arises on denial of the child's need to be special. All of these early dynamics precipitate the onset of shadow in adulthood.

An *exhibitionistic narcissist* adopts grandiosity in defence of the closet experience. "I'm better than others" is a reaction against "I'm not as good as others". This grandiose escalation can appear to be manic, and, as a consequence of the status of grandiosity and its relational energy and perfectionism, these people seek leadership positions: for example, they become psychotherapy trainers. Equality of relationship is not part of the world of the narcissist. To be senior to others prevents against feeling lesser than others, and this person may deny their own reality or tell lies, through fear, to maintain the illusions.

Difficulties arise when the elation is challenged. It can be punctured with one word (true manic elation is not shifted dialogically), and the defence against this shaming is to become toxic. A *toxic narcissist* will annihilate another, rather than face the pain of criticism, with "I'll do to you what's been done to me" as the unconscious life script. The toxic narcissist seeks the weak link person in a group and talks about them behind their back. When somebody says something negative about another group member, the toxic narcissist joins in the chase and enlists the others. The hidden transferential message is "kill the trainer" to survive.

DSM-IV (1997) describes the narcissistic process as follows:

> A pervasive pattern of grandiosity (in fantasy or behaviour), need for admiration, and lack of empathy, beginning by early adulthood and present in a variety of contexts as indicated by five or more of the following:
>
> 1) has a grandiose sense of self-importance (e.g. exaggerates achievements and talents, expects to be recognized as superior without commensurate achievements)
>
> 2) is preoccupied with fantasies of unlimited success, power, brilliance, beauty or ideal love
>
> 3) believes that he or she is special and unique and can only be understood by, or should associate with, other special or high-status people (or institutions)
>
> 4) requires excessive admiration
>
> 5) has a sense of entitlement, i.e., unreasonable expectations of especially favourable treatment or automatic compliance with his or her expectations
>
> 6) is interpersonally exploitative, i.e., takes advantage of others to achieve his or her own ends
>
> 7) lacks empathy: is unwilling to recognize or identify with the feelings and needs of others
>
> 8) is often envious of others or believes that others are envious of him or her
>
> 9) shows arrogant, haughty behaviours or attitudes
> [*DSM* (301.81:661)]

It is interesting that *DSM-IV* shows only one aspect of the narcissistic character, and it is important to realize that the polarity of this is also true.

The message to the trainer from a narcissistic trainee is, "I admire/idolize you", or "I ridicule/persecute you". The counter-transferential response from a trainer might be either (a) to enjoy the idealization (if the trainer is also a narcissist who was not allowed in childhood to feel special); this pitfall is that the trainer reinforces the infantilization of the trainee, or (b) to persecute, as a way of dealing with the induced self-doubt, rage, and fear of the trainee's rage, envy, and narcissistically wounded response of the trainer. The educational task is to make room for others without persecuting. Trainers who cannot contain invite rage. In training groups, closet narcissists comply, while exhibitionistic narcissists render the trainer not all right, and their entitlement knows no bounds. The narcissist swings from omnipotence to impotence, or uses one to hide the other. What is needed is to achieve an internal sense of potency.

Schmukler (1998) teaches that the primary educational task for processes involving identity formation is the containment of anxiety and aggression through the meeting of attachment–individuation needs. Our society is repeatedly fragmenting: wars, recessions, strikes, unemployment. The positive side is that grandparents are increasingly around, living longer. However, experience of the effects of institutionalization, migratory effects, being displaced and moving to inner cities, high-rise flats, fewer members in the churches, all contribute to reducing containment. Because these processes are inherent in our culture, each of us knows them. Work within trainings where these processes are obviously evident triggers all our own schizoid need to feel safe, borderline need to feel loved, or narcissistic need to feel special (Greenberg, 1998). Given Greenberg's understanding, we can hope that all integrative psychotherapy trainees will experience these dynamics as they work through their own early developmental experience; trainees who fear their own success are caught up in narcissistic process, success bringing the very thing that they fear! This makes the examination process a profoundly challenging and painful experience.

I realize personally how important it is to have a sound understanding of these processes in order to feel compassion towards any acting out shadow behaviour, which I might need to challenge supportively as a trainer. And, in recognizing my own narcissism, I can feel both shame at how I may have been overly judgemental as a trainer, both with trainees and with myself, aiming for perfection as narcissistic process invites from a defended place, and celebratory of the tenacity that my narcissistic energy has given me.

Striving for perfection, which is an impossible goal, fuels a determination to keep going against all odds. I know personally how narcissism certainly brings shadow into training groups.

Group dynamics

Bly (1999) recognizes how we are always faced with shadow phenomena emerging as the result of people coming together in group formation. Psychotherapy trainings incorporate many hours of group experience; how we make conscious the unconscious dynamics in this setting is a large part of the learning process. Bly acknowledges that it is often when we move away from individual to group experience and back that shadow behaviours escalate.

Developmental theory believes the essence of humanity to be social, understanding that we are all driven by our emotional needs, and it is the meeting of these needs and the defences we erect in not having needs met that shape our essence of self in the formative years. Most models of group dynamics honour that this shape, this history, is what each person brings to group situations and is what influences our behaviour in groups, some of this by choice and some not. Foulkes and Anthony (1971), Whittaker (1985), and Yalom (1975) recognize that some of the individual defences emerging in group situations are destructive.

Integrative psychotherapy theorists believe that each trainee brings uniqueness to psychotherapy training groups and, through interactions with others, our individual ways of establishing gratifying and enduring relationships are activated. Similarly, our history of difficulties in relationships emerges, and interpersonal behaviour, which destructs and disrupts social adjustment, can be explored, ideally without the feared consequences occurring. It is widely recognized that, in this safe arena, group dynamics invite the shadow. Whittaker's (1985) "focal conflict" model acknowledges individual and group psyche, addressing both creative and destructive elements of being human. It not only recognizes shadow dynamics, but gives sound principles for containing interventions; hence, it has specific relevance to the group-work employed in psychotherapy trainings and is a useful theoretical perspective for understanding shadow phenomena.

Focal conflict theory of group-work.

I choose to explore the focal conflict group-work model of Whittaker, as opposed to other models such as those of Foulkes and Anthony (1971), Bion (1961), and Yalom (1975), because it specifically acknowledges the fear aspect of human nature, which inevitably leads to aggression (fight) or leave-taking (flight), another variation of which is to wipe out the other person. The model is clear and accessible, honouring that individuals need to approach group-work at different paces and from different starting points. It fits well, then, with psychotherapy philosophy, which honours both individual and collective phenomena and developmental need.

The focal conflict model carries major concepts, which also marry well with integrative philosophy:

- an assumption that the origins of human conflict are in childhood, arising from experience of intense impulses and desires being met by obstacles, arousing fear in some form, e.g., rejection, abandonment, annihilation. This fear initiates other feelings like anger, guilt and rage. From this process of desire *vs.* fear and rage emerges the *nuclear conflict*;
- strategies are employed in childhood to deal with these conflicts. These are *personalised solutions*;
- in adulthood, these conflict situations are repeated in modified form, as *derived conflicts*: for example, a child fearing shadows as "monsters" might become phobic in adulthood. Personalized solutions also become modified, taking a more adult appearance: for example, a child who gained his mother's attention by acting the clown may, in adulthood, be the life and soul of the party;
- in psychotherapy training groups, where emotions are encouraged and developmental theory introduced, individual derived conflicts and personalized solutions merge together, through a process of *resonance*, which is transferential;
- through this merging of association, resonance, empathic attunement, through and between individual conflicts, *themes* emerge within the group and take on a life form of their own;
- resonant themes are indicative of the *group focal conflict* with which members are working in any given moment;

- a *restrictive solution* to the conflict is adopted by the group when they choose to focus experience on resonances with individuals' underlying fears, and then defensive personalized solutions, probably portraying as shadow, become figural;
- an *enabling solution* takes the members forward. This is the free expression of energy, acknowledging both the initial unmet need and the fears of perceived consequences of expression of one's original reaction to that need not being met. This allows catharsis of the whole range of creative and destructive emotions.

In a repertoire of solutions, some may emerge as favourite defences; rationalizing one's anger or transforming it into somatic experience. Other solutions emerge in interpersonal relationships, such as choosing a partner who is aggressive as a denial of our own aggression, or defences may determine our whole life-style: for example, becoming a night-club bouncer, or long-distance lorry driver to avoid intimate situations wherein anger may emerge transferentially. It may also be the case that people come into psychotherapy training to be a carer, splitting off and avoiding their own shadow.

Containment in the training group is, in part, the responsibility of each individual in choosing to reflect on dynamics and taking ownership of his/her own behaviour. For the containment of transferential processes, I believe the trainer takes prime responsibility. Bly indicates the importance of containment.

> Human self-esteem is a delicate matter, and not to be dismissed as infantile grandiosity. Our "mirrored greatness" as Heinz Kohut calls it, needs to be carefully honoured, neither inflated nor crushed. If a man's or a woman's "mirrored greatness" is entirely dismissed, he or she will be crippled, and a candidate for all sorts of invasions by the group mind. [Bly, 1990, p. 221]

Whittaker shows how the facilitator (trainer) has the role of problem-solver, catalyst for feelings, transference vessel, explorer of the unconscious, and interpreter, with the task of fine-tuning the balance between support and challenge for trainees. Intervening too little might leave trainees struggling with conflicts too intense for a particular stage of group development. Intervening too much might leave the group insufficiently challenged, with a sense of not having done the work for themselves. Containment by the trainer requires preconditions: one, that the trainer has undergone suffi- cient personal therapy themselves to be able to tolerate feelings emerging in the group, and two, that the trainer has a sound theo- retical base by which to understand the emerging group dynamics. Whittaker (1985), while acknowledging the value of practical skills in group facilitation, insists that a group facilitator needs a sound theoretical understanding in order to seize opportunities for effec- tive facilitation and to avoid hindrances to the group process. She believes that a more elaborate theory is needed to be able to predict the probable course interventions and deal with the consequences of such interventions.

The contemporary situation of training groups (resonating with family experiences) elicits derived focal conflicts, which vary immensely in content and intensity. If there is a group focal conflict of anger towards people in authority *vs.* fear of abandonment should anger show, the group might employ an enabling solution that anger towards people in authority is understandable. For trainees for whom this is an issue, an enabling solution lends cour- age, making them feel safe enough to explore the issue important to them. A restrictive solution might be for the group to displace their anger emerging transferentially towards the trainer on to one group member, often the quietest. Trainees who show the least of themselves can, in that dynamic, invite the projections of other members and people can get hurt.

Effective facilitation will highlight not only themes being dis- cussed, but also which topics get dropped, who interacts with whom, non-verbal behaviours, where silences come, contents of speech, intonation, and pace. A theme becoming focal for the group will be important to different trainees in differing degrees. One person may be unconflicted by a theme, but can contribute empathically. Those deeply affected by a theme may gain much growth from the explo- ration of it. Others might not participate overtly in a group, but might still be deeply affected from a witness position by what is going on.

Themes may emerge in several forms; *metaphorically*, "Who's going to take care of the building (us), when we're not here in the summer?"; *intellectually*, discussion of the degree of vandalism in inner cities (destruction in this group); *using third person*, one training group experienced being strongly affected by the death of

Princess Diana (someone close to me)—this was compounded by Diana being the name of the group trainer.

When a group member deviates from a theme, then group energy becomes focused on the deviant to bring him back into the fold. Typically, a group will first attempt persuasion, "Will you share with us?", and when the required response is not forthcoming the group then attacks; "Are you feeling superior?" This never works, because it is too important for the deviant to intellectualize at that time for him to cease to do so. The group then encapsulate the deviant, excluding him altogether, so that the deviant leaves the group if the facilitator does not address this dynamic. An enabling solution would be for the group to make it safe enough for the deviant to explore his resonance. McClusky states, "It is my belief that a person's confidence is shattered, and their sense of self eroded when their feeling experience within the family [group] is constantly denied, overruled or misinterpreted" (1989, p. 3).

In groups, it might well be this very experience that triggers both the defensive and intuitive shadow side of human nature. Jungians respect how we respond both to transferential phenomena relating to parents themselves and to parental archetypes. While the psychotherapy training group is not a therapy group, transferential patterns emerge just as powerfully in any training group process as they might in a therapy group situation.

Stevens suggests that, in today's society, increasingly an anti-authoritarian hostility is carried towards the patriarchal archetypal values such as, "maintenance of law and order, discipline and self-control, morality and responsibility, courage and patriotism, loyalty and obligation, the exercise of authority and command" (Stevens, 1982, p. 121).

He continues by noting that when an archetype is rejected in this way, it will persist as an unconscious potential seeking actualization in other subversive and antisocial forms. The psychotherapy training group, in search of protection to support the fear side of the derived focal conflict, often idealizes the trainer as an authority figure, activating the paternal archetype. Archetypes denied actualization will seek this in whichever form is available to them; attack may be seen as a form of defence, hostility is rationalized into "they are bad, he is bad, we/I have a moral duty to destroy". A group member may be receiving anger from the other members because the other members feel he/she "deserves" this, owing to moving too far away from group norms.

I am reminded here of an intervention I use when training psychotherapists of mixed backgrounds: race, culture, class, sexual identity. That is, to ask what it is like for trainees to be taught by a white, English, heterosexual person. Because of oppressive practice previously in their lives, I may represent a controlling autocracy, and, archetypally, this remains in their psyche. This factor needs to be made welcome in the group settings, as does the organizational structure and rules of some faiths, for example, the Roman Catholic or Mormon Church. If these issues are allowed to remain split off from group discussion, the aggression and often murderous impulses will make themselves evident in destructive ways against the more vulnerable members of the group.

In Whittaker's concept of *displaced target* dynamics, anger towards the trainer may be expressed towards another group member. *Scapegoating* involves shared guilt. (Leviticus tells how we put our sins on the goat and then sacrifice the goat to be free of our own guilt.) The term used for the profoundly painful experience of group rejection to the point of someone leaving is that the group has been "blooded" (Philippson, 1990). And for some groups, this experience sets a modelling dynamic that, sadly, actually makes the group life irretrievable.

Given the complicated way in which unconscious group phenomena emerges, or remains denied and yet powerful, it is not surprising that errors will be made by trainers/facilitators. I believe that this, to some extent, is necessary, so that individuals can learn to tolerate their own frustrations in life and to make possible the modelling by the trainer of permission to make mistakes and retrieve errors in a healthy way.

Many theoretical viewpoints support the idea that human experiences of aggression and destructive impulses are present and potentially available in everyone. Greenberg (1998) believes the borderline personality shows aggression behaviourally, while someone with narcissistic traits will use criticism, shame, and humiliation, and the schizoid form of rage is to annihilate, to render someone emotionally non-existent.

These three types of personality structures are part of developmental process, invited by integrative psychotherapy training, and so most trainees will experience at some time in their training at least one of the above personality patterns. The most fruitful group, I am remembering, is that where all of these styles of relating are evident.

Carkhoff (1969) acknowledges that groups can offer more than individual treatment, in that the group member can examine his or her relationship, not only to the facilitator, but also to other group members. As such, groups potentially offer the greatest amount of learning to the greatest number of people at one time.

Society shows how, in group settings, the individual can become lost to the collective. A socially responsible person resorts to hooliganism in crowds, or to behaving destructively in gang formations. In organizations such as the NHS, the agenda for which we joined, to care for others, becomes superseded by the agenda of maintenance of the institution. Stevens (1982) refers to the "soulless anonymity of traditional institutions". Psychoanalytic group models work only with what the group, as an identity in its own right, presents. The facilitator in this setting would employ "therapeutic abstinence", inviting transference. Phillips states that

> When refusing to answer questions is not traumatic for the patient . . . at its worst, and it is often at its worst in analysis, it merely repeats the childhood trauma of the inaccessible parent. [1995, p. 2]

Inaccessibility, I think, does not foster good containment and may well be motivated by shadow phenomena. Theoretical models show how group pressures and established belief systems can instigate change, aiming at individuals reaching maturity. This means recognizing loving feelings and impulses that previously have had no witness, and, equally, it means experiencing aggressive and destructive impulses allocated to shadow due to social learning. If fear is denied, then members leave the group unchallenged and unchanged, or even with maladaptive coping mechanisms reinforced. The human predisposition to fear, to extreme, is acknowledged by Phillips: "Caught between the harshness of the world and the urgency of his or her instincts, the child is born with a readiness for terror" (ibid., p. xi).

Groups are not always comfortable, but with an experienced facilitator they are exciting, alive, and fruitful. Belief in the power of psychotherapeutic group learning originates from Freud (1921c), who tells us that neuroses may diminish and even disappear when a powerful impetus has been given to group formation.

As each training group sets its own norms, a collective shadow emerges. Freud (1912b) conceptualizes eros, the life instinct, and thanatos, the death instinct (the drive towards destruction of our self or others). Jung, in his discussions on the murderer and suicidal within us, states that "A collective personification . . . is the product of an aggregate of individuals" (1932 [1959], par. 262).

Guggenbuhl-Craig refers to the collective archetypal shadow as "evil", stating,

> the collective shadow tries to demolish collective ideals [that] . . . must be subject to attack, since they are false and one-sided. Were they not continually being eaten into from the depths of the human soul, there would be neither individual nor collective development. [1971, p. 103]

Psychotherapy training groups are fertile ground for the emergence of shadow phenomena, and, depending on the trainer's awareness and tolerance of his or her own shadow, the training group is an ideal place for the potential working through of such shadow experiences.

The psychotherapist's shadow

> The more we strive to be professional helpers who have the best interests of our clients at heart, the more we are in danger of acting out of our power-hungry shadow. . . . Either we can admit them [shadows] into our work consciously, observe them, and learn from them: or we can hide behind our professional persona and force the shadow into the role of destroyer. [Haule, 1971, p. xiii]

I wonder if integrative psychotherapy is perhaps more at risk than some other therapeutic orientations in splitting the archetype pertaining to power: that is, the powerful other, seen as either all protective or all punitive. In integrative psychotherapy, we expect trainees to understand what it is to have experienced the childhoods they have known in order, one hopes, to change some of the patterns that they have learnt throughout their formative years.

How much do we have a right to the expectation that trainees will be introspective, will re-experience, will regress . . .?

What might trainees know of regression phenomenologically, before making a choice to enter into training? Greenberg (1998) talks of "paradise lost" when we reach the point of experiencing life beneath our defences with a sense of no turning back. How often do we inform our trainees, before they enter into training, that this might happen for them, and, even if we do, how can they make a considered choice about something that they have not yet experienced? Might the power that trainers hold become hidden beneath a pseudo-democracy?

The paradox of making personal therapy a training requirement is that in imposing such a requirement, not only are trainees vulnerable, but we as trainers are also vulnerable to the projection of our own unresolved issues on to trainees. This means that perhaps we could be meeting our own needs in our relationships with trainees in a vicarious way, with a sense of pseudo-satisfaction, or we may be denying our own needs (the former is also a form of denial), accepting a defensive stance of superiority, different from seniority, in an unhealthy way. It is only too easy to accuse trainees whose perception of a situation differs from our own of not owning their own process.

What happens to the trainer's destructive shadow dynamic in the power imbalance? It is not easy to admit that perhaps we are not the all-caring, containing, lovingly supportive professional to whom we have dedicated years of commitment in the form of time, emotional energy, money, and study. And all this in a culture where societies and Christian values are to strive towards a collective of anti-crime, anti-violence, anti-aggression and ridding oneself of what is socially unacceptable. Phillips states,

> If the aim of a system is to create an outside where you can put the things you don't want, then we have to look at what that system disposes of—its rubbish—to understand it, get a picture of how it sees itself and wants to be seen. . . . insouciance and recklessness . . . are not psychoanalytic terms in the way that trust and integration are. [1995, p. 19]

I have heard psychotherapy trainees be adamant that they will not be working with the perpetrators of abuse. Is it not also abusive to deny the people who are most in need of change and support the pathway for that experience? Psychiatric systems will seclude or discharge patients who show outbursts of aggression, when it is that very behaviour that is in need of attention. We can drive people out of therapy and of training for the very thing for which they turn to us.

Of course, if we consider our behaviour to be in the interest of society, it can then be moralized, and an excuse is made for using aggression to keep the peace. In psychiatry, rather than support the aggressive patient to enable him to express his aggression healthily, we seclude and medicate him or even refuse him admission to the ward.

> In daily life we often suffer pangs of conscience when we permit ourselves to be excessively motivated by the power drive. But these guilt feelings completely disappear from consciousness when our actions, whilst unconsciously motivated by a lust for power, can be consciously justified by that which is allegedly right and good. [Guggenbuhl-Craig, 1971, p. 8]

In psychotherapy trainings with rife transferential patterns, how does the power projected on to the trainer, in the search for protection, become acted out as persecution? In acknowledging the unwanted, persecutory experience, let us explore some roles of the therapist's shadow, first in the wounded healer archetype.

Haule (1971) recognizes that, by the very nature of therapy, we have a split between helper and helpless: trainer as powerful, all-knowing, and trainee as needy, lacking understanding. Trainees enter into training because the trainer has something that they want; the trainee may or may not know what that is, but expects the trainer to know. As soon as a trainer accepts the stance of being all-knowing, superior in ideas, rather than senior in experience, although only perhaps in psychotherapy, then the trainee risks becoming oppressed into having to learn in the manner in which this trainer wishes. "When the teacher splits the archetype and becomes only a teacher, the students are forced into being childish individuals who do not wish to learn and have no self-control" (*ibid.*, p. xiv).

The dilemma is that, in recognizing the importance of experiential learning, we must accept that if therapists want to help clients through their most vulnerable and painful places, then they first need to go to those places on their own behalf: the concept of the wounded healer. Is it oppressive practice to impose this? Or is it shadow behaviour as a trainer or trainee to attempt to avoid this? Bly posits, "No one gets to adulthood without a wound that goes to the core. And the boy . . . does not become King without that wound" (1990, p. 219).

In the story of *The Fisher King*, it is the person who has been into the gutter of life's experience who is able to support a fellow human being through his psychosis. In some "caring" professions, our wounds lie unacknowledged, even to ourselves. In the NHS I have witnessed doctors, nurses, and police hiding themselves behind a role and uniform that accentuates their power and denies their woundedness. As psychotherapists, we have no uniform, but we have our theory, our techniques of intervention, and our concept of transference. How often do we too readily resort to these in situations where we are required to face our own fear and inadequacies in the presence of our clients? Perhaps our trainee may need us transferentially to hold the power imbalance for a while. This is different to a situation where a trainer holds on to power for his or her own purposes.

Stern (1996) defines emotional contact as having three discernible phases:

- the *pregnancy phase*, where we realize that something is about to happen;
- the *decision phase*, when we have to choose whether or not to go along with something unknown to us;
- the *weird moment*, when we either face the fear of the unknown, or protect ourselves by hiding behind some intelligent interpretation or sharing a theoretical perspective with our clients to retain our own power.

Here, our theory, potentially containing and grounding, when relied upon too heavily becomes our "uniform" and our shadow lies vulnerable to acting out. In training situations, I offer a moving or disturbing film to my trainees. The aim of this is primarily to encourage free expression of emotion and identification with one or more characters in the film, practising attunement and becoming strongly affected by another's story alongside acknowledgment of the "bad guy" in themselves. Only secondarily do we come to the theoretical and psychological analysis of the film.

The potential to engage may be relative to the extent to which we are able to tolerate frustrations. Freud tells how *too much* maternal love leaves a legacy of difficulty in doing without (as of course does having *too little* maternal love). Emotional maturity incorporates the tolerance of those things in life that we cannot change (Evetts-Secker, 2003) and the emergence of adult responsibility. It is the Trickster archetype that portrays the resistance to initiation into the responsibilities of adult life, incorporating "a kind of divinely sanctioned lawlessness that promises to become heroic" (Henderson, 1967).

It might be that the trainee who portrays this archetype becomes "ring-leader" for boundary breaking in the group. The pay-off for this behaviour is a sense of pseudo-superiority, which denies the trainee's fear of responsibility.

As a supervisor, I have seen therapists insisting on all clients attending for weekly therapy, with the rationale being that fortnightly therapy is not sufficiently containing, with too big a gap for clients to hold the process. Following this is a six-week period in the summer months when clients have no therapy, because the therapist takes a break. Where is the rationale for weekly therapy now?

What seems to me to be similarly and unfairly irresponsible is a situation where the clients are expected to pay for missed sessions when they are obviously too ill to attend (not to be confused with avoidance), or when snow makes roads inaccessible. Is this the Trickster archetype at work, where professionals see themselves as above the ordinary everyday human situation and behave in a potentially exploitative manner? Erikson (1959) would accept this view of the subtlety of the Trickster, honouring that it can influence without the extremes of vandalism, hooliganism, gang warfare, and heroic inflation of the leader. Stevens (1982) acknowledges the impact of the over-possessive mother who resists and will not allow the child to grow into maturity. Whatever the family pattern resulting in the Trickster archetype, a denial of responsibility is experienced.

As therapists, we have a professional responsibility, incorporating the responsibility of being human. When denying the human element, perhaps we are hiding behind a role to avoid our own vulnerability, which can result in projection on to our clients and potentially practising from a Trickster archetypal pattern. The opposite is also true: that in being too human we deny the responsibility of being professional. And, I wonder, how much do we impose shadow upon ourselves as trainers or trainees, in accepting ethical rules without due consideration, introjecting them as our own, and simply accepting the mores imposed on us by the masters in the field. The dilemma between differences in ethical codes, the law of the land, human morality, and personal integrity is something with which a therapist must continually struggle in awareness.

> The task of confronting the brutal, destructive elements of the Shadow has become in the twentieth century the inescapable destiny of our species: if we fail, we cannot hope to survive. . . . There is an urgent biological imperative to make the Shadow conscious. The moral burden of this immense task is greater than any previous generation could have even conceived. Only by becoming consciously to terms with our nature—and in particular with the nature of the Shadow—can we hope to avert a total catastrophe. [Stevens, 1982, p. 214]

How much, through the one-sided striving for goodness in our training institutes, are we instigating our own downfall? How much are we contributing to the acting out behaviours of shadow in a society where many children know few boundaries and adults are finding it increasingly difficult to tolerate the frustrations of life, with expectations of immediate gratification and reliance upon the state for their future? In a society where perfection is encouraged, with surgical interventions to halt the ageing process, the effects of ageing and evidence of wisdom is being eroded. I wonder how this societal change shows itself in the training institutes, as they must naturally be affected by changes in the field.

Do we acknowledge the wisdom of an older, more experienced trainer in a contact-orientated way so that we can use their encouragement of our own potential to healthily take charge of our own learning, or do we idealize the older trainer and expect to be fed information and containment throughout our training time? How many trainees, when first working with clients, expect not to have to find those client training placements for themselves? When does guidance from a trainer become rescuing of trainees, and, hence, also become persecutory in that the trainer might be implying to the trainee, "You need me to do this for you".

Guggenbuhl-Craig (1971) believes that, transferentially, the vulnerable partner (trainee) initially projects on to the more powerful person (trainer) the image of magician or saviour. Kohut (1992) names this the idealizing transference, considering that whether or not the trainer adopts this projected role and becomes confluent with the grandiose image is dependent on how much he has come to terms with his own narcissistic needs.

Guggenbuhl-Craig states,

> Training analyses in particular are subject to this danger. The trainee may remain an "apprentice" for the rest of his life . . . or he may try to become a master, sorcerer, himself, which leads to bitter recriminations between old master and former apprentice. A father projection which has not been withdrawn is often not enough to explain the friction which arises between a training analyst and his professionally matured trainees. [*ibid.*, p. 34]

In integrative therapy, we respect the co-creation of relationships. To see every dynamic between trainer and trainee as transferential process on the trainee's part is a denial of the responsibility of the trainer in the co-created dynamics, and this might well be triggered by the trainer's lust for power, or unresolved narcissistic process in his or her need to be idealized (special).

The polarity to the role of "saviour" Stevens (1982) sees as the role of "charlatan". This can show itself in trainings: for example, in fee paying and through sexuality. When training fees are high, this unconsciously suggests that the standard of this training is better than that of another organization. For example, counselling training offered at a local college is substantially less expensive than that at a private training institute. The local college is supported by government subsidies and can afford to offer cheaper trainings, and, while there might be some truth in the comparison of standards, assumptions are made out of awareness.

With client work

> It is remarkable how often psychotherapists find it necessary to emphasise that the fee is itself a therapeutic necessity for

promoting the healing process. May this not be, among other things, a shadow statement? The fee . . .is there to permit the therapist to live in a manner appropriate to a man of his level of education and training. [Guggenbuhl-Craig, 1971, p. 36]

I have heard it said, "If I charge more, people will think I'm good at what I do". This is the charlatan, the false prophet, at play. I have also heard it said that in order to do the sometimes deeply painful work that we do, we need a standard of living that is nourishing of ourselves. I would encourage, here, the reflexive consideration of our own value systems in life and what it is that is really nourishing to our professional relationships.

One dynamic supporting this role of the charlatan is that of not acknowledging the paternal shadow. Symbolically, in the transference, the trainer may assume the father role. In transferentially separating from father (trainer), if the trainer's shadow lies unaddressed in that the trainee "escapes" rather than turning around and, prior to moving away, facing and dealing with this dynamic of the relationship between himself and his trainer, the trainee (new trainer) may well not acknowledge his own shadow. The paternal transference in the training situation is likely to emerge towards the end of the training period, when the trainee is leaving the comfort of the training group and going independently out into the professional world.

Bly (1990) suggests that in society today a father image is often coloured by associations of workaholism, weakness, submission, isolation, abusiveness, evasion, cowardice, addiction, and alcoholism. Many sons do not address or fight this, but defensively strive to rise above it.

The son, flying towards the sun will not see his own shadow, for his shadow falls behind him as he flies. He has seen his father's shadow, but his own remains hidden. [*ibid.*, p. 101]

To see and flee, Bly believes, is not enough. Trainers have a responsibility to encourage open and free exploration of shadow phenomena, and especially so within our current society of increasingly "missing" fathers. "Society without the father produces these bird-like men, so intense, so charming, so open to addiction . . ." (Bly, 1990, p. 104).

I have experienced that, in defensively abandoning my own shadow as a reaction to my father's shadow, we become what we avoid. This pattern is not reserved only for sons and not daughters.

The seducer

Regarding sexuality, it is hardly surprising that, given the very intimate nature of the therapeutic relationship, some therapists find themselves caught up in the breaking of sexual boundaries. Of course, as we strive to understand the likely dynamics of this, we must not in any way make right this abusive process of sexual relationships with clients and trainees.

As Moursund and Erskine (2004) state,

> While it is normal and natural for a client to feel sexually attracted to his therapist, or vice versa, there are no circumstances under which it is appropriate to act on those feelings. . . . A client's sexual invitations must be respectfully declined and the client invited to discuss his response to that refusal. [*ibid.*, p. 189]

In a training group that I knew, there were very clear guidelines that for the period of training there was to be no sexual contact between trainees. When one female trainee challenged a male trainee, in the group process, for seducing her (she had responded willingly), another three female trainees joined the challenge! Despite the training agreement, five group members had engaged in breaking a sexual boundary. The human concept of *prohibition as invitation*, which invites the unconscious to break given rules, makes questionable the practice of imposing a rule of no sexual contact between trainees in training situations. Might the practice of addressing sexuality in the group and inviting a more considered rationale for this group guideline not prove to be more fruitful and empowering in group situations?

In today's society, a troubling process is emerging. It is increasingly possible for an adopted child to trace the birth mother and family of origin, with the difficulty arising that, in a disturbing number of instances, sexual contact is happening between adopted adults and members of their original family. This has become known in the field as genetic sexual attraction. Mathes discusses this powerful experience, describing the transferential component as "Something you long for and need [the infantile genetic attraction] has swiftly become something you fear and are ashamed of [genetic sexual attraction]. . . . This depth and intensity needs expression and connection" (2001, p. 1).

Recent studies show that this incest has resulted in the breakdown of many otherwise happy marriages. In working with those suffering the effects of such incest, I am made aware, as developmental theorists advocate, of the need to merge between mother and child in the very early days and weeks. In the process of adoption this need lies unmet and carries on into adult life, both for the mother and the adopted child. The human need to merge in childhood is satisfied customarily in the symbiotic union between mother and child in the early weeks of life. The human need to merge as an adult is served in sexual union between partners.

Some adopted children with early needs unmet reach adulthood without an awareness of the difference between maternal intimacy and sexual intimacy, and the unconscious drive with which the merger process seeks actualization is extremely powerful. Because it is a need that initially emerges prior to the formation of the sense of self, then the most basic of animal nature is experienced with very little ability to respond to rational thought.

My thinking is that in the therapeutic relationship, the therapist symbolically, in the transference, becomes the missing parent for the client. It is hardly surprising, then, that sexual feelings are rife in an adult psychotherapy relationship where early symbiosis has not been attended to and where the emotional age and chronological age of the client may differ. Indeed, this is also true for the therapist who has not yet fully worked through the very early, unfinished situation of his or her own life experience. One might assume that boundaries are broken, for the most part, because we have a therapist who is unaware of either the shadow side of being human, or of his or her own needs to merge not being met. A therapist who is recently disengaged from a partnership, or who is without sexual contact, is particularly at risk in therapeutic relationships, as is a therapist with a history of being sexually abused or working with a client who has been sexually abused. "People who have been abused as children or adults struggle to set limits in intense emotional situations" (Post Adoption Centre, 2002, p. 6).

Gilbert (1999) believes that when we have two people emotionally vulnerable or regressed in an intense relationship together, there is no one sufficiently adult to take responsibility for maintenance of boundaries, and boundaries get broken not because we have a bad therapist, but because we have a vulnerable therapist who is unaware of the full extent of their own need. Emotionally we have two "children" in a relationship.

When we consider human maturity to be the ability to live with the tension between opposites, good and bad, structure and freedom, we might also see sexual feelings as the symbolic union of opposites of male and female. Jungian philosophy supports this view, seeing erotic feelings between analyst and patient as healthy while recognizing the dangers of destructive acting out of sexuality.

Guggenbuhl-Craig believes a therapist who takes refuge in only working with the symbolic nature of sexuality and fails to address the fantasies of either himself or his patients

> . . . destroys certain possibilities of relationship and spoils an opportunity of dealing with possible destructive tendencies in himself and his patient. . . . Though sexuality is ultimately a symbol, it can only be a living symbol if it is truly experienced. [1971, p. 57]

To reject the addressing of sexuality in the psychotherapy training programme rejects an important part of the identity formation of our blossoming therapists and leaves them unprepared for this aspect of client work. If, as Stevens states,

> Domineering mothers are particularly effective at promoting sexual deviations in their sons through their exemplification of womanhood as something too dangerous to be approached with any degree of trust or desire for intimacy. Deprived of its normal goal, the boy's sexuality is forced to seek other modes of expression, such as exhibitionism, transvestism, fetishism, sado-masochism or homosexuality. [1982, p. 131]

then we can see the risks involved transferentially of not addressing sexuality in a healthy way in psychotherapy trainings, both for our trainees (and their spouses) and subsequently for their clients.

Stevens (1982) suggests that denial of aggressive impulses in the therapeutic relationship can lead to unacceptable aggression becoming eroticized, in that the two forbidden impulses, sex and aggression, achieve a shared discharge in sado-masochistic fantasies and practices; he sees sadistic experience as eroticized aggression directed against more vulnerable people, and masochism as eroticized aggression directed against the self. I believe that sexual abuse is certainly just as much about power as about sex. From my experience in forensic psychiatry, I know that many rapists believe that they are inadequate sexually and incapable of "normal" sexual relationships. The power feeling in rape is for them a defence against the vulnerability of their perceived sexual inadequacy. Here we have another reason for inviting and addressing the shadow in psychotherapy trainings.

And this process must last the lifetime of the therapist, as Guggenbuhl-Craig emphasizes: the psychotherapist

> ... must wrestle with the dark, uncanny forces in himself and others. It is only through repeated confrontations with the shadow that he can fulfil his task. He cannot, like the biblical Isaac, spend just one night wrestling with the angel to win his blessing. His struggle for the blessing must last a lifetime. [1971, p. 142]

To summarize this chapter, the material shared reinforces the firm belief that the notion of shadow is of paramount importance in psychotherapy trainings. Also evident is the deeper realization that energy from shadow experience not only needs addressing to prevent harm, but needs addressing to promote growth. Human growth encouraged without shadow is phenomenologically superficial, ungrounded, and potentially short-lived. The energy used in the repression of shadow, for example, in retroflection, depletes our sense of vitality and availability for relational contact.

It seems that shadow is a profoundly complex process of organizing and experiencing relationships that exists both within and beyond the level of understanding. It incorporates the whole of our life experiences, in every walk of life and across the years; it involves dynamics occurring intra-psychically, between two people and within group situations, building upon both inherited and learnt behaviour; it can be damaging and hurtful, and yet can also provide the energy with which to empower people to positively change their lives.

The question of determining what is and what is not shadow is not so black and white as to suppose that either quality or intensity of behaviours alone will constitute shadow. Human experiences become shadow when the tension between growth and destruction is too heavily laden towards the latter. Shadow is a highly complex process phenomenon. Maslow emphasizes that

> There is no substitute for experience, none at all. All the other para-phernalia of communication and of knowledge—words, labels, concepts, symbols, theories, formulas, sciences—all are useful only because people already knew them experientially. [1966, p. 45]

While exploring shadow phenomena has paradoxically reinforced my faith in human nature and the courage with which people subjected to the most horrific of shadow experiences can find the strength to rebuild their lives, as Maslow posits, understanding alone is not enough. The heuristic process is that which enables each one of us to include our own intuitive experiences and tacit knowledge, employed throughout the process of psychotherapy practice and study. Moustakas honours this tacit knowledge, which grows out of direct human experience, believing that "When we curtail the tacit in research, we curtail the possibilities for knowing" (1990, p. 22).

West supports Moustakas's belief in heuristic inquiry, referring to "passionate research" (1988, p. 60) that benefits from the use of the researcher's involvement in the study, both as a source of data and in the process of researching. He points out that counsellors are already familiar with the use of self in their work; they have learned to trust their own countertransference responses and these data, in relation to subject's experience, bring an added richness at an holis-tic level, heuristically involving body, mind, emotions, and spirit. West advocates researchers personalizing the research process and fruitfully using the way in which this process affects them.

In considering shadow, I have incessantly been drawn to personalizing concepts, been reminded of situations from my life experience, and been increasingly aware of my own phenomeno-logical reactions to concepts. Research, like therapy, seen only as an intellectual pursuit is dry and stunting. Husserl (1975) teaches that there is no evidence that objects are real, except for our subjective experience of them. Heuristic enquiry then must be the method of choice for understanding shadow experience.

I am pleased to be an integrative psychotherapist, welcoming how this model uncovers and supports human potential alongside a corresponding increasing realization of the valuable contribution that Jungian understanding can offer to integrative psychotherapy.

Invited experiment

You will need paper, a paper cup and paper plate, and coloured pens.

Allow yourself time and a comfortable space to sit and reflect, without interruption.

1. Think of a nursery rhyme. Take a paper cup and pens and create something to represent the first character that comes to mind for you from that nursery rhyme.
2. Take a sheet of paper and write freely, without censoring yourself, as if you are that character.
   Begin with, "I am . . ."
3. Take a paper plate and pens and create the character whose personality is opposite to the first character you thought of.
4. Take a sheet of paper and write, without censoring yourself, *to the first character, from the second character.*
5. Now, take a different coloured pen and underline the words that stand out for you, on each of the sheets of paper.
6. Now, take the written sheet with the most underlining and read this out loud to yourself, as if you are that character.
   Be aware: how many of these characteristics and qualities can you easily identify with? Which sit comfortably for you and which not?
7. Consider your relationships and allow yourself to notice how these qualities might show themselves in these relationships.
8. Ask yourself: what might I need to change to be more comfortable with my own shadow?

CHAPTER THREE

Charting the waters

"Do not force feelings of any kind, least of all the feeling of conviction"

(Ferenczi, quoted in Phillips, 1995, p. 25)

This chapter considers the approaches that might be best used for a journey of exploration into the experience of being human. How are we going to embark on this journey? What philosophical stance might support our journey well?

In my original study of shadow, the data gathering methodology included various stances of intervention, all interconnected by the philosophical base of phenomenological inquiry. This philosophical base, underpinning each mode of intervention, provided the consistency and grounding for the various approaches to be usefully employed alongside each other.

Given that the phenomenological enquiry approach honours the uniqueness of experience, then having a range of potential stances of intervention reinforces this principle, in that people need differing levels and types of support in order to enhance phenomenological experience and make sharing possible. Throughout the data gathering, I used whichever aspect of the considered approaches was most figurally pertinent to subject need, in any given moment. The methods of intervention were,

(a) focus group, using the focal conflict group process model;
(b) in-depth interviews using phenomenological inquiry, supported with attunement, involvement, and interpersonal process recall;
(c) discovery of my own process, using in-depth interview, dream analysis, and personal critical reflexive evaluation.

I chose the relational approach of phenomenological inquiry, which surpasses all other approaches of data gathering in honouring individual truth, alongside heuristically honouring my own truth and integrity. This proved enormously valuable and nourishing in my client relationships and my friendships over the years of study.

This philosophical base for relationships necessarily deserves acknowledgement in a book such as this, because it models a way of being in the world and a way of relating to our own reading experience. Each reader, in personalizing this experience, will deepen their own understanding and felt experience of shadow in their own way.

Phenomenological inquiry

The *Award Compact Dictionary* (1975) describes "phenomenon" as "*a remarkable and unusual experience*". Phenomenological investigation is an inquiry into what is both remarkable and unusual, indeed unique, human experience. We cannot measure the quality, intensity, or depth of human pain and passion from an objective stance. Being human is so inextricably complicated a process, ever in a state of flux and fluidity, that to use measurements that seek sameness and generalizations would be impractical and detract from the individual's truth of experience. A deeper understanding emerges from a more uniquely detailed and emotionally and somatically felt experience. For example, Oppenheim (1992) tells us how Bowlby may show that maternal deprivation in childhood correlates highly with painful attachment patterns in adulthood, but we cannot possibly meaningfully know the quality of that pain for the individual sufferer without phenomenological inquiry. Oakley (1981) supports this view, claiming that in research, depth interviews result in data that are more valid in exposing the subject's true feelings and opinions than structured interviews.

Moustakas (1994) tells us that the question in phenomenological research emerges from the researchers intense interest in the topic or problem being researched. As such, the excitement of the researcher and his or her curiosity inspire the research and, hence, the heuristic inquiry into the phenomenological experience of the researcher adds richness to the data. The definite characteristics that Moustakas believes to be incorporated in a human science research are as follows:

- It seeks to reveal more fully the essences and meanings of human experience;

- It seeks to uncover the qualitative rather than the quantitative factors in behavior and experience;

- It engages the total self of the research participant, and sustains personal and passionate involvement;

- It does not seek to predict or to determine causal relationships

- It is illuminated through careful, comprehensive descriptions, vivid and accurate renderings of the experience, rather than measurements, ratings or scores. [*ibid.*, p. 105]

The research method of phenomenological investigation in the primary study was enhanced, where appropriate, through the processes of interpersonal process recall and inquiry, attunement, and involvement. Any informal, interactive process of inquiry may be supported by the use of a "series of questions aimed at evoking a comprehensive account of the person's experience" (*ibid.*, p. 114). These open questions need to be designed in such a way so as not to lead the recipient. They are an invitation to enhance the subject's own phenomenological awareness and the researcher must forfeit any assumptions about what or how the subject is experiencing. The questions may be varied or altered to assist the process of sharing, or might not be needed at all if the subject is in free-flowing sharing. Spontaneity, then, is a goal of this method of inquiry.

As Oppenheim states,

> In depth interviewing, every effort is made to get respondents to express their own ideas spontaneously in their own words. It is only too easy for an inexperienced interviewer to ask questions which are subtly leading. [1992, p. 74]

When topics are suggested with one word, and this stimulates a train of thoughts and associations for the subjects, this avoids the danger of the researcher leading or pre-determining a response. "In a depth interview that is going well, there should be hardly any need for questions as such" (*ibid.*, p. 73).

Interpersonal process recall was used only if necessary, and to promote holism and further the process of inquiry.

Moustakas suggests that the phenomenological inquiry process involves

1. Discovering a topic and question rooted in autobiographical meanings and values, as well as involving social meanings and significance;

2. Conducting a comprehensive review of the professional and research literature;

3. Constructing a set of criteria to locate appropriate co-researchers;

4. Providing co-researchers with instructions on the nature and purpose of the investigation, and developing an agreement that includes obtaining informed consent, insuring confidentiality, and delineating the responsibilities of the primary researcher and research participant, consistent with ethical principles of research;

5. Developing a set of questions or topics to guide the interview process;

6. Conducting and recording a lengthy person-to-person interview that focuses on a bracketed topic and question. A follow-up interview may also be needed;

7. Organizing and analysing the data to facilitate development of individual, textural and structural descriptions, a composite textural description, a composite structural description, and a synthesis of textural meanings and essences. [Moustakas, 1994, p. 103]

An alternative methodology would have been to conduct a case study of my own training organization from a grounded theory perspective. This would have given me unique evidence very useful to my own organization, and the results, potentially coloured by the influence of fewer trainers, trainees, and cultural mores, might be less generalizable. For example, the results might have been coloured by the level of social of awareness of the area in which the training institute resides, which is not at all cosmopolitan and can be quite concrete in its thinking and tunnel-visioned in attitude at times. Differing methods of data gathering, for example, exploring minutes of meetings, questionnaires, and field notes, as well as phenomenological inquiry, might have given cross-validation of method. However, this would be very time-consuming, and I ask how ethical it might be to stir up shadow experiences in an institute when there may not be external consultancy available to contain institute dynamics. External consultation to an institute is as personal therapy is to the individual.

A more generalizable approach would be that of a survey using questionnaires. However, it would prove more difficult to structure questions in such a way that invites the emergence of unconscious experience than it would using a phenomenological inquiry approach, where the researcher is able to respond to the subject's pace, intonations, and energy levels. The containment engendered in a relationship involving contact is not possible with questionnaires. Although it is commonly accepted that the questionnaire return rate is often no more than 33% I would be interested to see whether this might have improved for this particular theme, given that subject energy and general interest was high, from which one could assume that a higher than usual return rate might be due to the importance of the theme to psychotherapy training.

To interview senior international trainers gives a much broader perspective of experience.

The rationale underpinning phenomenological inquiry

Self

Schmidt (1992) states evidence that "Jungian studies referred to the shadow as a catalyst for individuation and self-actualisation as well as a doorway to the deeper inclines of the personal and collective unconscious" (p. 141)

If we are to perceive, as Schmidt suggests, healthy integration and individuation towards the sense of self as inclusive of shadow phenomena, then qualitative methodology, which affirms the phenomena of "self" and measures subjective experience in relation to shadow, is the most appropriate methodology for the task.

Comprehensive recall

The empirical phenomenological research approach "involves a return to experience, in order to obtain comprehensive descriptions that provide the basis for a reflective structural analysis that portrays the essences of the experience" (Moustakas, 1994, p. 13).

Interpersonal process recall not only invites that return to experience, but does so in a way that supports a holistic and, hence, comprehensive view of the subject's experience at somatic, cognitive, emotive, behavioural, and symbolic levels. This marries well with Erskine's view of integration and support for wholeness in welcoming all the aspects of self.

Search for meaning

The interpersonal process recall (IPR) question, "What does that mean to you?", supports the philosophy underpinning the empirical research approach, which is to search for meaning. "The aim is to determine what an experience means for the persons who have had the experience and are able to provide a comprehensive description of it" (*ibid.*)

This question is important in the reduction of potential for the researcher to superimpose his or her own interpretations on interview data. It is natural for human beings to seek completion, to create meaningful "wholes" of their experience, and when a subject might be struggling in understanding his or her experience, then it can become so easy for a researcher to want to complete that experience for the subject and make assumptions.

Price (1953) tells us that when we read a piece of text, we cannot possibly hold together all the words at the same time. What enables us to "hold together" is the general meaning of the text. We apprehend the unity (whole) prior to recognizing and differentiating the parts. Using IPR, with its differing facets of human experience, facilitates the creation of an organizing "whole".

Subject involvement

Strupp, Hadley, and Gomez-Schwartz (1977), following their work on the Vanderbilt Psychotherapy Process Scale, believed that client involvement is an indicator of the *alliance*. Greenberg and Pinsof (1986), in considering the alliance, state that "Most, if not all, psychotherapies and psychotherapists acknowledge the importance of the relationship between the therapist and the client" (p. 10).

In phenomenological inquiry, the level of subject involvement is high, and the alliance between subject and researcher is enhanced through the skills of applying IPR. The part played in human growth of the psychological environment, that is the witnessing of one's experience, as in the IPR responses of listening and exploring, supports recall. This alliance between researcher and subject creates a setting where subject involvement can be high, whereas the more structured research approaches deny the free-flowing awareness of experiencing. Silverman, in his studies of sociology students, refers to their introjection of sets of paradigmatic oppositions, believing that "so many undergraduate sociology courses actually provide a learned incapacity to go out and do research" (1993, p. 203).

To introject restricts the potential of people to discover their own inner truth. I ask myself, does a truth need to be generalizable for it to be true? In integrative psychotherapy we are taught "Beware he who believes he knows the truth" (Evans, 1998).

Phenomenological inquiry supports the view that there are as many truths as those experiencing them. While, of course, there are limits to human experiences, there are no two exact configurations of experience, and each of us knows our own truth. As such, phenomenological inquiry is merely a study of possibilities and potentials, and some potentials are yet to be discovered. In-depth inquiry values human experience and, rather than being truth seeking, is individual reality seeking.

Integrative psychotherapy carries a flavour of the romantic, without sentimentalization of experience, in its spiritual dimension. Buber (1923) tells us that the understanding of another human heart is the ultimate spiritual experience. We cannot fully understand matters of the heart without a qualitative approach to research, which supports the welcoming of self and one's own truth as unique.

Interpersonal process recall

In referring to shadow phenomena, Guggenbuhl-Graig suggests that "If he manages to open himself up to this dimension of existence" [i.e., if he has learned to encounter the unconscious] "then his development can proceed" (1971, p. 142).

Interpersonal process recall (IPR), as developed by Kagan and Kagan (1990), uses questioning as a methodology inviting the encountering of unconscious material, and so is likely to illuminate shadow experience. Kagan and Kagan's assumption is that opening up communication and appreciating what has meaning and heart for each individual will help them explore their own understanding, thus enhancing their own phenomenological awareness. In IPR, participants have the experience of relational knowing as well as semantic knowing. Stern (1985) states that in "semantic knowing", which develops as the use of language develops, we can rationalize, make considered choices, judgements, and decisions, and, hence, make sense of our own felt experience. His concept of "relational knowing" encompasses unconscious processes, intuition, creativity, and spontaneity. This way of knowing honours our own phenomenology, gut reactions, and emotional and somatic awareness.

IPR is excellent for noticing and exploring, without being evaluative. In the inquirer creating the space in which to learn through phenomenological experience, Kagan and Kagan posit that subjects will employ self-enquiry quite naturally. An advantage of IPR is that it is a way of experiencing in the present that which might have been experienced at an out-of-awareness level, or might have been forgotten, from the past, whether the immediate past or the distant past of years. This method is based on the belief that experience that is out-of-awareness wants acknowledgement, and this fits well with the philosophy of integrative psychotherapy. Recall, clarification of human experience, provides an area for structure and for self-understanding.

Ethically, the researcher takes care not to inveigle the subject to drift into therapy mode. If feelings that emerge need containment, then it might be necessary to step outside of the method temporarily, with mutual acknowledgement of this, to reduce anxiety to a level where the method can be resumed.

Kagan and Kagan denote four modes of response to the subject from the inquirer: exploratory, listening, affective responses, and honest labelling. Exploratory and listening responses are those employed by the researcher. The latter two may blur the boundary between research and therapy.

The process of recall invites inquiring questions to the subject to allow elaboration, as shown below.

1. What do you feel?
2. What do you think?
3. What happens in your body?
4. What did you do?
5. What would you rather have done?
6. What would be the risk of that for you?
7. What images come up for you?
8. Are there any associations here for you?
9. Is there anything else?

The researcher asks these questions in listening mode, but with little or no verbal response and always with the assumption that the researcher does *not* know: hence, the follow-up question of "What does that mean for you?" Such questions as these fit well with the model of integration described by Erskine and Moursund (1998), and they seek to explore subjective experience as uncoloured by researcher suggestion or bias. This overall process remains inductive in that the focus is exploration of experience rather than to prove assumptions. Qualitative methodology honours complexity rather than the linearity of quantitative research.

Literature supporting the use of IPR

People find ways of blocking experience when the environment makes it unsafe to know. We have considered already how "shadow" lives in this blocked realm. Communication through symbols and imagery makes it possible for the client to share what they "know" internally, without being subjected to archaic imposed messages; that is, shadow phenomena become more available.

Bollas (1987) refers to the "unthought known" as that which does not become available to cognitive awareness until it has been either affirmed by another, or experienced outside of the self: a mirroring process. In childhood we may have internalizations of (ways in which we have been affected by) a relationship, and we may not have *consciously thought* this yet. The feedback loop, in having witness to our phenomenology, mirrors unconscious experience to make knowledge available to the client's organismic experience. We create the image because we do not have the words, and, as we create something in the play space and explore it, we begin to find the words.

Oaklander (1978) tells how the creation of images often brings about not only a change, but an intense change in subject awareness of their internal state. Greenberg and Pinsof (1986) show, with reference to the experiencing scale, that peak indices, indices of intensity, seem to be most predictive of the outcome of a psychotherapy process. This acknowledges their importance. In my experience, working with symbolism and imagery often brings peak moments of change; they become a *critical event*. I believe this to be because the visual senses are stimulated as well as auditory sensation, enhancing *immediacy* of experience. And if the symbolic image can be formed in plasticine, then the olfactory sensations are also stimulated. With creation of images, the degree of involvement of the subject is high and a developmental learning stage is experienced. Daniel Stern refers to the developmental advantage of symbolic experience, saying that

> With this new capacity for objectifying the self and coordinating different mental and actional schemas, infants have transcended immediate experience. They now have the psychic mechanisms and operations to share their interpersonal world knowledge and experience, as well as to work on it in imagination or reality. The advance is enormous. [Stern, 1985, p. 167]

Price (1953, p. 306), in considering symbolism, tells us that it is able to show itself in language: "The emotion appropriate to the story (the 'feel' of it) gets attached to one key-word". Lacan supports this view, in his concept of *signifier*, one key word, with a dual meaning, which encompasses a whole range of experiences. He states

> That is why we move on . . . [a process] in which the necessity of integration in the imaginary is recognised. What must emerge is not simply understanding of the signification, but reminiscence properly speaking . . . passage into the imaginary . . . to reintegrate the sequence of significations which had not been recognised into this imaginary continuum, which we call the ego . . . to integrate it into his biography. [Lacan, 1954, p. 320]

Through imagery, we have a more direct access to the influence of the past in the present. It is often when I try to think about what I want to recall that I have the most difficulty in recollection. In his major point, "thought overflows symbols", Price (1953) is saying that we have a general sense of a concept that is more primary than our thinking of it. The unification of something underpins the discriminations. It is natural for human beings to seek completion, to create meaningful "wholes" of their experience. As Perls, Hefferline, and Goodman tell us

> In order to get a reality at all, there must be an abstract thinking process to add up the parts and reconstruct a whole. In this construction, all of the parts—isolated percepts, propriocepts, habits and abstract purposes—are grounded in inhibiting the unity of spontaneity. [1951, p. 219]

All the elements of a clients experience will be unified by a whole; we experience pressure for closure, and symbolism is one medium by which movement from thinking to feeling is enhanced and closure is enabled. The value of creating symbolic images is two-fold. We may have a thought about our past with little access to the corresponding emotions. In creating the substitute (symbolic image) for an experience, the fuller memory of that experience becomes available. *Immediacy* replaces mere recollection, or even makes recollection possible. And this supports the way that the formation of images frees clients' thinking, because it enables them to regain contact with the "whole" of an experience. "When we use symbols understandingly, there is an activity or process of under-standing along with and different from the process of producing the symbols" (Price, 1953, p. 312).

Let us also realize here that people have preferences in their ways of relating, and symbolic imagery may not be useful for everyone; hence, the relevance to this study of the whole range of IPR questioning.

Inquiry, attunement, and involvement

> These three aspects of the therapist's behaviour—inquiry, attune-ment, and involvement—compose the essence of a successful thera-peutic relationship. With careful inquiry, sensitive attunement, and authentic involvement, the therapist will be experienced as depend-able, consistent and trustworthy. Experiencing such a relationship, clients can begin to reintegrate the parts of self that were split off in response to trauma and neglect; and with reintegration comes the possibility of full contact with self and with others, of true rela-tionship, of being in the world as a whole person again. [Erskine, Moursund, & Trautman, 1999, p. 17]

Evetts-Secker (2004) tells how individual shadow is the place where we put all that is forbidden or denied by society. Inquiry, attune-ment, and involvement will free research subjects to become aware of that which they themselves have relegated to shadow experience.

Inquiry is underpinned by the belief that, as researcher, we know nothing of the unique experience of the subject. The researcher is striving for respectful investigation into, and understanding of, the subject's phenomenological experience. Through this empathic process, hidden and undiscovered experiences are revealed and internal phenomenon become figural in awareness. Inquiry, then, begins with an attitude of mind as well as specific intersubjective choices of interaction. The basic stance adopted by the researcher, either verbally or in spirit, is "What is it like for you?"

Attunement deepens this process, with a communication to the other person of a fully felt awareness of their process, a kinaesthetic and emotional sensing of the subject's experience. The subject becomes aware of another who not only witnesses their phenomenological experience, but is strongly affected by this. Attunement is conveyed as much by facial expression or body movement as it is verbally. Hence, this experience is understood at both a semantic landscape level and a relational landscape level (Stern, 1985). In therapy, at this stage, we might meet with client resistance, described by Erskine (1993) as a process of juxtaposition, which arises because of an individual's natural ambivalence towards his or her subjective experience. With experienced research subjects, who, by the nature of their experience have already undergone years of personal therapy, this stage of juxtaposition is less likely to occur.

At a time of re-experiencing, which is evoked with the use of inquiry and attunement, the underlying need is for the isolation of the original experience not to be repeated, and here subjects might need a degree of involvement from the researcher, although again this is less likely with experienced subjects. Involvement is the researcher's validation of the significance of subject experience, and, through this experience, the normalization and diminishing of any sense of pathologizing counters societal messages.

These three modes of intervention both promote and support the research subjects to allow to emerge into their awareness aspects of shadow experience that they have encountered over the years. This is a model befitting those subjects involved in the study: psychotherapists who engage deeply with their own phenomenology in their work.

Heuristic process

In allowing myself also to engage deeply as I progressed in my original journey of research and became increasingly curious and aware of the shadow dimension of my own process, I felt a need for support and understanding, as reassurance that I could explore such material without disintegrating emotionally. On reflection, I believe this to be because, in today's society, as shadow phenomena are relegated to the depths of the unconscious, below the level of rational thought, they often appear in bizarre forms of symbolism and metaphor accompanied by emotions, primarily fear, too painful to tolerate. Or they may seem phenomenologically to come from outside oneself, or from some entity experienced as more powerful than oneself. Shadow is rendered unconscious because of the very nature of the quality of its experience. Its intensity showed for me in my dreams, both waking and sleeping.

My own critical reflexive evaluation was in the form of a record of my dream process, what I learned of the issues in my life with which I was then struggling: that is, my own phenomenological experience in relation to the study itself. While a degree of structure in my thinking grounded me well, I needed a process that would allow me to reach more deeply my own phenomenological experience. I embarked on a period of dream analysis and gave myself over to my own personal shadow life becoming a large part of my awareness. I became a heuristic researcher.

The heuristic researcher engages in the process of research in six phases, which enhance the "deeper currents of meaning and knowledge" taking place "within the individual, through one's senses, perceptions, beliefs and judgments". This requires a "passionate, disciplined commitment to remain with a question intensely until it is illuminated or answered" (Moustakas, 1994, p. 18). This is also a holistic approach, focusing on understanding human experience from the perspective of honouring human creativity in "vivid, alive, accurate and meaningful language" which may be "further elucidated through poems, songs, artwork and other personal documents and creations" (*ibid.*, p. 19).

For myself, this occurred primarily in my dreams that enhanced insightfulness via symbolism and metaphor. In accepting Husserl's concept of the "path of universal self-knowledge" (1975, p. 39), we are recognizing the valuable experience of the researcher as part of the research field data. The kind of knowledge in human science gleaned from a deep empathic understanding of someone else's experience, alongside awareness of one's own phenomenology, underpins both heuristic research process and the integrative psychotherapeutic aims of attunement and contact. The mess, ambiguity, ambivalence, and confusion of the human condition was more fruitfully utilized for me in this tentative, emergent model of heuristic inquiry.

I think of Stern's (1996) concept of the phases of engagement: the *pregnancy phase*, when we are aware that something is about to happen and we know not what—this phase carries both excitement and anxiety; the *decision phase*, when we choose either to seek structure to contain our anxiety, perhaps with a plan or theory, or to stay with the uncertainty into the third phase of the *weird moment*, when we allow ourselves to remain with our uncertainty and become attuned to the co-creating of experience. Moustakas's (1990) model of heuristic research offered me more spontaneous and creative access to the data from a phenomenological reality. This quality of capturing a more lived experience sat comfortably with me. The model is as described in the sections below.

Phase 1: initial engagement

Moustakas states, "Within each researcher exists a topic, theme, problem or question that represents a critical interest and area of search" (1990, p. 27), and in this first phase "One encounters the self, one's autobiography, and significant relationships within asocial context" (*ibid.*).

It is within the context of my professional work, over years, that my curiosity in shadow has emerged. This has been a natural, evolving aspect of my life, before ever I decided to embark on this research study.

Phase 2: immersion

Following my decision to research, and again on deciding to write, I found myself reading shadow material, dreaming shadow material, noticing shadow behaviours both inside and external to the psychotherapy profession, in a myriad of ways. Shadow became and is figural in my life.

> The researcher . . . enters fully into life with others wherever the theme is being expressed or talked about—in public settings, in social contexts or in professional meetings. . . . Primary concepts for facilitating the immersion process include spontaneous self-dialogue and self-searching, pursuing intuitive clues or hunches and drawing from the mystery and sources of energy and knowledge within the tacit dimension. [Moustakas, 1990, p. 28]

I heard of evil pertaining to religion on Sunday morning radio; I found myself introducing this theme into professional discussions, and I seemed to be in a new phase of learning and personal growth in my own life's journey. From this self-searching emerged my decision to go into Jungian dream analysis.

Phase 3: incubation

My struggle here was to sacrifice my striving to learn and examine in order to allow myself to follow the philosophy that supports me, the "paradoxical theory of change" (Yontef, 1993, p. 21). Yontef believes that the more we strive towards something future orientated, the more difficult is the process of reaching it. If we stay open to our immediate experience, then we arrive naturally at where we need to be. As I found myself striving, I accordingly learned to let go and come in and out of the process of awareness of shadow, without trying to capture something. My supervisor's support here was invaluable, with his advice to "slow down, learn to wait".

Incubation is

> a process in which a seed has been planted; the seed undergoes silent nourishment, support and care that produces creative awareness of some dimension of a phenomenon or a creative integration of its parts or qualities. [Moustakas, 1990, p. 29]

Phase 4: illumination

First, illumination is "a breakthrough into conscious awareness of qualities and clusters of themes inherent in the question", and second, illumination "may involve corrections of distorted understandings or disclosure of hidden meanings" (*ibid.*, p. 29).

I commented, in my psychotherapy supervision, on my momentary sickening experience of horror when I viewed a large mural of a woman with angelic wings and the distorted face of a gargoyle. This mural had been in my supervisor's office for the duration of my relationship with her and I had previously desensitized myself to it. On becoming open to shadow, it found its way into my awareness.

I visited a synagogue in Prague, built in memory of the holocaust victims. I wept during my visit there and was aware of feeling rage towards a group of American visitors who were chatting and laughing as they walked through this very sacred space. This phase of illumination rendered me more sensitive to my own experience in relation to the outside world.

Phase 5: explication

> Perhaps the most significant concepts in explicating a phenomenon are focusing and indwelling, where concentrated attention is given to creating an inward space and discovering nuances, textures and constituents of the phenomenon which may be then more fully elucidated through indwelling. [Moustakas, 1990, p. 31]

It was at this time that I began to search for answers and ideas from within my own experiences of internal and external awareness. I felt awash with material, and any attempts to group and organize information increased my confusion. In this phase, where the researcher recognizes that meanings are unique and distinctive to internal frames of reference, grouping information into pre-set boxes left me feeling constrained, and I felt freer using heuristic inquiry, with a choice to submit to the impact of shadow phenomena upon my self. My heuristic journey brought for me a sense of being a vessel, in relation to each subject and the theme as whole, through which something was being co-created. I was engaged with, and impacted by, the co-creation at many levels and at all times. Both the research and myself were in a process of growth and change.

It was as if all aspects of the research metaphorically became the baking ingredients of a cake and my sense of self became the oven, providing the environment for the baking. This was a place of fertile void, rather than a place of disempowerment.

Phase 6: creative synthesis

In creative synthesis, the researcher enters into the process thoroughly familiar with all the data in their major constituents and qualities, and the themes and details of the experience as a whole. Moustakas points out that

> creative synthesis can only be achieved through tacit and intuitive powers. . . . Knowledge of the data and a period of solitude and meditation focusing on the topic are the essential preparatory steps for the inspiration that eventually enables a creative synthesis. [1990, p. 32]

I was fortunate in having access to an isolated French farm, where meditation and introspection seemed to be naturally induced and solitude was much a part of the ambience as was the peaceful quietness and a sense of being closer to the elements. It is there that I prepared for the final stages of the study, holding the tension between my fear of "What if nothing of significance emerges?" and my excitement at the prospect of discovering new insights. I hoped to relinquish the shadow of my temptation to read too much, to seek new insights, rather than learning and growing through immersing myself in the data to allow insights to emerge.

I dreamed of myself shaping green "Slime", a play-dough that my grandchildren enjoyed. Slime (dictionary definition) is "mud, mire, to soil with mire". Like human shadow, this malleable jelly-like substance can cling, can soil, can never take the same form twice, and is ever-changing. When handled within boundaries, it can also bring pleasure.

Shadow is not a thought or idea, but a metaphor that exemplifies human energy, bringing a whole range of human experiences. The term "shadow" represents interrelational dynamics; the in-between of people, of polarities, current tensions, human history, hopes and dreams, and the very nature of how people flourish or not.

Shadow is a process: not a concept, but a paradigm.

In writing this book at this time in my life, I am not simply considering what I already know, but, more importantly, I am in the process of discovering new insights as I write. The writing of this book is a heuristic journey in itself.

Reflective activity

Consider the following questions.

1(a)   Would you take prescribed antidepressant medication if your general practitioner recommended this to you?

1(b)   Would you work, as a client, with a psychotherapist who was taking prescribed psychiatric medication, antidepressants, say?
If not, then why not?

In making your decision, whatever that might be, what assumptions could you be making about this therapist and as a generalization, and, hence, perhaps not seeing the person concerned?

1(c)   What values are important here for you in considering this issue and in determining and honouring your own professional integrity?

Consider why you chose the orientation in which you trained.

2(a)   Which orientation might you certainly not have chosen?
2(b)   Why not?
2(c)   What positive attributes does this orientation have to offer?
2(d)   What can you learn from them?
2(e)   What values are important here for you in considering this issue and in determining and honouring your own professional integrity?

CHAPTER FOUR

Navigating a route

"Midwives and winding sheets know birthing is hard and
dying is mean and living's a trial in between"

(Angelou, 1994, p. 228)

B
efore beginning any journey, it is wise to have some idea of
the route. This is not to say that one might never set a course
in a different direction at any time. In the journey of understanding of human experience and potential, grounded theory
offers a sound baseline of categories that, together as a whole, cover
the wide range of human capacity. Grounded theory serves as a
good model from which to begin.

I use grounded theory to begin to consider the data available in
the transcribed interviews of seven experienced psychotherapy
trainers. I identify meta-themes and consider them at length,
perhaps with sub-themes emerging, as they come to mind for me.
In this way I acquire information that elucidates the experience of
the trainers in relation to shadow dynamics occurring in training
institutes.

The initial reading, open, axial, and selective coding model used here is suggested by Strauss and Corbin (1990). Seale (1999) refers to Strauss and Corbin, elucidating how they focus on showing researchers how to apply a well-established method by using some well-tried procedures. In principle, their method involves closely examining the data to name and categorize phenomena that are then broken down into discrete parts prior to being compared and contrasted using a questioning stance. This process challenges assumptions about the phenomena and allows newly discovered data to emerge. Following this, each single category is allocated intensive work with the aim of "seeking to explore its conditions, contexts, action/interactional strategies and consequences" (Seale, 1999, p. 99). The advised sets of coding are:

1. *Open coding*. Strauss and Corbin (1990) posit that here the researcher forms "initial categories" of information about the phenomenon being studied from the data gathered. Within each category, several sub-categories ("properties") are sought and data are explored in "dimensional extremes" of these properties, to show the range of variation, including extreme possibilities on these continua.

2. *Axial coding*. This involves assembling the data in new ways after open coding. A *coding paradigm* (or a *logic diagram*) is developed, which
   - identifies a *central phenomenon* (i.e., a central category about the phenomenon);
   - explores *causal conditions* (i.e., categories of conditions that influence the phenomenon);
   - specifies *strategies* (i.e., the actions or interactions that result from central phenomenon);
   - identifies the *context* and *intervening conditions* (i.e., the conditions that influence the strategies);
   - delineates the *consequences* (i.e., the outcomes of the strategies) for this phenomenon.

3. *Selective coding* involves the integration of the categories in the axial coding model. In this phase, conditional *propositions* (or hypotheses) are typically presented. The result of this process of data collection and analysis is a *substantive-level theory* relevant to a specific problem, issue, or group.

If we accept the understanding that the core of the material being analysed originates at a collective unconscious level, it can be argued that whatever the researchers own reactions to data might be, they will also have a valid meaning, at an existential level, to other people. Moustakas affirms that subjective experience can also hold meaning for others, saying, "The heuristic process is autobiographic, yet with virtually every question that matters there is also a social and perhaps universal significance" (1994, p. 17).

While Moustakas is not a grounded theory researcher, but rather supports heuristic inquiry, the subjective experience of the researcher is supported with the integration of aspects of heuristic inquiry into this grounded theory analysis.

Although one could argue that this data holds themes which are (a) no more than the views of only seven people in the whole of the integrative psychotherapy profession, and (b) may well be coloured in some way by my own understanding of meaning, it is worth noting that this profession is currently relatively infantile in its growth and the subjects chosen for the study are very experienced people in this field. Also, much of what is to be studied is rooted at an existential level, and so, while the uniqueness of individual ways of relating to collective phenomenon is primary to this study, there is a pertinence to the collective of that individual experience, given that existential issues are common to us all.

Initial reading and absorption of data

I had chosen to type the transcripts myself. This allowed further familiarization with content in the process of listening and re-listening to aspects of the tapes that were difficult to decipher. Once transcripts had been typed, I sat quietly and simply read through the material without any attempt to absorb the content. I noted my awareness, figure from ground, of what I was reading. I then slept overnight to allow my unconscious to work on what I had read before repeating the reading. This process is in accord with my beliefs as an integrative psychotherapist that awareness emerges and grows over time, as with the incubation phase of heuristic inquiry, and it cannot be acquired under pressure. At subsequent readings, I highlighted what became figural for me, noticing my immediate responses at a cognitive, emotional, somatic, and symbolic level. By this time, I had a sense of the recurring themes emerging, prior to embarking on open coding of the data.

Methodologically, I allowed myself to notice ideas and concepts beginning to form, seeking examples and verifications; noticing that which supported ideas I already hold and that which stimulated new thinking and suggestions. For example, my initial assumption that shadow always emerges was reinforced; some of the dynamics beneath a process of "bursting out" or "seeping out" were new to me. I surrounded myself with notes, lists, memos, and records of different categories of experience, struggling with overlap and information pertinent to more than one category, until a degree of clarity emerged and links and causal factors proposing an idea became evident. Moustakas (1994) describes this experience, referring to Strauss (1987). Moustakas tells us that during the process "the researcher puts down theoretical questions, hypotheses, summary of codes" thus "keeping track of coding results and stimulating further coding, and also a major means for integrating the theory" (p. 22).

> [P]rocedures for discovering, verifying and formulating grounded theory . . . are in operation all through the research project and . . . go in closed relationship to each other, in quick sequence and often simultaneously. . . . Memos are likely to become increasingly elaborate, summarizing the previous ones or focusing closely on closing gaps in theory. [Strauss, 1987, pp. 23–24]

The amount of time and energy invested in this process fluctuated and varied over a period of months, according to practical considerations and also dependent on my clarity of thinking and level of emotional engagement with the task. At times of potential confusion, I allowed myself "time out" from the study in order to return to it refreshed, more objective and clearer in my thinking. This allowed for the incubation period supporting awareness. Moustakas acknowledges how

> Each research project has its own detailed sequences that depend on the data available, the interpretations and experience of the researcher and the contingencies that influence and guide the research, both personally and professionally. [1994, p. 5]

The recognition of the uniqueness of each qualitative research study fits well with the philosophy of uniqueness being experienced in phenomenological inquiry and invited in integrative psychotherapy.

Generalized open coding

Let us begin, for example, with the category of definition of shadow. When referring to their understanding of the term, trainers described how they thought shadow experience was formed and/or originated: that is, on the one hand, experience may have once been known to us and then repressed due to its quality, or experience may be in shadow because it has never been known to us. One trainer refers to the "unwanted bits which are in the shadow because of the systemic forces, they've become relegated to the darkness", and also the "unborn bits that have never been there", and another states, "The shadow is really not just what we don't own but what we don't even know."

With reference to the levels of dangerousness of shadow, I am told "something that includes actual evil but also something which includes the murky and iffy and problematic . . . aspects of human resistance as well."

The codes in Table 2 were taken from the data in this way.

Generalized axial coding

Wiener successfully used this model of analysis in her studies of rheumatoid arthritis. She believes that "conceptually specifying behaviour will strengthen its applicability as a guideline for health professionals" (Seale, 1999, p. 97).

Seale (1999) refers to Geertz (1993) who used the term "thick description" to portray the good practice of writing which revealed and built upon many-layered interpretations of data, so that rich descriptions and detailed understanding might make possible several meanings for particular events. Part of the richness of his studies involved the use of symbolism and metaphor. The process of visiting and revisiting data in the light of new awareness and

Table 2. Open coding of the shared experience of trainers.

Initial category	Property	Dimensional extremes
Definition of shadow	Aetiology	Repressed material *vs.* undiscovered material
	Level of dangerousness	Problematic aspects of human resistance *vs.* actual evil
Cognition	Introjection	Compliance with dogma *vs.* critical reflection
	Ideas	What springs to mind *vs.* repression
	Thoughts	A level of recognition *vs.* blind spot
	Symbolism	A chosen metaphor *vs.* unconscious dreams
Behaviour	Degree of willingness to address this.	Invited *vs.* censored
	Collaboration	Responsibility *vs.* destructiveness
	Acting out	Self harm *vs.* harm others
		Leave-taking *vs.* exacerbate position
		To ignore *vs.* physically attack
Somatization	Discussion of	Avoid bodily references *vs.* freedom to be me
	Pain	Avoid the issue *vs.* acknowledge
	Illness	Immediacy of "feel sick" *vs.* long-term illness
	Body	Used for support *vs.* retroflection
	Object of violence	Retroflection *vs.* attack other
Emotions	Hurt	Feeling concerned *vs.* feeling attacked
	Shame	Embarrassed *vs.* gutted
	Anger	Resentment *vs.* furious
	Fear	Fright *vs.* terror
	Sadness	Disappointed *vs.* devastated
	Nurtured	Stimulated *vs.* encouraged
Attitude	Approach to psychotherapy practice re shadow	Tune in carefully *vs.* not looked at
		Model disclosure *vs.* abstinence
		Political correctness *vs.* name differences
Course design	Structure	Primarily theory *vs.* primarily practice
	Place for shadow	Space for negativity *vs.* Tactics of denial
		Teach it *vs.* manipulate it
		Be open and invite *vs.* be closed and deny
	Differences	Allow and welcome *vs.* Attempt to resolve

(*continued*)

Table 2.   (*continued*).

Unconscious process	Self-awareness	Unexplored depths *vs.* bringing to the fore
		Encouraged *vs.* blindness
		Subjectivity *vs.* objectivity
	Defences	Denied *vs.* worked with
	Transference and countertransference	Supported *vs.* challenged
Group process	Splitting	Protection of abuser *vs.* consideration of splits
	Scapegoating	Disown and project blame *vs.* banish other from group
		Ownership of *vs.* lynch mob
	Boundaries	Watertight *vs.* ethical breaches
	Responsibility	Ownership of *vs.* caught up in dynamics
	Conflict	Work with *vs.* impossible to handle
Power	Use of	Oppression *vs.* acquiescence
		Call the shots *vs.* give power away
		Dominance *vs.* insecurity
		Hierarchical stance *vs.* becoming equal
		Overwhelming *vs.* addressed clearly
Field dynamics	Organizational issues	Dominance *vs.* managing power
		Rivalry *vs.* consideration
	Stereotyping	Labelling *vs.* bring out prejudice
Containment	Conflicts	Hold the tension *vs.* imposed change
		Struggle with *vs.* polarization
		Challenge *vs.* support
	Responsibility	Trainee responsible for containment *vs.* trainer responsible for containment
	Support	Systems in place *vs.* lack of support

exploring interrelational dynamics (that is, antecedents to behaviour, how one behaves and the consequences emerging from behavioural aspects, and how these colour and influence one another) is all discovered in the phase of axial coding. Seale proposes that axial coding "involves intensive work with a single category, examining how it connects with other categories and seeking to explore its conditions, contexts, action/interactional strategies and consequences" (1999, p. 98).

While the term "thick description" is usually applied to case studies, it is also pertinent to any study where data is repeatedly visited and revisited to allow the emergence of detail. A general axial coding paradigm arising from the total transcripts of this study might look as is set out below.

Central phenomenon: presentation of shadow

1. Understanding of the term.
2. Behaviour exhibited, both interpersonally and in field dynamics.
3. Emotions experienced.
4   Metaphor and symbolism employed in the use of stories and dreams.
5. Somatization

Causal conditions: influencing the central phenomenon

Predisposing factors:

1. Culture, including litigation.
2. Religion.
3. Philosophical beliefs: fluctuations in fashion, including orientation.
4. Bias and judgementalism.
5. Human nature

Precipitating factors

1. Group process: power dynamics.
2. Course design: paradigms employed.
3. Transference and countertransference: power dynamics.
4. Trainer personality type, including personal history and unresolved issues.
5. Trainee personality type including personal history and unresolved issues.
6. Assessment procedures: shame.

Specific strategies: resulting from central phenomenon

1. Illness.
2. Sexual breaches.
3. Shaming.
4. People leaving.
5. Money issues.
6. Re-traumatization.
7. Resistance.
8. Group behaviours: splitting, scapegoating.

Contextual and intervening conditions

1. Approach and attitude underpinning training.
2. Thoughts.
3. Course design: boundaries.
4. Levels of awareness.
5. Trainer support systems.

Consequences: outcome of interventions upon strategies

1. Containment.
2. Working through.
3. Ownership.
4. Responsibility.
5. Therapeutic effectiveness.

Later stages of analysis clarify and detail the mutually influencing factors proposed in the data. Suffice, at this stage, to exemplify the paradigm in the trainer statement:

> Some of it is about a mixture of fear and a kind of exhaustive weariness that change, change in our field, and our work is so very difficult to achieve, because the degree to which this person held on to power and success, the invariable success, in my experience, with which she managed to evict the others, used as a scapegoat which eventually included me, was quite remarkable.

Here we have example of the central phenomenon as behaviour exhibited, i.e., "she managed to evict the others", and the emotion experienced, "fear", with the somatization of "weariness". Pre-disposing factors of "the degree to which this person held on to power and success" and the precipitating factors of both "change in our field" and the unconscious process of "scapegoating" are stated. The trainer continues to share strategies he adopted result-ing from the central phenomena. That is, "I did three things succes-sively. I reckoned from the start that it was impossible to defeat her, or influence her in a head on battle. . . . I supported her at that time, because I thought that the institution overall, was good, and I felt it would be destroyed if this battle wasn't won", and "I just put on rhinoceros hide and went about my own business."

These processes are alive alongside each other and not occurring in a linear fashion.

Moustakas quotes Strauss (1987, p. 12) in stating that "Scientific theories require first of all that they be conceived, then elaborated, then checked out" (Moustakas, 1994, p. 7).

It is the interrelational component of these three processes, which validates the grounded theory model. Given that in the elab-oration and checking out of theories, new conceptions may occur, information needs visiting and revisiting. This process stops when what Moustakas (*ibid.*, p. 94) refers to as "theoretical saturation" is reached.

While the potential for new knowledge is limitless, saturation means that no new information or additional data are being found at this time, with this study. However, it may be that with a differ-ent approach to data analysis, a more tacit, intuitive approach, say, new or more detailed ideas may emerge.

CHAPTER FIVE

Weathering the storm

"I learned what every dreaming child needs to know, that no horizon is so far you cannot get above it or beyond it"

(Markham, quoted in Gallman, 1991, p. 1)

Dream analysis

In any qualitative research programme, or any writing of a book which so powerfully invites one's own phenomenological reality into the arena, one must inevitably, in being open to phenomenological experience, be aware of an ever increasing movement from unconscious to conscious process. And the most powerful of human transitions from the unconscious to conscious experience is through the process of befriending our dream process. Wholeness of the psyche is encouraged as we make room in our current lives for all the experiences we have defensively needed, at some time in the past, to deny into awareness. Dreams are a gift to our souls.

Hence, I am bringing into this arena several of the most striking dreams that I have experienced during the process of my analysis.

I shall take these dreams in chronological order as I worked with them and spend some time recounting the story of each dream prior to discussing the personal meanings of these dreams to my own psychological growth. I am bringing twelve dreams in all and I chose these as a few which became figural for me from many I had previously recorded. The symbolic representations are my own, as opposed to generalizations.

Dream one

> It is evening. My married daughter, A, is living in a house and I am with her. She decides to set fire to the lounge in order to claim some insurance money; not a lot, but enough to have some treats. The intention is to ring the fire brigade and have the fire extinguished quite quickly, so that only the lounge needs redecorating and the insurance will pay for this. I feel uneasy but do not challenge her. She senses my uneasiness and reassures me "Mother, don't fuss. It will be fine."
>
> As the furniture begins to blaze, I ring the fire brigade and cannot get through. The whole house is soon alight and the children are in bed. We hurriedly get them outside and notice that a draught has taken the flames the full length of the roof void in this row of terraced houses. All are ablaze.
>
> We stand in the street. I'm frantic for the fire brigade to arrive and worry about the old people asleep in their beds, as sparks shoot off from the roof to land on properties in other streets. Soon the whole town is alight. I feel terrified, faint, and wake.

In this dream, my intention is to destroy prior to renewing, from a manipulative and dishonest place, but in commencing this process it becomes more powerful than myself and all boundaries are lost.

My intention is to remain in control (of my own shadow), yet the draught, something outside of myself (projection of my power), disempowers me. Again I seek power from outside of myself (fire brigade) to correct the situation. In the dream I fail to empower myself by challenging my daughter. In not challenging my daughter (symbolically my younger self), I am not reworking my earlier life experience.

Fire here symbolizes the total destruction of life form, at least temporarily, and in this dream the young and old (a whole life span) are at risk. Shadow is total and all consuming.

My dream reminds me that as a child I learnt to manipulate because asking up front was not productive. It tells me that the objects of my projections are not going to rescue me and I have to begin to ask openly and honestly for what I want, own my own destructiveness, and face the consequences of my own behaviour in life.

Dream two

> R and I are planning the workshop where he will co-train with me. We stand beside a table on which is a pile of white chocolate rose petals, each bearing the name of a trainee from the training group. R and I take a petal each, alternately and this tells us with whom we shall each work as therapists on the workshop. Behind this pile of petals is a pile of dark chocolate, broken chunks, also bearing the names of trainees, which I am aware of avoiding. I want to give these chunks (trainees) to R to work with, and know that this is unfair. I wake, struggling with my dilemma.

This dream indicates a splitting process in the training group for whom I am Core Trainer. The split is invited in welcoming a new male trainer (R) to the group. I am aware of how I might have favourites and preferences among trainees. Some of this process emerges from the shadow side of my own personality, in that the rose petals signify my "rose-coloured glasses" and chocolate my black-and-white thinking, as opposed to the integration of grey. In some way, this might also be invited, or more powerfully, induced, by certain trainees, following the changing group formation. In reality, I hate dark chocolate.

The dream tells me that R and I need to discuss how we shall work together in containing the anxiety beneath the new form of the splitting dynamic within the group process. It alerts me to consider how I might induce or enhance this process in an uncontaining way. This is a countertransferential dream.

Dream three

> I am invited to a party and am about to leave with my partner. I am carrying a silver tray from his kitchen, on which are several (I think

seven or nine) fried eggs, with a spoonful of baked beans in the corner. I am puzzled that this is what I am taking.

This dream is intra-personal to me. Symbolically, the silver tray (silver as in moon/feminine) supports my maternal nature, as does the number seven, which is the number of grandchildren I have. Eggs powerfully represent life force. However, in the dream I am both puzzled by and displeased with what I carry. I am struck by the number nine, and understand this to be the largest number one can have without involving another numeral. I notice that this dream occurs when (a) I am bringing a second trainer into the training group, and (b) I am introducing a new Head of Institute as I sell the business. Beans are able to grow (as in Jack and the Beanstalk) to unlimited heights.

Here, I think the message to myself is to stop mothering and engage in the world and the training group/institute in another way. I am introducing two male people into the training environment. Having recently sold the institute to a colleague, because of illness, I have to make room for my new colleague and must learn to work alongside someone else (two numerals instead of one; a working though of my narcissism). The institute has recently been awarded UKCP status for the trainings and can now reach unlimited heights! I, too, have to grow in this new training situation.

Dream four

> I am somewhere unfamiliar to myself and I notice, hanging close by me, a very large, hairy, dark, but not black, spider. It is torn, ripped down the middle, and one half of its body is just hanging on to the other half by a piece of skin. I feel curious and sick, as if I am about to be consumed, and I wake.

Mythologically, the spider is creator, womb, container. The splitting element of this dream is threefold: in part, the institute splitting process in members' normal reaction to the recently introduced enormous changes; in part, representative of my recent surgery and large abdominal suture and my coming to terms with that and the unfamiliarity with my body that this brings; and in part, my arachnophobia as a child, which was projection of my fear of my father's sudden change of stance with me, all loving or all punitive. I knew what it is like to feel emotionally ruptured, torn, in relation to my father and inconsistencies. An element of this dream is countertransferential to the institute changes. I am containing members' anxiety.

The dream process is also aiding me in the ongoing discovery of my own healthy male energy. In previous years, my unhealthy identification with my father has shown itself in the institute setting as control and dominance, and I have worked continuously hard over years to promote a democratic culture. This is being reworked with the introduction of a new male Director of Training at the institute.

Dream five

> My new colleague's family and friends are staying in my castle. They obviously do not want me there, giving dismissive and shaming/belittling glances. H is doing his best to mediate. Small children are running about and I am trying to be friendly, but resent having to keep these children safe when my colleague's friends are not bothering at all. Three children fall out of windows (those from which arrows would have been sent in medieval times) and no one is caring. Suddenly, it becomes important for us to leave—other people are arriving and we are not safe. As we depart, my colleague's relative pushes a yellow envelope in my bag and I casually pretend I do not notice. This is what the new people, investigators, are looking for.

The castle was the old logo used to represent the training institute. Castle is "fortress", which both protects and imprisons. In this dream I struggle with the Apollo and the Hermes in myself as internalizations of my father, of H, from whom I am now divorced, and of my new colleague.

I am aware that a new dream often continues on from work done in a previous session. Apollo, archetypally, is rigid, structured, ordered, the god of music, and thinking rules the musical scale. When we push Apollo to extreme, he becomes a tyrant, as was my father when he became aggressive on feeling threatened by my separation from him and his having to relinquish control of me.

Order should serve the kingdom and not the kingdom serve the order. The structure and dominance I employ at the institute must be in relation to the institute's need for containment and not in relation to my internalized need for control.

Hermes, archetypally, is the God of freedom. When we push Hermes to extreme, he becomes anarchic. It is interesting that I had married someone who was archetypally polarized from my father. My Apollo (rigidity to my father complex) was moderated by the maternal in my psyche. In my current work of giving up the maternal (my dream warns me of my potential to rescue by hiding the yellow [cowardly] envelope), I must take care not to run Apollo to extreme and be imprisoned by this internalized controller. My work includes allowing myself to internalize the healthy male psyche of my new colleague, to allow him to penetrate me emotionally and not defensively attack this new relationship from a shadow place.

The "investigators", symbolic of UKCP, are looking for some mutual support between myself and the people introduced to the institute by my new colleague.

Dream six

> I am in a very large, many-roomed building, like an old cinema/ theatre. I know there are several floors (layers) to the building and several exits and stairs/corridors leading to exits, but I do not know where the exits all are. Everywhere I go is unfamiliar to me.

> I am with a few people (no children) and one of them is an ex-client (a policewoman). Her brother is with us (he looks like Ian Beal from Coronation Street). The brother has been taking cannabis and harder drugs and I find the evidence. I sense there are other people in his group somewhere, hiding away in the building (I hear voices in distant rooms and smells come to me), and I want to alert the police and I sneak off to look for a telephone.

> The building is full of treacherous stairways and high places with no safety rails, and sometimes I have to take serious risks to get around. I wake in panic, struggling with one of these stairways up the edge of a room to the next floor. The stairs are inches wide, so only my toes will rest on them. The stairs are curved and narrowing as I progress and the hand rail is getting lower and more unreachable as it rises. I fear falling and feel relief on waking.

The building in this dream, the cinema or theatre, is the place where dramas are acted out. I am reminded of my holiday visit to the catacombs, a visit to what is buried. Here, the Apollonic appears as female, the policewoman symbolizing order and containment. I am aware that the Apollonic leaves no place for creativity, and in this dream my creativity is unhealthily represented in the Dionysian image of the orgy, the drugs. This polarization of control (Apollo) and freedom (Dionysian fantasy) appearing in the same dream is seeking integration.

The lack of support for feet brings a memory of a childhood fantasy I had, that an Indian Chief lived beneath my bed and would remove my feet with a tomahawk if I were to try to escape. The mother of the night puts her child to sleep securely then faces her own fears? This was not so in my family. My internalized maternal psyche (lack of support, attunement, on which to find a "footing") and paternal psyche (police control) are both present in this dream, in the process of acknowledging shadow in search for transformation.

Music and poetry (and dreams) integrate the creative tension between freedom and order—even in free verse and dream process there is structure. I am currently teaching the structure–freedom continuum in relation to psychotherapeutic intervention. This dream, then, also carries a countertransferential component.

Dream seven

> I am in a one-storey building, a workplace, like a school, and I find a room resembling a chemistry laboratory with machines and worktops around the walls. I see this through a glass door and enter, curious to find myself wading through waist-high fluid, almost gelatinous fluid, and I wonder why it has not leaked through the door frame or begun to pour out of the room when I opened and closed the door. I sense something "electric" in the air and realize that the machines standing in this fluid are electrically operated and working, and I am very aware of the dangerousness of the situation. Other people are somewhere in the building. I realize that nothing bad is happening and imagine that is because there must be some solution in the water that maintains safety. All becomes dark and I wake.

I have always understood water in my dreams to be representative of unconscious process. This dream, then, is telling me that the solution to conflictual dynamics with which I have been recently working is in my unconscious dream process. The feel of the fluid in my dream brings mercury to mind, and Mercury is the agent of transformation. Also, what comes to mind is that alchemists worked in a laboratory, so this dream is a transformation dream. My feeling accompanying this dream is one of fear and, as a girl, my fear of the chemical world showed itself in high-school chemistry, where I had my lowest marks. I was reasonable at everything else, so why so bad at chemistry?

The associations here for me are that, at that time, what was projected on to the chemistry lab, with its smells, tastes, and somatic experience, was my sexuality and my relationship with my father. I remember his sickly smile, not genuine but invasive, leering when I reached my adolescence. My dream chooses a school subject at which I did poorly. I know now that what I projected on to my ex-husband was my intelligence (which my father shamed me into believing I did not have) and, in embarking on research and the retrieval of my mind and reconstructive energy, I am owning my own intellect and able to free myself from an unhealthy way of being in a relationship, both with my internalized ex-husband and internalized father. Owning my own intelligence promotes my confidence as a trainer, especially for this next academic year, when some of the material, though not new to me, is something I have not previously taught.

This whole dream is a metaphor for containment, in that the fluid neither leaks nor destroys.

Dream eight

> I am in a cottage with another woman, an artist, and she is showing me a work she has just begun, a white moon hiding behind some trees, with branches, over some water. The picture is sketched out in pencil and she is painting from top to bottom systematically, first some white paint for a portion of the moon, then black for tree branches (silhouette), then white, then black, etc. I think, "I can do that, but I'd paint the whole moon and then superimpose the branches with perhaps a little foliage to give it some life."

> Then, I am painting the same picture, but in daylight time, dusk, with shades of pale lemon in the moon and greens in the trees and blues in the water with reflections, and pinks and orange in the sky.

I am then leaving this room. A friend, V, has come to visit and I go to make a coffee in the small kitchen. On opening the door I find a slug on the floor, then a host of small creatures, like miniature rabbits, squirrels, dinosaurs (quite cute, furry) all over the floor with slugs and worms (quite horrible, rough and slimy). I am frantically grabbing kitchen roll and gathering them all up and putting them in the bin. They keep coming from under cupboards, etc. V thinks that it is a shame to hurt the cute ones, so I open the back door to let them out (free) and there's a small narrow pathway between the door and next door's hedge. I am surprised at how narrow a pathway this is, and wonder if the creatures are coming from next door. I am woken by the alarm clock.

The process of painting in this dream clearly explicates the movement from black-and-white (concrete and lifeless) thinking to a more integrated whole picture (view) of life. It goes from concrete thinking to discrimination (of colour). The maternal (moon) leads to creativity and wholeness. The move from night to day signifies movement from the unconscious (sleep) to conscious experience.

The coming out of hiding of the creatures brings to mind that I have recently discovered that my father had war wounds. Wound = vulnus, and I am recognizing my father's vulnerability as opposed to his aggressive control and wonder how much of each of these aspects I have carried for him over the years. I remember his infantile facial expression in my wedding photograph, a time when I am archetypally delivered from his house and his tutelage. The "coming from under cupboards" brings material from beneath where it is stored; again, this signifies movement from the unconscious to conscious experience. This is an integration dream.

Associations here for me, between the feeling state of this dream and my history, are the times when my father took his belt to me as a teenager with some, though minimal, naked sexual exposure, prior to his returning apologetically and in tears; a confusion, I think, between sexual and emotional vulnerability. As I write, considering the Apollo of my father, the term "Apollo" as *signifier* (Lacan, 1954) indicates my learning to apolo-gise without being paternally shamed for mistakes I have made. This experience very much has enhanced my stance of openness as a trainer and how not to react from the paternal introjects of my shadow side.

In previous dreams "house" has symbolically been paternal for me. In this dream, "cottage" is maternal. Maternal space tolerates both symmetry and irregularity. The dream invites the "cute" and the "horrible"; dinosaurs inform me that some of what I have to "clear up" is archaic, and the futility, that when we try to discard something it comes back stronger. I need to work with myself at the instinctual level. How do I relate to men in my life at a female instinctual level and not from shadow introjected history?

Dream nine

> I am in Scarborough, walking along the south sea front and an attractive man approaches me and asks me to go with him. He wears a raincoat with a belt. I feel sexual and attracted and then slowly begin to realise I'm in danger. So I run, along the sea front and up Eastborough. As I turn the bend, the road steepens powerfully and increasingly, I become very
>
> breathless and much slowed and think that I'll have to go up the slope on my hands and knees soon. I am afraid that I am too slow and he'll catch me.
>
> I am then in a tall narrow house, standing by a counter and a man approaches me, again wearing a coat and belt, with a syringe and needle and wanting to persuade me to have his injection to help my painful back. He says he'll have to stand behind me after administering this (he made pelvic thrusting movements) whilst I lean over the counter, to help the injection work. He leers a sickly smile and I feel fear, powerless and trapped. I grab the syringe from him, as he begins to try to inject me, and I thrust it into his thigh through his trousers. He reels backwards and I run. I run upstairs to collect my belongings before escaping the building. I realise then, that the only way out is down the stairs past where he is probably pursuing me and I wake panicked.

In this extended dream, when I free myself from the pursuer by running upstairs, I actually do not escape him because I have no way out, and so in the dream I cannot separate myself from him. And this supports my belief that in all of my dreams the representations are my own, even when they are also universally understood.

I am aware of having witnessed staff in a secure mental health unit administer injections through a patient's trousers when he has made an attack on staff and is about to be secluded. I remember feeling appalled at this practice and isolating myself from other staff in speaking up about this.

In writing this now, I feel the significance of the belts in the dream and remember my father taking his belt to me as a child, if I were to be up-front and open about my mistakes (theme as in 8). I learned to be devious. Symbolically, I relate "front" to up-front, open, and honest, and "behind" to shadow, unseen, deceitful, and dishonest.

The compass points, South and East, I associate respectively, to slavery, oppression (South) and Hull (East Riding) from where my parents originated. My mother was compliant with my oppressive father.

In the dream, the feminine is at risk of losing her voice and para-doxically, the "escape" is in the turning and meeting (addressing) my own potentially harmful masculine energy and my sexual energy.

The message to myself in this dream is to say "No" to penetra-tive oppressive masculine energy and not to fear the healthy masculine energy in myself, in order to claim my own power in relationships. The tall thin building is the institute that I have recently sold. I have profound uneasiness in the father complex I know already, and I need to take another stance. Differences between my father and myself were not allowed. Differences between my new colleague and myself are being worked through. In the dreams, as always, in getting away I do it the hard way—uphill and alone!!

Dream ten

> My colleague is showing me around his home and sharing his posses-sions with me. We reach the bedroom and we make love in the most beautiful way I've ever made love. Yet I wake feeling uncomfortable.

My discomfort is in the concretization of the symbolic, in that my colleague is a married man and I have a partner, and hence this dream is of a forbidden act. Previous dreams have informed me of my need to be spontaneous and in considering this dream in a concrete thinking way, that need remains very evident. Jung sees libido as psychic energy (not specifically sexual as with Freud), which flows towards other, ideas, friends, children. Making love is symbolic of the creation of life, with intercourse as the greatest metaphor for union without fusion. This dream then, holds the symbolic meaning of female and male ego uniting in the unconscious, in my unconscious.

I am aware of the enormous strides (given my history story, not room enough to portray here) that this dream encapsulates of my owning my own sexuality without shame. The phallus is symbolic of the masculine principle of insemination, and I am taking on board a healthy male ego.

Often, when our energy has been spent in survival, we need to access our shadow energy (that which is socially unacceptable) to bring about change. Shadow is necessary in any emotional growth.

Dream eleven

> I'm in a meeting place and H arrives with LC and introduces me to her. They discuss the UKCP meeting they've just attended together and L is attempting to comfort H, telling him that she never realized he was so vulnerable and had such a hard time looking after himself. "They really went for you in that meeting." H was a bit flustered, and defensively trying to make light of it all, acting with bravado.
>
> I am then outside of a hotel building with H and his male friend/ colleague. A 4×4 arrives and a man and woman get out and the man says something to H that H doesn't understand. H comes across as insolent, and the man attacks him. I realize that this is going to be brutal; H is totally defenceless and mouths a scream, saying, "Help me". The woman and H's friend stand, detached, and look on at this.
>
> I am on the hotel steps terrified, frozen, and thinking, "I must ring the police but can't leave him, and by the time the police get here he'll be dead."

In this dream, innocence gets caught. The death of an aspect of someone can show in a dream as the death of the whole person. Each aspect of a dream may be our own quality but may also be a quality that we see in someone who is very close to us. I am acknowledging here that I have separated from H and am feeling the pain of not being able to rescue (rescuing was my stance in our relationship). I need to feel this despair in order to be able to let go.

In this dream, the urge to destroy is localized to one aspect, innocence, of someone with whom I have been in relationship, and. in acting in a mature way. I am moving on from my own unhealthy innocent way of being in relationships, with the accompanying idealizing transferences that I bring from my childhood.

The archetypal existential destruction as in dream one is now broken down to a specific attribute. As shadow phenomena are worked with in dreams, the archetypes lose their power and show themselves in more detailed form. While I do not wish to lose my innocence, it must be integrated into the adult, healthier, more responsible aspect of my personality.

Dream twelve

> I have three babies/children in a pram, my children. There is no one about. The world is isolated and feels cold to me. Although I am in a street of houses, the feeling is of emptiness, almost eerie, and we are to get away, though not quite urgently. I am to take them away from this place to somewhere else. I notice that the middle toddler has diarrhoea on his/her hands (I am unsure of the sex of the children), then realize that another toddler has this also. I imagine a full nappy, which they have been playing with, then realize that the baby is the same. I am concerned that I must clean them all up to make them comfortable, and then see diarrhoea coming from the baby's nostrils. I am concerned now that they are infected and may soon become dehydrated, and there is urgency for me to get them to somewhere with people before they each die. I wake extremely anxious.

Freud relates human excrement and sphincter control, that is, what is inside and what is outside, to boundary formation. Faeces are the first thing a child creates, and hence dreams of faeces can be profoundly creative. However, in society in general, shit is unwelcome, and can indicate the shadow side of our society's sanitized psyche. I was brought up in a sanitized, squeaky-clean household. To have diarrhoea is to have no sphincter control, but the important factor is whether or not the diarrhoea is infected, or affected. The contaminated aspect is how we let our shadow influence us. Although in this dream I become aware of risks of dehydration and lack of nourishment, I take steps to counter-balance this.

Life is at risk in this dream. I relate this to early schizoidal process, whereby the baby is emotionally deprived of the right to spontaneously exist.

I am reminded of dream seven, and consider how the goal of the alchemist is to transform shit into treasure. Christ was born in a stable; the greatest-born in the lowliest place among cattle and in a base container. My mother attempted to transform her "shit" by becoming confluent with a Baptist, almost Pentecostal, religion. And my father, in his grandiosity, repressed any characterological shit he carried and strived in an obsessive–compulsive way for cleanliness.

For my consideration is, "What parts of myself have I written off as shitty?" If we are willing to receive, repression becomes unnecessary.

Below, relating the dreams (numerically) and my understanding to my work as a psychotherapy trainer, I conclude:

1. Own my own power, including the potentially destructive aspects of this.
2. Negotiate the training stance needed to contain the splitting process.
3. Do not "mother" trainees unhealthily. Learn to work alongside the new Director. Acknowledge the success of UKCP Registration and adapt to the changes this will inevitably bring.
4. Find my own healthy male energy as well as learning to acknowledge a healthy male presence in the Institute.
5. Ongoing process of discovery re new institute dynamics, re new Director and UKCP presence. Be aware of the positive and negative aspects of the structure/freedom tension in my training approach.
6. How am I both controlling and permission-giving with trainees? Acceptance of my own structure and creativity in teaching this material to them. How can they bring their own negative energy to the group and have me contain this?
7. Owning my own intellect enhances my stance as a trainer. I can be more appreciative of containment as it occurs cognitively in seeking meaning, as well as how it occurs emotionally, somatically, or symbolically in my dreams.
8. Confirmation of my beliefs about shadow experience—I do not have to be narcissistically perfect as a trainer. Inviting

and welcoming shadow experience into the training group is necessary.

9. Where is the place for male energy in the countertransference? My role in the training group is more than that of symbolic mother! In acknowledging this and owning my own healthy male energy, I reduce the potential of trainees to "split" myself and my colleague. Marriage (transferentially as in a male and female trainer) is one institution where two halves do not make a whole. Each trainer needs to own both their male and female qualities.

10. Inviting sexual expression and exploration into the training process is healthy. Shadow energy needs welcoming in the training milieu.

11. In selling the institute I am no longer the womb, symbolically, and am freeing myself from the maternal and from my prone-ness to unhealthy rescuing. In owning my own maleness, I remain open to discovering new ways of relating to trainees and to SCPTI.

12. Bring the shit to the training group. Currently, trainees are still in conflict about how considerate (safe) we are in this group *vs.* desires to bring aggression. My role is to balance, offering nour-ishment without infantilizing.

Overview of the six-month dream process and analysis as whole.

Initially, in my dreams, shadow presents as destructiveness, which is all consuming, existential. Later, discrimination occurs, and shadow images are broken down and related to specific qualities in myself and individuals with whom I identify. Destructiveness shows in the form of fire (passion) and penetration (sexuality) and, partway through the analysis, the concept of alchemy (transforma-tion) is introduced and fire then becomes portrayed as strengthen-ing (as in firing china to reinforce) and sexuality becomes related to healthy union of male and female energy.

My own process of making shadow welcome is being paralleled in the training situation, or theirs in mine. The training process and my own process are mutually influencing of each other, and my dreams, then, are in part containing of my own intra-psychic growth and in part containing of training group dynamics counter-transferentially.

Invited experiment

Remember to keep a small notebook and pen at your bedside.

As you go off to sleep each evening, give yourself an invitation to remember your dreams. Remember that this process cannot be forced. As you become more and more open to remembering, the memories will stay with you.

As each dream wakes you, make a note of three key words or a picture, which will prompt your memory in the morning.

When you have a half hour free time, find yourself a comfortable, quiet and uninterrupted space to contemplate your dream.

You may wish to

- draw a picture of your dream,
- write down the story as if you were telling your dream to some-one else,
- write down the story as if your dream is happening right now,
- consider, if your dream was a televised programme, what title would it carry?

It does not matter if you cannot remember all of your dream. Allow yourself to remember what you can.

Allow yourself to notice what is figural for you in your dream. What aspect of your dream is it that takes most of your time, energy and interest at any given moment? What are you curious about?

- Take each of these aspects in turn and, in a relaxed place, allow yourself to identify with what is figural for you. Begin your sentence with "I am—" and stay open to whatever emerges for you. For example, if you dream of a briefcase, you might think, "I am made of the very finest leather. I am softer on the outside than on the inside. Only I have the code to access what's inside me," etc., or you may think, "I am very old and worn. I have been handled a lot and done a lot of work. I carry important things inside me." Only you can know what message is hidden for you in the identification with what has been projected into your dreams.

- You might choose to take each key word and free associate the meaning for yourself. The process of free association stimulates a train of thought, which enhances awareness and the making of connections between symbolic meaning and phenomenologically felt experience. For example, the word tart may signify something pleasant to eat and bring back a memory of baking with your mother, or it may signify a woman whose sexual boundaries are loose. You might then ask yourself, where is the mother or the tart in yourself?

- This process can also be adopted with numbers occurring in your dream. What does each number signify for you? What memories or associations arise from the numbers presenting in your dreams?

Over a period of time, you may notice recurring themes in your dreams, or you may have a memory of a recurring dream or nightmare from your childhood that you would like to work on and understand more fully by exploring it in one of the above ways.

If you wake before your dream feels complete, you can suggest for yourself an appropriate ending for this dream. This is particularly valuable if your dream is a nightmare.

Above all, realize that frightening and disturbing dreams are normal, common to us all (even if we do not remember them) and these dreams carry important learning for us, just as the more pleasant dreams do.

CHAPTER SIX

Life at sea

"I want to know if you can sit with pain, mine or your own, without moving to hide it, or fade it, or fix it"

(Oriah Mountain Dreamer, 1999, p. 35)

I n this chapter, we have evidence of shadow dynamics from the training field, as the actual experience of senior trainers. Direct quotes from trainers are in italics. To maintain anonymity and respect the confidentiality of the owners of the statements and of specific training institutes and organizations, I have chosen to use only the material by which the trainers themselves and their training environments cannot be identified.

Those of you who read this chapter and recognize your own contribution and influence, please accept my deepest appreciation of your willingness to have your experiences included in this way, as potential learning for fellow professionals and for us all.

In an attempt to present this complex material with as much clarity as is possible, I have chosen to use the following headings:

- the presentation of shadow;
- the influence of past on present—the personality we bring with us into the training environment;
- current field dynamics;
- containment.

The presentation of shadow

The question of shadow? *Well, it's a big question—I can contain a belief in the central importance of the shadow as possibly the most demanding and possibly the greatest characteristic of human nature that we know.* This shows how enormous shadow dynamics can be in training groups, where human nature is at the core of the work undertaken.

Within the broad understanding of the meaning of the term, and the wide range of experiences that this term covers, shadow can be understood as, *something that includes actual evil, but also something which includes the murky and iffy and problematic and tricky and pain in the butt aspects of human resistance as well. And I think it shunts back and forth between those two dimensions.*

The quality of shadow in the form of evil can show itself as *Oppression, cruelty, malice, torture, scapegoating, lynching, persecution, destroying the soul of other human beings and destroying the body of other human beings.* I would add to this the process of retroflection, whereby shadow can also be turned against the self, against one's own body.

The essence of human nature predisposes both aggression and destruction. Reference is given to *all that conflictual, aggressive side of what it is to be human* and *it is the nature of envy that when it comes out of the bag, it seeks to destroy.* While certain circumstances precipitate aggression and destructiveness, the predisposition to these experiences is seen as a core human quality in each one of us, and envy is one example of this.

Both the enormity of shadow experience and its place in the unconscious are acknowledged with *It's a big question. I mean, the shadow is really the disowned bits isn't it? The things we don't say of our imagination. Or even the things we don't know about. The shadow is not just really what we don't own, but what we don't even know; what we cannot even begin to accept.*

There are *problem issues I've found really difficult and struggled with as a trainer*. Examples are given of trainees' shadow experience, such as when they breached boundaries by being late coming back to the training group every lunchtime and after breaks. When trainees were challenged about this, *their reaction was completely irrational and they engaged in acting out behaviours*. Their aggression was to such a degree that this trainer would be unwilling to ever become a major trainer again. Some of this acting out behaviour was in the form of people not being reliable in paying training fees and *playing games around this*. A correlation is made between acting out behaviour and *Shadow can emerge in the form of regression*. This will be explored further when transference is considered.

In considering shadow in his own experience as a psychotherapy trainee, one trainer recognizes the shock of first finding out that trainers had problems with each other. In early training experiences, this trainer felt stimulated, nurtured, and encouraged, and the realization that alerted him to the dangers of malign and malevolent forces being released in the background came later. What then followed were lots of experiences of people cutting out, in terms of mistrust and self-righteousness and censoriousness.

In shadow being assigned here to the breaking down of relationships within training institutes, it is acknowledged that most of the reasons for this were about power and status, about who called the shots, about who really had the say, about who takes centre stage. This is qualified with the trainer's experience of being in a highly charged situation where healing of this was really impossible. Alongside the issue of who holds the power is the issue of who gets slagged off or stereotyped. Although this trainer believes that all of this was in awareness, he also reports leakage of shadow experience that was out of awareness.

Evidence of the "out of awareness" component of shadow is given as shadow is defined as described by Robert Bly (1990), that is, "The black bag into which we put a lot of negative things in our lives". These negative things incorporate that which is considered *less honourable, sometimes shocking, somewhat persecutory, distant and austere, highly critical, maliciously viscous, wanting to destroy, diminishing and rubbishing*. This shadow *lashes out, disempowers, exercises an abusive part, badmouths people, denigrates* and makes *potential enemies*. This evidence supports Guggenbuhl-Craig's (1971, p. 31) belief that the shadow is "always somewhat destructive, operating negatively upon the positive ideals taken up by the collective or the individual". Shadow experience leaves the black bag in one of two ways; the bag leaks, or it bursts. The people whose shadow leaks, *kind of seep things out of this bag all the time*. When the bag bursts, this happens because someone who appears on the surface to be very *sweet* is suddenly faced with another aspect of his or her personality, which surprises them, as well as those around them.

Sometimes shadow shows verbally in what is said or in how it is said, *some of the things he said, and the way he said it, were really personally quite hurtful*, with behavioural implications in which *people try to split key figures in institutes, by feeding them information, often in the most innocuous way, but nevertheless it's quite deliberate and malevolent*. This dynamic can be considered metaphorically with the story of Othello and Desdemona, where an envy-based murder takes place for someone to be displaced and replaced by the person who envies. Both Oaklander (1978) and Stern (1985) honour the advantages of metaphor and symbolism in the process of raising awareness.

The longevity of people's defensive strategies in relation to shadow is acknowledged with reference to ageing, suggesting that it is possible to see the effects of ageing in two ways: *And then as we get older and the bag gets fuller, people keep it under wraps, even from themselves, for years and years and years*, and, when shadow emerges, *when it does come out, it's quite shocking*. This implies that the longer shadow remains unacknowledged, the more powerfully it might show itself when it does emerge. But, also, the statement of *I'm aware that I must be carrying things in my bag that come out from time to time* recognizes a willingness to engage in a healthy level of self-awareness. Awareness brings with it a reduction in the internal pressure to relegate experience to shadow aspects of personality. In believing that *there's something about getting older and not giving a damn so much*, this trainer seems to be saying that, paradoxically, growing older increases potential for shadow to leak only if one does not engage in a process of awareness, which in itself reduces the impact of shadow.

Being part of the psychotherapy profession is seen as a predisposing factor in itself to shadow potentially emerging. Belief is expressed that *in the psychotherapy profession, because we are very sophisticated interpersonally . . . we do have the capacity to reach in and hurt people where it hurts them most* and an example is given of a trainer who, *out of awareness, was using the therapy/training situation to exercise an abusive part.* Again, the value of awareness is acknowledged.

The impact of such abusive conduct is exemplified as one trainer shares his *anger at the way I was treated* and *indignation at the way both staff and students felt themselves having to acquiesce in . . . quite oppressive conduct.* His phenomenological experience on the receiving end of this shadow behaviour, which he conceptualizes as *what we're inclined to dump on other people and make them carriers of it,* he describes as *anxiety, fear* and *weariness.*

He reflects that *There's always a power aspect to any psychotherapy training process that people chafe with, both at the level of students, trainees and at the level of people running the trainings and at every level of that, some of that comes out as shadow.*

Another trainer contemplates shadow. *Phew! It's out there! Power and sex. They're the two. They're the two aspects of shadow; they're the two that come to mind.* And *What I think about power is that we don't see it when we've got it. That I don't see it when I've got it and they* [trainees] *don't see it when they've got it".* Regarding sexuality, in one training group, *Anything that leads to some of what we offered, just on having sex, led to almost giggles and laughter. And that is not sufficiently part of what we train on sexuality. We are much more comfortable doing it about the sexual difficulties or problem; vaginismus, or whatever it might be, that some clients bring, and not enough of the experiential aspects of sex".*

A trainer alludes to male sexuality with, *It's easier to see the man's shadow than the woman's shadow. Man's shadow sticks out,* and *being seductive* is also referred to as part of shadow process.

I am remembering a psychotherapy training group where, despite the directive not to have sex with other group members, several people engaged in sexual activity with each other. For some people, it is part of their developmental process that, paradoxically, and perhaps unconsciously, prohibition is seen as invitation. Analytic theory suggests that there is no negative in the unconscious.

We have all known the small child who, when told not to touch the sweets when Mum is out of the room, will automatically do that very thing. His intellect is insufficiently developed for him to think rationally and understand concepts of "because" and "not", and, hence, what he hears is "touch the sweets", because that is what he wants. Regression and transference in the training situation will be discussed more fully a little later. And we cannot deny their existence. Perhaps what is needed is not an imposed set of ground rules but, rather, a healthy discussion for each group to determine their own ground rules with as minimal trainer authority as possible. Imposition, I think, engages the child ego state in the trainee to either conform or reject.

With the issue of shadow emerging as petty theft from an institute or from a colleague, I wonder whether, in some cases, the need for souvenirs or mementos can precipitate this behaviour. Winnicott (1969) discusses the concept of "transitional object" that is useful in the development of object constancy in personal growth, in that the taken object becomes the representative of the valued other person, and it is adhered to until the other person has become sufficiently internalized by the person who took the object. With items going missing from an institute, one would hope that someone might respectfully request the possibility of removing something small to act as a transitional object, as happened with one of my trainees who took home a small ornament. In my willingness to allow her to do this, she felt loved by me and other group members learnt that I care about my trainees. However, given that this is often a developmentally needed request, while not condoning the behaviour, we can be compassionate with those people whose process, at this time in their lives, makes asking impossible.

Another dynamic at work here, of course, might be theft as an acting out of aggression directed at a trainer, with a sense of "I've got one over on you". And I am reminded of the early developmental process of individuation between mother and child, when the child learns to undo a confluent situation by having a secret. The experience for the child of "I know something that you don't know" builds his or her sense of self as being different from the parent. It would be even more understandable that transferential dynamics such as these happen in an institute where trainees have not only their training, but also their therapy. In expecting trainees to work through transferential issues and increasingly bring their adult ego state experience into the training situation, we are acknowledging that transferential issues can arise or leak into arenas outside of therapy. And if the trainee's transference is blocked by the trainer too soon, then it is more likely to become acted out in the environment.

It is human nature that people in a less powerful position might seek to disempower authority figures. The power that senior trainers have can be attacked by more junior people in the ways in which juniors play one senior member against the other, trying to "split" them in an innocuous way, as we have seen, by feeding them information. This is considered with *I think it's a malevolence in the shadow that comes out and seeks to destroy through splitting.* Klein (1989) suggests that projection of a split-off aspect of the self occurs as a relief from the internal anxiety of feeling split and in pieces, and that this process may well be below the level of awareness. It is not only the junior members of an institute who bring their transferential patterns to authority. *Misuse and abuse of power* among trainers themselves is also discussed. The *snobbery involved in psychotherapy trainings* is likened to being *formally heady*, and results in the experiences of aggression, jealousy, and envy that the attitude of superiority stimulates. Another pertinent dynamic is when someone attacks, not the authority figure themselves, but someone close to the authority figure, so that the authority figure is hurt by displacement.

Again, the "out of awareness" nature of some shadow material is considered, alongside an acknowledgement of the more pleasurable aspect of shadow, when it is defined as . . . *a delightful thing and a really very painful encounter; maybe the unborn bits that have never been there, but there are the unwanted bits which are in shadow because of the systemic forces; they've become relegated to the darkness.*

This trainer responds to the question on shadow spontaneously with *to go with what immediately comes to mind with . . . a strong feeling*, and her initial sharing of her shadow experience is in reference to gender bias. She shares, *That was very strong*, and explains that this issue was *just on the nether regions of my unconscious or preconscious.* In this experience, a male trainee had challenged her about her attitude towards him; he was angry and behaved in a very hurtful way. She perceived, *It was destructiveness.* She continues to acknowledge the primarily unconscious nature of her shadow, with *So, there's the blindness and the themes and the areas where maybe I get caught*, and again, in reference to trainees, *that's another little catch net which takes them by surprise.* Named themes are sexuality, envy, and jealousy as underlying emotions, which this trainer believes contribute to shadow behaviour, in particular about competitiveness in training groups. Shadow also shows itself, she states, in the form of labelling. Labelling becomes a *hot potato*.

She seems to be saying that shadow comprises unconscious motivation to behaviours and, once an issue or experience comes into awareness, then painful encounters might become a delight, and this is hard work. She refers to the time with trainees when *You're kind of knee deep in it and you think, Oh shit! Is that really a part of me? So, I mean it brings up themes which surprise them at first, and then they can own them.* This marries well with Zinker's (1977) concept of the "uncomfortable delight" of discovering oneself.

The positive attributes to be utilized from shadow energy that is in awareness is recognized with, *I suppose I just think of shadow as so self-limiting, which makes it almost such a waste, not realizing, not just turning over those sods of earth which are the shadow, so as to actually just capture that energy there. So, part of the shadow, I suppose, is actually thinking here that shadow is bad and awful. But I like to think of shadow as lost energy, or energy to be found.* And, in the training group, *There was something of having to be really open to hearing and open to . . . hurt and destructiveness. But, if I could let some of it in, it might be quite useful.*

Another trainer makes a distinction between shadow that is enjoyable, and shadow that is not; *There's part of shadow that becomes enjoyable, which is the shadow that's in the light. The shadow's shadow, that can sneak around and cause trouble.*

It seems, then, that acknowledgement of shadow is good practice. What is clear is that *We've got it. It's one of those things*, and, as professionals, we need to take responsibility for working with it. *Who knows who's going to do the most damage? It's hard to know. How do we even know our place? How do we know what place we actually have? We are, at the end of the day, human, with our limited abilities, with our democratic criteria.*

With the shadow comes something that is fantastic.

The influence of past on present—the personality we bring with us to the training environment

We have considered that shadow can leak, or it can burst. In the situation of shadow leaking into someone's current field, where the persecutory behaviour seems to others to be part of someone's personality, when conflict arises in this person's life their ego is insufficiently strong to contain the emotions, to protect themselves against the conflict. These people function from a place of introjection of an aspect of someone in their past. They have identified with abusive power in their family or social world and, when conflicted in adulthood, will do to others what was done to themselves as children. So, one could surmise that predisposing factors would be the original relationship with authority figures and an underdeveloped ego, and the precipitating dynamic is how this original relationship colours current experiences of conflict. This is evidenced with the understanding that *they tend to be persecutory from their Parent* [ego-state] *. . . it's almost like they reach out and strangle the Child* [ego-state], *so people get very frightened or intimidated by them, beyond all proportion.*

The other dynamic that leads to this reaction is when someone phenomenologically feels vulnerable, behaving in a supportive way to people in authority and thus projecting his or her power. The authority figure sees this person as supportive, shares their own vulnerability, and hence denies the projection of power, leading to the projector, unconsciously, being left holding their own power, which is expressed as punitive because that is what they already know from authority figures in their early past. The underlying emotions here are given as envy and jealousy. *Envy not only wants what you want, it's prepared to destroy you to get what is wanted.* An example of how this is portrayed is as the envy that seeks to rubbish a colleague's professional ability and to denigrate their published work, a kind of stealing of reputation *in a moral high ground fashion.* This is one example of what Cashdan (1988) describes as the unhealthy process of projective identification. I believe that this can show itself in different forms, according to the personality style of the projector.

Personality styles are seen as potential underpinnings for shadow in relation to power dynamics. For example, when trainers feed on their image of importance and allow themselves to be the subject of adulation, this is shadow at work. It is suggested that it is the excitement of this that invites them to allow it to happen and continue. This is indicative of the grandiosity associated with the narcissistic personality.

It is recognized that some training institutes are founded by very charismatic trainers. Indeed, this might, in part, be necessary, because institutes need someone with an air of confidence who feels they really do deserve an institute in order for them to make it happen. The negative side of that is that these trainers can take all the authority and power and others around them allow that to happen, projecting their own power on to the leader. People feel beholden to the leaders and then not in a position to challenge them, which, from a shadow perspective, can lead to quite serious loss of skill. One trainer acknowledges that, for him, interrelationships between trainers were difficult, in part because he, at that time, felt insufficiently in touch with his own strength and authority, and the other person involved was not able to handle conflict and be challenged. Hence, getting to the resolution of difficulties was impossible. We have a realization here that although to be in touch with one's own strength paradoxically allows for vulnerability also to be welcome, this should not be so much so that our strength becomes lost. Strength and vulnerability go hand in hand.

The unhealthy strategy for one trainer, in dealing with his/her own narcissistic vulnerability, was to become controlling and monopolise all the power. The strategy of those around this person was to conform and project. And a colleague realizes that, at that time, even if he had been more open and welcomed unexplored depths rising to the surface, because of the inability of the other colleague also to do this, the relationship would still have broken down. We can see that for relationships to be deep and open, both parties must have the willingness to engage in vulnerability.

One trainer found herself vulnerable as a result of her cultural background differing from that of her trainees. In reference to this, she states, *It has brought up themes. I rather suspect that it was my different cultural upbringing. I often felt, when I came to live here, that what shadow was for me there, is in the light here. So, culturally, there's an obverse situation, which has been advantageous to be able to capture.*

This trainer qualifies the polarity of this with an example of the different way in which success or failure is treated in each country. She states, *So, there, what would be hidden is failure. Success, you display success.* Having been supported earlier in her life to behave in a certain way, she is open to noticing the avoidance of this in her trainees. *So, I think that opposite or apposite has been useful in catching that aspect of really having to tease out of them owning their success. Getting trainees to say, almost getting a competitive edge up, saying with the training, "I'm really going to do well" was like, What!! I never actually thought somebody would come out with that!! So, I mean, there's the envy, of course, and the jealousy.*

We can see here how owning one's skill and the competitiveness in the training environment can bring uncomfortable feelings that, when influenced by cultural introjects, might lead someone to discount and belittle their own abilities, perhaps in the form of retroflection, withholding of energy. Introjection is the process that, in this instance, is responsible for supporting lack of ownership of one's power. "Don't boast" is a typically British parental attitude.

We have already considered how the process of narcissism, an over-preoccupation with the self, can lead to withdrawal and a fear of being seen: either to be seen as successful or to be seen as a failure is experienced as excruciatingly shaming; this is the closet aspect of narcissistic process. The experience of shame can result in shadow evidencing itself in several self-limiting ways, for example, in turning negative energy towards the self in the form of withholding and withdrawing self-celebration and abilities, for someone who might otherwise be really bright and excel in our field: *the terrible, terrible fear* [in] *steering away from being too clever* and *It seems like that asymptotic approaching of a point of really being somebody outstanding. But how much of the pain here is of just touching into their superego of "too clever, grandiose".*

A sad and painful example, which the subject shares, is her memory of a trainer who would have had all these attributes, but no one ever honoured his outstanding capabilities. His strategy was to assume a stance of becoming alcoholic (retroflected shadow) rather than seemingly abuse people by overshadowing them. This is the shadow of running from oneself. When our phenomenological experience is not affirmed or mirrored, we have a sense of being too big, too much for other people.

In the grandiose aspect of narcissism, of course, the opposite is also true, and the pain of failure is defended against with the strategy of "I can do anything on my own", this moral high ground being part of the narcissistic inflatory defence.

One trainer refers to a trainee with narcissistic process: *he took very few notes in workshops . . . was fairly dogmatic in his statements*

. . . found reflective self-criticism very difficult . . . blamed the trainers for an average mark. The trainer continues to say that when this trainee chose to end his therapy abruptly, telling his therapist, "You're a waste of space", and was respectfully reminded by his therapist of a verbal contract for an ending of one month, he denied the contract. When his therapist informed the training organization, as he was ethically obliged to do, the trainee refused conciliation and took out a complaint in a malicious, vicious way, wanting to destroy the reputation of the therapist. This is the toxic aspect of the narcissistic personality. The effect on the therapist of this behaviour was to feel *quite gutted, diminished and rubbished.* We have evidence here of how narcissistic process can both predispose and precipitate shadow.

The three aspects of narcissism, closet, grandiose, and toxic might not all be in someone's awareness, as demonstrated by intrapersonal denial, *There's a whole side of their personality which they're actually not in touch with,* or inter-personal denial, as in the above example (*We never had such a contract*) between therapist and client, and this unawareness leads to toxicity, as in this case, where the trainee attacked through an accusation of unethical behaviour: *he got extremely angry and took out an ethics charge.*

In my experience, for the narcissist idealization offers a transferential position both potentially projected and personally adopted in the countertransference, and the unmet need in childhood is that of feeling special (Greenberg, 1998). Hence, sharing and equality are intolerable. A situation, fuelled by such jealousy perhaps, is *I heard of a situation where a trainer was criticizing other trainers in the training group.* Here, the "grandiose sense of self-importance" referred to in *DSM-IV* (1997) is achieved through belittling the other, as the trainee who had forgotten his verbal contract had to do to his therapist. The necessary learning from this situation is that written contracts are far more protective of all concerned than are verbal agreements.

Trainers and trainees alike can also become caught up in a negative way in the dynamics of the training group: *. . . this particular programme leader, when trainees talked about their therapy in the training group, he encouraged them to be highly critical, making judgements about their therapists.* Trainees *in this training group were feeling disempowered. They felt their trainer had favourites.*

When this was addressed with the trainer by a senior institute member, *it was completely out of his awareness. His first reaction was to be very angry, then he began to cry . . . said he would deal with it . . . within a matter of days he'd written a letter saying that everything that was said about him was a lie and he wanted to resign.*

I wonder if this is likely to be a narcissistic group leader, who became toxic when his defensive sense of grandiosity was threatened by his perceived criticism. His closet vulnerability was too much for his ego to tolerate.

Another trainer addresses the interrelational process of shadow experience in an organization in which he held a senior position. He discusses his own personality pattern of relating, learnt in childhood, and also the personality of the manager with whom he relates. He refers to his manager as *someone whose leadership was extremely insecure and rather restrictively dominance based,* and who *overrides all considerations of fairness in pursuit of her own power, and scapegoats people who don't conform.* He uses metaphor to exemplify this, with the American saying that *You can't fight City Hall,* suggesting of the manager that *in this institute, she was City Hall,* and she was very good at what he terms divide and conquer, which meant that she managed to hold on to power for many years.

In this particular situation, for a period of time, he was supportive to his manager. Difficulties arose when she perceived him as not being so. This happened, she thought, in the way in which he related to trainees, following his own integrity rather than what his manager wished to impose. He then, in his experience, *became a marked person in my turn,* and he *just put on a rhinoceros hide where she was concerned.* The interrelational dynamics here of the manager using her powerful position to control, in defence of her own vulnerability, and then behaving toxically when feeling her control threatened, again fits well with narcissistic process. The receiving trainer's cognitive defence of using understanding to self support, his vulnerability to shame and humiliation and being adversely affected at the level of terror, his learning to wait and to watch, reflects what Greenberg (1998) would understand as schizoid personality process. This might also be evidenced by what one might consider a masochistic aspect to his personality, in that he *didn't mind being the battered scapegoat.* This trainer values his awareness of his own potential to shadow and the usefulness of reflexive practice as he states, *lest I, in my turn, am projecting and dumping my own totalitarianism on this person.* We have evidence here of how schizoid process and narcissistic process can both predispose and precipitate shadow dynamics becoming acted out.

The transferential aspect of this situation is acknowledged as he shares, *I have difficult relationships with women of this kind of temperament* [powerful women]. *Some of those go back to school days.* The power, intensity, and impact of the memory of boarding school evoked in the manager–trainer relationship suggest that there are transferential phenomena at work here and the trainer acknowledges that. *That pattern goes back to my experience of prep school and there have been other variants on it since.* The fact that the trainer says that he will be able to access issues relating to the shadow better if he *doesn't go down that for the moment,* and then he continues almost immediately to talk at length and in great detail about *that,* the original incident leading to his awareness of *the fact that not all adults were to be trusted,* is further evidence of how transferential experiences can very easily and powerfully invade current thoughts and relationships.

His childhood experience, which gave him *quite an intensive sado-masochistic strand in my personality* with the positive effect of having *radar for these kinds of people,* also rendered him vulnerable in power imbalance situations. He acknowledges that his childhood experience *does have a bearing for the moment . . . I had to learn to be able to repress my immediate reactions,* which he later qualifies with memories of his early years as *the humiliation was far worse than the actual physical punishment.*

A *terrific amount of competitiveness* in the field is seen by a further trainer as underpinning shadow behaviour. When she herself was leaving the training due to illness, despite being offered other trainers, the trainees all engaged in leave-taking, *It was, I felt that it was, for me, very much the shadow side coming out. They got ***. They got ***. They got somebody else to work with him. You know, it was like, we'd done lots and lots of things in Adult* [ego-state], *here and now, to prepare them, but still they acted out.*

The subject tells how she had *gone to a lot of trouble and self-sacrifice for them* and they *had absolutely no understanding of that . . . I think that was the other bit that wounded me.* Other experiences she endured were those of feeling *furious, wounded, and disappointed.* At an organizational level, the subject believes that people *can be quite ruthless* and that things remain unchallenged because *people must be scared*. Indeed, in her institute, . . . *they were all so angry with me, they went to another training institute.*

She gives, as a contributory factor for trainees moving across to another training programme, the charismatic personality of one of the trainers at the second institute. She reports that, despite the fact that the other trainer does very little teaching, he has written books, and this attracts trainees. This possibly is an idealizing transference dynamic on the trainees' behalf, potentially invited by the narcissism of the charismatic second trainer.

A further trainer considers transferential process linked to the leadership style of the narcissist, where he sees hero worship and adulation inviting idealization of the trainer by trainees. This collapses eventually, when the trainee feels internally rejected or done over. And then, once the trainee becomes uppity and breaks out of the transference, the narcissistically orientated leader withdraws their favours and, from a shadow place, diminishes the trainee. Interestingly, he considers a paradox: that the more narcissistic the trainer, the more he or she needs the grandiosity and illusions, and this is not good. Narcissistic leaders need the blunt truth, and, again paradoxically, they actually cannot hear it. He believes that the only hope for containment is in modelling alternative ways of being, persistently, and not buying into their depiction of their worlds. They need a change of thought that can be invited when they observe other ways of doing things than their own. Appreciating difference enhances democracy, and potentially transforms transferential idealization into genuine admiration and respect.

Transference

The transferential aspect to the training process is recognized with *we attract what we see in the world around us*. Transferentially, we see/expect what we already know; we can even behave in such a way as to set others up to give us what we already know, despite an intense desire to have something different. With reference to trainees, one trainer shares that difficulties have arisen because of trainees' projections on to herself, and also hers on to them, with the transferential dynamic emerging of: *Their behaviour is as if they're back at school with a teacher, which I think is the shadow side. They're actually all adults, mostly in their thirties and forties, professional people,* and yet, *A part of the shadow is that as soon as people get into a training group they regress to about eight years old.*

When considering shadow experience, a trainer shares, *obviously, what springs to mind is the transference and countertransference, as negative, but also positive,* yet acknowledges *that positive transference and countertransference carries a negative side to that, because neither of them are real. But it's very powerful.*

What astounds me is that, over a period of many years as a psychotherapist and as a trainer, I never cease to be strongly affected by the transferential process. This is the undeniable evidence of its power. We never graduate from the impact of transferential dynamics. Of course, without the transference we would be denied one very valuable pathway for exploring the experience of past relational dynamics. And I would argue now that, without transference, no real in-depth therapeutic work can be done. The healing is in the move from unconscious to conscious experience, from illusion to reality.

The importance and influence of transference has been noted in the very paradigm that underpins integrative psychotherapy philosophy, that of reworking our childhood experience, and also in addressing the potential idealization, which is displaced from childhood on to charismatic psychotherapy trainers. A trainer tells us that . . . *other people catch my shadow. People that I'm thinking about . . . some students are more visible than others. I mean, that seems unfair both to them and me. They don't ask for attention, while others are more pushy, I would say. My shadow is this; how people fit into my planning. So, they become special for reasons in my own countertransference and then there's a sense in which they're in my thinking and others aren't.*

We see how this trainer relates to her own aspect of the transferential situation. Transference dynamics emerge from *both* parties of the relationship, the trainee and the trainer. They are co-created. Transferentially, when a student gets forgotten in the training group it might well be that this is what has already happened in his or her childhood, or, as Greenberg (1998) states, the unmet need of the narcissistic personality is the need to be special. If a trainer makes one student special, it is likely that the trainer is responding to a developmental deficit, and, in my experience of training, when one person is perceived as special in a training group, then others may feel a sense of rejection or of being forgotten. This trainer acknowledges the impact of transference in training relationships as she says of trainees, *Their history might somehow intercept.*

To make one trainee "special" is paradoxically shadow, because it singles out this trainee from his/her peers. A trainee whose husband was friendly with the Director of the institute at which she was training was invited with her husband to a Directors' party. The envy and jealousy that was directed at her in her training group emerged as a verbal attack; as shadow dynamics at work. Some trainees perceived the Directors' invitation as shadow in itself, as setting up a situation where the whole training group would be obliged to work with this issue. They felt that their training time and space had been invaded.

The position where a trainer reserves the right to *openly* discriminate between trainees in a healthy way, honouring their differences and uniqueness, is usually more relevantly employed towards the latter stages of training, when individuation and separation is figural in group process. The trainer, of course, notices differences from the commencement of training programmes. How much openness is offered here depends on the needs of each trainee, and the timing of interventions is imperative.

Transference shows itself, in varying degrees, in every relationship we have. It is not peculiar to psychotherapy but is always very present in psychotherapy training groups. *When I had a group of people I was training, a four year training . . . I decided that I couldn't continue running the course. I wasn't feeling well at that point and it was actually quite hydrating and I wasn't feeling well and I was feeling very tired and I knew I had to pull out. And I saw them through to the end of their fourth year and I told them I was pulling out, but I would still be running the ongoing exam-prep for them after the four years. And they were all so angry with me.*

This trainer's serious illness might be seen as an unconscious way of her experiencing shadow phenomenon through retroflection; the anger of the trainees was also a strategy for dealing with their own perceived hurt. The trainer sees this as shadow behaviour evident in the transference. She welcomes the strategy of open discussion for containment of feelings; however, on this occasion, discussion was insufficient for the difficulties between the trainees and herself/colleagues to be resolved. She states, *I think we did everything we could. You know, gave them plenty of opportunity to talk about it, express their feelings, deal with it transferentially, went down the transferential line. And I think, very often, the powerful nature of the transference just overwhelms people. The shadow actually comes up and engulfs them.*

It is interesting to note that the timing of intervention here was determined by the trainer's illness and not the trainees' developmental need. This is the power of unconscious process. This trainer sees her responsibility, as a trainer, as being in charge, maintaining boundaries, teaching trainees things. There is a tension for all trainers between the trainer behaving as a parental (transference) figure and, at the same time, wanting trainees not to behave as children. Trainers have a constant consideration for how much of the trainer–trainee relationship is transferential and how much is about other aspects of relationship, such as training alliance. Of course, in group process terms, all trainees are individual and in different stages of developmental relationship with their trainer, with different transferential needs. It is also widely known, and evidenced in my own experience, that at the end of a training relationship, early patterns re-emerge and issues become reworked through at a different level.

This trainer comes to the conclusion that, despite her beliefs that *meditation tells us that we attract what we see in the world around us* and her owning parts of herself that she saw in the trainees, regarding shadow, *It wasn't just me. It was also them. I couldn't say they were just reflecting me. They were doing their own thing too.*

Shadow dynamics and behaviours are activated in the in-between space of relationships of two or more people, and each person in the training group is vulnerable to transference, which so easily attracts shadow. The movement from illusion to reality involves a disappointment in the client/trainee, and this disappointment is an inevitable part of the working through of transference.

The following story gives evidence of the complicated nature of transference.

We have a trainee, Jenni, who perceived a sexual breach towards herself by a guest trainer, David. He had *kissed her on the cheek, patted her on the backside* and *leered at her*. Jenni felt as though the trainer was *touching her up*. When new co-trainers, Sara and John, arrived at a subsequent weekend, and Jenni shared this experience with her group, their response was to tell her that she had *asked for it*, with, *It's your fault*. They implied, rightly or wrongly, a belief that we cannot assume to be correct but must remain open to, that Jenni may have had some part to play in the event occurring. Jenni did not arrive the following day.

Sara asked of the group that she be given Jenni's telephone number so that she could contact her. The response was *She's chosen not to come* (angrily) and *We don't want her back*. It is imperative that we ask here who has the ultimate responsibility for holding of such boundaries in training situations?

When transferential situations occur and trainees unconsciously attempt to repeat their early negative history, in the hope that it will *not* be repeated, and that reconfiguration of the field *will* occur, then the object of the transference, in this case, David, is responsible for his own response to any transferential invitation. The purpose of Psychotherapy Codes of Ethics is to very clearly support this stance.

What followed in the group was the idealization of John, as David had been idealized. The group split John and Sara with John actually being referred to as David, and the group shared their dislike of Sara, initially in a displaced way, with, *We don't like your terminology*. Sara had challenged both David's behaviour and the trainees' idealization process of him.

Sara was eventually given Jenni's number, because, as one member said, *We're not going to get any work done until we give it to her*, and Jenni did return to the group and sat beside Sara. However, the group verbally attacked Sara and Jenni with challenge that claimed that it was not all right to dismiss David from his professional organization (which subsequently happened). The group continued to attempt to dismiss Sara from their presence and John became confluent and reinforced that happening. Despite their being given information that David had seriously transgressed sexual boundaries in the past and that this was currently under investigation, comments of *Don't blame him* and *You can't ruin a man's life like that* ensued. It was so profoundly painful for trainees to have lost their idealized transference object. Transferentially, Jenni and David had repeated a situation evident in Jenni's childhood. Waelder (1956) suggests that this happens out of awareness and Cashdan (1988) argues that it is the transference object who holds the responsibility to deny the projective identification. So, the ultimate containing of boundaries lies always in the hands of the trainer.

Containment of this situation was made easier for Sara than for John by the fact that she had never met David, as John had. *I think it was probably easier for me because I didn't know him and I hadn't been charmed by how he was. People were saying "But he's magic", so I think there was this charisma about him that other people had unconsciously not resisted.*

While acknowledging that she had no direct experience of this relationship dynamic occurring in a training group setting, Sara did have associations from her childhood of having undergone a similar experience as Jenni, which gave her some understanding of the relational processes at work here. Sara suggests that a sexually leering look holds a *weakness, an infantile vulnerability,* which seduces people into *Don't challenge me, because I couldn't bear it.* When the sense of self remains insufficiently developed (i.e., infantile), the merger transference may be at play and this becomes a fertile ground for breach of sexual boundaries.

In this group process, when the anger and rage had been expressed, the group worked in a fruitful and very moving way with their pain and welcomed Jenni back into the fold. So we can see, here, that the transferential situation serves two purposes. Its advantage is that it gives insight and understanding from a place of having already had an experience, a "radar" for situations. We can more easily recognize something that is already known to us. It also provides a medium for maintaining hope that things will be different, and hope is a very necessary factor in the human survival of trauma. In the working through of transference, a new experience emerges.

Problems occur when a transference is not worked with; for example, when a trainer becomes confluent with a trainee's idealization process, or when transference is too easily seen only as a block to contact; which it is, but, nevertheless, it is also a search for contact. And I do not believe that contact is ever possible until the transference has been sufficiently worked through.

Transference takes us back to our most painful life experiences at times in our lives when we were probably at our most vulnerable. Hence, it holds the strongest possibility of inviting shadow dynamics than any other aspect of relationship, and also the strongest pathway for exploring that shadow and transforming its energy.

Current field dynamics

For clarity, this section will be divided into two parts; environmental factors with their influence on the psychotherapy profession as a whole, and group process dynamics. We must recognize, of course, that all aspects of field experience are mutually influential.

Environmental factors

Political correctness is figural in today's society, and this is seen as having a role in determining what can and cannot be openly discussed within a training group. The importance of trainers needing *not* to be politically correct is emphasized with the belief that openness enhances a feeling of being much more sound and much more careful with one's choice of communication terminology.

I have some suspicion that there's a dance that goes on about being politically correct and gender issues. Gay issues bring it to the fore more than anything else. . . . And to name some of those things that, I suppose in a very simplistic way, that in the world there's litigation and it will be considered politically incorrect. So that is pervaded into psychotherapy as well. We really avoid these issues, which might be ethnic, which might be bodily references and relate to sexual preferences.

This statement accepts the fact that, although we create and honour the boundary of the therapeutic frame, we cannot help but exist within a wider field than psychotherapy and we are influenced by society's norms, for example, the current field of litigation and the vulnerability of not only the client but the trainee therapist and trainer.

It is suggested that, given that discrimination can lead to litigation, in order to avoid being stereotypical of others, we resist discussing certain issues, and we have already noted how that which we avoid becomes relegated to shadow. In order that relegation to shadow does not happen, one trainer believes that, *It's important for me to name somebody who is too fat, too big, too tall.* She continues to differentiate between naming and labelling. I see both the act of "not naming" and the act of labelling as shadow attitude/ behaviour.

One position is to become too constrained in the training field by society's expectations, and the polarity is not to be sufficiently aware of society's influence. One trainer wonders whether a part she might play in being surprised by shadow phenomena in training situations is that she can become confluent with the expectation of the sanctuary and safety of the training environment: *What can happen is that we can get caught up in the sanctuary of the safety of the temenos . . . the outside world becomes too far away. I can be so respectful of the boundary of the therapeutic space that I imagine there's no connection to the outside world, but there is.*

What is needed is for trainers to engage in a process of osmosis of awareness between the levels of socio-political field conditions, the psychotherapy field conditions, and the training group process, with all of its transferential positions.

One trainer sees integrative psychotherapy as invariably underpinned by the philosophical paradigm of *mother and baby*. And, while this is significant, in that the integrative psychotherapy process involves a recapitulation of our early life experience, she explains how we can use this philosophy to undermine male influence on the experience of being human and on being in psychotherapy training. She shares, *So, my example is like playing a game of tennis, mixed doubles, and if the man serves to me and he serves as well as he can, I'm going to say "What a maggot, is he showing off?". And if he serves softly to me, I'm going to say "The maggot's patronizing me at this stage".* So, in a profession that is for the most part built upon the maternal archetype, maleness takes a back seat. This is shadow experience being directed towards male trainers and trainees. I know many mothers who have felt their relationship with their child threatened by the child's love for father. These dynamics are pertinent to transferential process in whole training groups and organizations. I have experience myself of this issue being pertinent in training groups where that is how men experience the mother– child paradigm. It is interesting, too, that new clients to an institute invariably ask for a female therapist. This suggests that we need to address this dynamic, to *bring it out a bit more* in the profession, perhaps to pay more attention to the transference *at a father level*. Once again, the suggestion of bringing it out honours the value of awareness.

The caring professions also are moving increasingly towards an openness to the benefits of new-age practice, with a philosophy that moves on from thinking and analysing to more intuitive, sensation work. One trainer struggles with wanting to honour *the serendipitous, the synchronistic, the awe, the transpersonal and spiritual dimensions of writers, theorists, people that I encounter*, while not wanting psychotherapy to be moulded into becoming another institutionalized religion, whereby we rely on psychotherapy too heavily, as we might rely on our faith, for personal well-being. As psychotherapy and new-age methods are increasing, the congregations of our churches are growing smaller and many churches struggle to survive. The effects of religious beliefs, in reference to owning shadow, are that *Christians are taught not to* [own shadow]. And another trainer shares his childhood experience, in which elements of what his religious grandfather required he should be *meant that I've put things in shadow which could have been more helpful in my life really.* The *Pentecostal, bible-thumping, very austere* attitude of his grandfather supported a process of introjection, which has taken *years to get over.*

And psychotherapy, with its invitation to feeling responses, is compared with Buddhism: *It's as if the Buddhist would say, "Don't get attached", in relation to affection responses. OK, in therapy, you know, we pant, rush after them. In Buddhism, they're irrelevant. Let them go. And in psychotherapy, "Let's look at that", and not let it go. So, the Buddhist perspective, as it were, casts a shadow on things, some things in psychotherapy, deeper feeling.*

The question here for this trainer is whether or not to *open the box* and let shadow in. She considers that if she does that, will she be good enough? I imagine her to be asking how much shadow she can contain. We have here another example of how life presents us with the structure–freedom continuum; the tension between allowing ourselves to experience the pain of shadow, and seeking strategies to avoid, rather than contain, it. Ethically, for any psychotherapist–trainer, especially in relation to powerful shadow experience, one question is, how much human pain can my client, my trainee, myself contain at any one time? One might ask, is the assumption that therapy must be painful, shadow in itself? I have heard it said *No pain, no gain,* and *Therapy hurts, but it hurts good.* The question would be, how much right do we have to make clinical interventions that we know will invite clients' pain into their arena?

Another trainer shares how differences in religious belief can influence group process, in that, in her psychotherapy training groups, where there is a cross-section of people ranging from those who are comfortable in their churches, perhaps being ordained, to those whose expression of spirituality takes a very different form, there is potential for polarization and splitting dynamics to occur. This experience in training groups happens in a culture where religion is very much alive and still carries an element of authority over people's lives.

This trainer believes that containment of group process is enhanced by inviting facilitators from outside the training arena for the group-work component of the training. *Having a group process that is completely water-tight from the rest of the course is a help.* There is no feeding into the course from the two group facilitators and confidentiality applies if someone shares. Group facilitators hold that confidentiality. Problems can occur when trainees who might wish to bring something into the training group arena are expected to hold confidentiality and not bring certain things to this group.

Another trainer considers how the need for psychotherapy stems from a rise in loneliness in our culture and the social structure, which supports psychotherapy as an industry. He believes that this needs recognition. An important point he makes is that, as psychotherapists, we are in a privileged position; we get a lot of respect and get paid for what we do as well. He suggests that shadow emerges when we do not just think about what we are doing and be clearer with ourselves. After all, psychotherapy is not only a way of being in the world, it is our livelihood. At a practical level, we are running a business. The social need paves the way, I think, for projection of power on to the therapist.

And one effect of idealization is linked with money; quoting the Bible, "The love of money is the root of all evil". It is suggested that if psychotherapy becomes all-powerful in a religious way, a culture of self-sacrifice may emerge. A grandiosity in reverse, I think, with a stance of, "Look how good/saintly I am, to make sacrifices to pay for psychotherapy training". It is believed that *There's even a little bit in psychotherapy trainings and being around this idea of sackcloth and ashes; being so awfully hippie-ish and doing the training and living on the edge.* In the UK, most people who undergo psychotherapy training are self-financing, and this is an expensive training. So, while there may actually be a *sackcloth and ashes* philosophical stance to a trainee's financial state, there is, very often, also a reality factor. This trainer suggests that, as trainers, we have a responsibility to urge our trainees into self-care, with *Listen, there's some practical stuff, if you want to be a psychotherapist. Make sure that you might hang on to the day job and support your children well.*

She notes the self-limitation of trainees just throwing up everything and having a crusade into psychotherapy, not looking after their own where-with-all and the well-being of their own families. The profession itself then becomes an unhealthy transitional object for the trainee.

Owning our own investment in, and practical reasons for, becoming a psychotherapist reduces the potential for our own needs to colour our client relationships. As a supervisor, I have had to challenge supervisees who, already working to their full capacity, take on another client for financial gain; for example, to repay the loan for a bathroom extension.

And those of us who enter this profession primarily for financial gain are likely to find that they overstretch themselves in a very unhealthy way, because this attitude never really provides the satisfaction for which striving for wealth becomes a substitute.

Contracts between psychotherapists and organizations that finance emotional support for their employees request that therapists make referrals for long-term work to colleagues rather than to themselves. This prevents any therapist's unconscious wish to inveigle clients into long-term work for the wrong reasons. The sadness, of course, is that this safety factor, in place for the protection of clients, also denies them the right to choose the therapist they may feel most comfortable with for their long-term work. And, we must consider here, might there be some narcissistic grandiosity in a therapist believing he or she is the only therapist, or the best therapist, for a client?

Another shadow dynamic in employee assistant work might be that some firms send employees for therapy for the wrong reasons.

Often, in the guise of care and support for employees, people are offered counselling when the real reason for the employer might be either to keep someone at work and prevent sick leave, or to expect the therapist to deal with inter-organizational issues or staff conflicts without the organization itself having to look at its own dynamics and be responsible. Shadow invades the therapeutic space from without. And I have known clients' shadow to emerge in the form of, "Of course I'll keep coming. I'll make that manager pay!"

It is interesting to note that the fee levels for psychotherapy training in this country vary enormously between institutes; more so, that is, than one would expect due to difference in locality. And the financial state of any institute is often misperceived. A trainer tells of when she went into partnership with a colleague: *He'd run trainings for the local authority. That's different. He kept saying, "There's lots of money in the bank." He didn't think, "We'll need that for the mailing, the printing, and the advertising in April, May". And he wasn't going to know that until he'd been through it once. People see you earning all this money but they don't understand the huge expenses; even if you do it all yourself.*

As psychotherapy becomes more recognized in the field of medicine, and psychotherapists are given the esteem of psychologists and psychiatrists, we can expect that psychotherapy will be remunerated at the same pay scale. Government legislation for our profession will ensure this. And this, too, will bring some people into our profession for the wrong reasons. Personal therapy and good supervision will never cease to be important in addressing these issues.

We can see how religion, finance, and sex, the three things that cause the breakdown of most marriages, are also the most difficult issues to deal with in psychotherapy training institute dynamics.

Group process

The management, or containment, of group dynamics *involves maximizing people's freedom to express the diversity of their views, cultural preferences etc., while at the same time, ensuring the face to face norms of respectful behaviour are maintained.* The task of the psychotherapy group trainer is to, moment by moment seek the optimum balance between support and challenge for each group member. Without challenge, no growth will occur and without support no challenge will be fruitful. Paradoxically, for a trainee who has spent most of his or her life without support, then support is challenge in itself. Each time a trainer encourages a trainee to take one step further on his or her journey of development, one step beyond their comfort zone, we have a whole group of other trainees who, through witnessing, are also strongly affected by the behaviour of the trainer. And perhaps the level of challenge needed by one trainee might be very scary for another. This complicated process of whose needs get most attention at any one time invites sibling rivalry, jealousies, and splitting dynamics into the arena of the group.

We all know that in the heat of the moment, in the midst of powerful exercises, where there are time constraints and where there's competition for communication and expression of what needs to be communicated and expressed by various people, it is extremely difficult for everyone to get a fair slice of the loaf in those situations.

In group process terms, the individuals internal splitting process itself can become projected, as a relief from anxiety, and colleagues are 'set up' to act out our internal process for us. This invariably leads to one half of the group members feeling empathic towards the protagonist and others feeling a degree of distancing or hostility.

When working with both individual dynamics and group dynamics, learning to balance the right amount of support with the right amount of challenge is a precarious and unique process. One trainer tells us, *I had in fact taken great pains to be delicate and supportive in the manner I did this and with hindsight, perhaps a bit too much,* and even with such delicacy and understanding, when trainees *lashed out towards us—it was a very painful experience.* This evidences the responsibility for containment by the trainer and also the dilemma of, as Laura Perls posits, the importance of supporting as little as possible and as much as is necessary. It is also necessary for trainers to support themselves. A risk of not doing so is that they feed their own narcissistic needs from the trainees by ingratiation rather than genuine support.

Each group member carries the dilemma of "How much can I be myself in this group situation and still be welcome?" and "Is it OK here to be different?" We are told *When somebody stands out from the group and their behaviour evokes these processes, that will then put them into script, so they will exacerbate their position. At the same time as one might want to challenge what they are doing to bring this down upon themselves, that challenge in turn could get sucked in to create an expression of the lynch mob itself. You can lose your balance in these moments.*

This phenomenological experience of being ungrounded disturbs not only the trainee, but also the level of containment offered by the trainer, and this leaves the group vulnerable to unconscious dynamics such as scapegoating and projection. One trainer compares this training group process with society's norms. He refers to the *preoccupation with torture and physical abuse of all kinds* in society, and considers the political aspect of fundamentalism, which involves a *recognition that people lynch other people emotionally in groups and in institutions—and that too is a form of seriously abusive conduct.* The betrayal aspect of trauma in group dynamics is seen as far worse than physical abuse.

This is taken further in reference to the experience of lynch mob and polarization that takes place in training groups, with the belief that people feel terror at how to handle someone who does not fit into the majority of norms in the group, resulting in humiliation of that person, in moderate and in extreme versions. One trainer shares how, when he chose an alternative stance in his teaching to that of his manager, he was accused of splitting, because there was no culture in that organization where diversity and difference were welcomed. He believes that *there is a very grey area here about how one manages those situations.*

And the culture of the training organization colours this process. That is, cultures where *this person held on to power*, where sides were taken *in the conflict that was unfolding*, where the culture is about *adhering to the party line pure and simple.* The transferential aspect of this experience is honoured with reference to his school culture, where *suddenly the goalposts had moved*, and where one was expected to *take your punishment, put on a brave face . . . you held your head high and behaved with dignity* and *fit in with how one was supposed to be.* So, vulnerable people in autocratic groups and institutes often have to deal with their early life memories as well as what is happening in their current professional situation

And this situation implies a sense of inner isolation. A trainer compares her sense of isolation as a trainer with her actual enjoyment of her own training process as a trainee; that is, *I enjoyed the camaraderie of it.* It seems that, once qualified, she was held in the tension of knowing that the organization to which she belonged maintained a hierarchical stance, and the only way for her to really belong was to become a trainer, despite her own lack of desire for this. *I wanted to feel . . . to be a really full member of the ***, and there's a sense that you're not, really, unless you're a trainer.*

Such a hierarchical stance as this goes against the humanistic philosophy underpinning integrative psychotherapy and I would suggest that this emerges from shadow phenomena and the power issues associated with grandiosity, which are experienced at an organizational level.

And at an inter-organizational level, splitting occurs as the unpleasant, shadow side of being human gets projected outside of the group and into the field. It is unethical to criticize or demean a fellow professional, and yet, one trainer relates, *I got the most venomous letters, several letters from another trainer, about me poaching, which wasn't the case.* This trainer was being accused of shadow behaviour, which was actually coming from the other trainer in the nature of the content of the letters. The written attack was precipitated by students making the choice to move across from one organization to another. If we are to assume that shadow is *usually from a transferential place*, it could be that sibling rivalry, in inter-organizational process, was being experienced here by the first trainer.

This rivalry can occur also within individual organizations, where several generations of trainers are present. In terms of status and equality, as trainees qualify and become a second generation of trainers and researchers, meetings occur in which trainers encounter ex-trainees attending. A struggle emerges here as to who holds the power. Even when this dynamic is processed, some of the initial trainers in an institute might feel senior and still, archetypally, hold a grandparent figure image. It is suggested that one way forward would be for the senior staff members, the elders, to withdraw and allow the new trainers to become more powerful in their own right and the training team to become a more equal group.

A strategy for developing equality might be for the elders to model honesty and vulnerability, to model self-disclosure in being completely open. When institutes avoid talking about things openly, they become slightly defended and plotting; one trainer describes this lack of openness as *having an incredible shadow side.*

The influence on one training group process from another training organization is also considered. Given that the code of confidentiality to which we subscribe involves not discussing information given in other settings, where confidentiality has been agreed, this in itself may constitute a problem. A trainer says, *Talking about it hasn't always been possible because things have come in from the outside world, that have been . . . where you can't talk about it. And that's hard. It meant that there was simply something in the group that was unaddressed, that everybody ignored. But at some point I said, "Let's call it the X thing", at which point there was relief, because I'd named the X thing. They knew so little that they didn't even know there was an X thing. But for me, there was something . . . going on.*

Shadow behaviour emerged in this group when someone actually named something that one of the members of another group had told her in confidence. This constitutes a breach of boundaries.

The trainer here recognizes the restrictive aspect of confidentiality, which, paradoxically, is expected to promote a safe learning environment. A conscious choice may be made to maintain confidentiality, but this gives an unconscious message to the group of *Some things cannot be addressed in this group*; this can, in turn, put brakes on group process. When might the holding of boundaries of confidentiality paradoxically enhance a splitting process? Borderline process is viewed by this trainer as something else with which trainees have difficulty in holding their boundaries. Borderline process, she says, *may be explained and addressed in the areas of sadism and omnipotence and we have to look at these.* It causes *the splitting process.* Whether splitting occurs between training groups in the same institute or between organizations, it is seen to be invited, as people are branded by whom they trained with and their style of working. This brings institutional rivalry, and associations with particular institutes might underpin this. We are told that new trainees who idealize their training can become quite dismissive of other theoretical models.

The purpose of a splitting process is often to defend the person, or the group, from painful feelings. The philosophy underpinning psychotherapy training, which encourages us to be attached to feelings, is held responsible for the fact that, in training, *groups can crank up the energy levels . . . with addictive, seductive qualities. This is what it means to be living with these . . . attunement to profound feelings really.* This trainer implies that it is healthier to have shadow feelings addressed than not, with reference to her trainees experience of her own shadow, stating, *And it's come to awareness because it's caught their perception strongly enough for them to confront me about it. They confront me as to how I teach, with differences. It's what they haven't confronted me with . . . there's no avoiding it . . . there's shadow.*

And even when a group begins to confront and work with a shadow theme, there is often an initial defence, which, if allowed to run its course, paves the way for more open discussions, and when shadow emerges, what is useful is humour. In reference to her own shadow and how the group used a metaphor for this, a trainer tells us *That's one of the things that became sort of a running joke, which was very helpful.*

In any group process, the conflict for each individual is how much to remain involved and how much to withdraw; this process dynamic is evidenced by whose issues gain the most attention in time and energy from the group. And one way of both presenting a theme and also keeping an element of distance and a sense of safety is to use humour to reduce the seriousness of the theme.

Laughter is seen, for the most part, as healthy. *In many psychotherapy cultures, there's a fear of laughter, and it's considered that laughter is an avoidance of some kind. It is not just avoidance and it can sometimes . . . it's a lubricant of group processes, of a quite extraordinary character. And if it's permissible, it leads to the enhancement of diversity, while at the same time permitting a great deal of free expression to happen in a good-natured way that doesn't invoke the lynch mob in groups.*

In training groups, as in life itself *The most fundamental problem facing human beings is between the problem of why human beings are so evil some of the time and secondly, what, if anything, can be done about it? I do think that the psychotherapeutic training processes have the potential to give people access to a kind of live laboratory study, with the potential formation of evil and also that very much on a knife edge, that double edge between creating a culture in which the potential for evil is free to occur and where, yet, sufficient protection against its consequences is put in place so that it's a safe experience.*

Over time, it is hoped that the safety factors in a group make possible the open and honest expression of shadow in such a way as to permit the phenomenologically felt experience with optimum damage limitation.

Containment

We need first here to understand what is meant by the term "containment". What is ever increasingly apparent to me is the many ways in which those of us in the psychotherapy profession have to continually monitor the depth and intensity of our behaviours, because at one level they can be healthy and permit growth, while at another level, or in different circumstances, the same quality of behaviour might be termed shadow and detrimental to relationships and to others. This monitoring function can only happen with, first, awareness of our own relational processes and dynamics, and second, with our access to appropriate external support and use of healthy self-support systems, and this goes for both parties in a relationship.

For all professionals and clients, containment is the healthy balance of support and challenge that renders phenomenological experience tolerable, whether this is in the form of new experiences and growth or the welcoming of previously intolerable past experience. And containment may be a function that we can, for the most part, carry out for ourselves, or it may be experienced through healthy projective identification and deep empathy from another. Containment is the psychological recognition of, and willingness to be with, our own or another person's phenomenological state.

Just as in any other caring profession, when the challenge/support balance is wrong, in the short term people can suffer emotional or somatic pain, and in the long term, people suffer burnout, with chronic emotional distress, physical symptoms, and an inability to cope with their everyday life. *It's as if I'm tireder and tireder, and that's not good to be in. And yes, I have seen trainers collapse. We're a very hard-working bunch.*

Greenberg (1998) points out that the primary therapeutic task in psychotherapy is the containment of anxiety and of aggression. Professionally, "containment" is what we do, as integrative psychotherapists. This is underpinning the very purpose of our work.

We have already considered how the raising of awareness might become a healthy strategy for containment of shadow. *If I can let it into my awareness, then it's not trapped in the bag.* What can happen when awareness is not strived for is: *All the while, there appears to be*

building up, a resentment and envy and a jealousy, which is out of aware-
ness and tucked away inside the bag. So that, suddenly, all the jealousy
and envy then comes out and they can actually be quite vicious, sometimes
in a controlled way and sometimes in an apparently caring way.

Without containment, what can happen is *she managed to evict the*
others and *that person left the training as a consequence of what*
happened.

And trainers share their own phenomenological experiences
that need containing:

I feel kicked . . . that night I was down.
I was physically shaking. I felt sick in the room.
Furious, wounded, disappointed.
I felt it was too much for me . . . felt it was too much. All the avenues
I explored to try and share it, all came to dead ends.

And if these are the experiences of trainers, with all their previous therapy, clinical practice, and understanding, then how much
more impact might lack of containment have on trainees?

Containment can incorporate all aspects of human experience:
cognitive, emotional, behavioural, somatic, social, spiritual, and the
common factor that enhances optimum access to all of these is the
element of choice. What is important is to remember that none of
us is perfect and only optimum containment can be our goal. Containment is the ability to stay with the inner tension of newly
emerging, previously denied, or mixed, emotions. One trainer notes
his attitudinal change with *I don't have to be perfect all the time. That*
is something I've learned as a trainer and therapist. He acknowledges
that the more pressure we put on ourselves to be "good", the
greater the shadow becomes.

Greenberg (1998) sees the question of needing to be "good
enough", or perfect, as part of the narcissistic process. Most narcissists are unsure of when a realistic level of containment is reached.
From a closet place they tend to project their own needs on to
others, and then satisfy themselves by proflection. This can bring
a sense of being infantalized or suffocated for the recipient, who
then might withdraw and, in doing so, invites the toxicity of the
narcissist.

Sometimes containment is less possible than at other times,
depending on the amount of stress we carry in our lives in relation

to our own support systems. And Winnicott (1969) is clear that "good enough" parenting, and transferentially good enough containment in psychotherapy, is all we can hope for, and this is ample.

Cognitively, our philosophical beliefs and theoretical understandings bring a feeling of being able to make sense of our experience, which provides structure and normalization as containment for chaos and uncertainty. Even when, paradoxically, to remain uncertain and not try to "fix" things is our philosophical stance, a sense of understanding and having a rationale for the process supports this. Understanding brings containment.

One of the good things about the integrative psychotherapy movement is that is seeks to draw in what's useful from a range of different schools, assuming that no one has a monopoly on the truth. An integrative trainer appreciates what she learns about containment of shadow from a different theoretical orientation to her own with, *The training group; it may come under analytic theory because shadow is explicitly addressed.* She uses her theory to inform her training syllabus, with successful introduction of shadow phenomenon early on in the training programme. She explains that *In our first year, which would be a foundation year, there's a lot of work in the shadow. I am just marking essays at the moment and I can really freshly relate to them writing about the steps and working through the shadow, suffering through shadow areas.*

And for trainers themselves, having theory and reading the experience of other trainers who have been in similar situations to their own is appreciated. This can be usefully found on the Internet: *I got the abstracts of various papers and said, this is what happens. Other people know about this. It is powerful. It hadn't come up for me before.* So, what is valued here is the mutually experienced types of situations shared with other trainers, a reduction in the sense of isolation.

To have one's own understanding, in and of itself, may be enough for some, but not all, trainers. One trainer recognizes that *a cognitive understanding of a situation is containing,* in owning that he *may have handled a particular situation more efficiently had I reached the level of recognition of her characteristics and functioning that I came to later, earlier in the process.*

In a situation when trainees did not understand, the trainer was hurt. This trainer tells how she had *gone to a lot of trouble and self-sacrifice for them* and they *had absolutely no understanding of that . . . I think that was the other bit that wounded me.*

Another trainer alludes to his wish to understand a situation where *someone could come to exercise that kind of dominance over a whole society.* The strategy that he adopted for dealing with being on the receiving end of the shadow of a senior colleague was to primarily remain cognitive and to seek understanding, to have *curiosity about the process that was going on, how these things happen in the field.* Having *reckoned* [cognition] *that it was impossible to defeat her,* he supported her in the interest of the institute overall. He continues to note that in situations like this one, he had previously learnt that people could be unjust and that to survive this he learnt to employ repression without breaching his inner integrity. He learnt to keep silent and watch and wait. Zinker (1977) refers to the silence of waiting and thinking as usefully allowing for the incubation period to lead to new awareness. Openness to this process guards against the times when *Dogma in the shadow overwhelms rational critical reflection.*

Understanding might also come in the form of metaphor, which is seen as playing a part in the containment of shadow with *It's like the smile on the face of the tiger.* This trainer tells the sci-fi story of a man chased by a monster, and how it was in the turning round and facing this monster, rather than continually avoiding and running scared, that the healing took place. In reference to this story, and to his own experience, containment is in the invitation to address the more negative aspects of humanness, in owning our projections. And humour can support the process of "owning", as with the trainer who appreciated her trainees noticing her shadow, affectionately, as *a running joke.*

Containment may come in a dream; for example, metaphorically, in the form of a dream of a hen run, surrounded by chicken wire in which the trainer was entwined, supporting the boundary. This symbolic image emerged for the trainer in the group process itself and in her dreams. *I think the dream was telling me that I must do some containing here.*

So I have a theory that is containing; that if we can turn round and accept the shadow, we can make some kind of friends with it. Because, for people who are scared of anger, the anger in the shadow can be quite useful if it is owned. If it's not, it's destructive, so everything there, I suspect, everything in there is potentially valuable if we can harness it and not deny it.

And this process takes time.

Containment was attempted in one group through *having discussions with them, discussing the infantile dynamic, how they felt about parent image*. Despite the fact that this group trainer shared her views that she did not see her trainees as children, she saw them as colleagues, they were stunned by her perception and remained angry. The degree to which a trainer can see trainees as colleagues and hold them primarily responsible for their own containment depends upon the developmental need at that time, for that particular group, in their particular stage of training.

Further reference is made to the containing factor in training groups of actually addressing and discussing the shadow experience, with *I think we offer the students the best something about shadow we can ... when I teach it ... explicit ... saying, "Stop and talk about what's happening"*.

The trainer is seen, within the training setting, as having some responsibility for containment, as does the therapist and the supervisor: *And I'm used to containing some things. They also have, within the course, containment in their own therapy and in the supervision.*

Trainers, of course, have a responsibility for their own support systems, which make containing possible. The amount of stress involved in running a training institute is acknowledged with *I felt very, very resentful that the amount of work was disproportionate to the rewards. Now you put up with that to begin with because you're hoping it will build up.*

One might ask: what happened to that trainer's resentment, over the years?

The issue here is that the running of a training institute, for one person, is simply too much hard work, and one particular resentment, which intensifies the dissatisfaction, is that the remuneration is not enough. Discrimination is made between working for a statutory body, where administration and financial concerns are not part of the trainer's role, and working for private organizations, where everything falls into the lap of the trainer.

We can see that taking on the role of trainer, manager of an institute, administrator, and also taking private clients, plus a part-time job (all of which I know from personal experience), can soon lead to burnout. This workload is, however, necessary at first, because there are no financial supports for someone starting out in running a training programme. In educational settings, trainings are, in part, government funded, and this makes the load so much easier. To prevent psychotherapy training from becoming an upper-middle-class venture, one must make training financially viable.

There's been a kind of culture to try and make the training as available as possible to people, therefore costing as little as possible. The problem is, if you are wanting to make a living out of it, you're simply not being paid enough.

One trainer believes that low fees are one way in which trainers and psychotherapists do not look after themselves, with *I think it's a way in which we don't take care of ourselves. We're not realistic.* Given the very intensity of demands made upon us in our work, balancing this with a lifestyle that nourishes and supports is imperative. And, in founding an institute, we need the financial means to be able to bring in an administrator, a cleaner, and to have the necessary time out, or time away, which enhances boundary keeping and maintaining a separation between professional and personal lives. This involves also the realization that what we deal with as psychotherapists has actually been dealt with for aeons by others: *clergymen, teachers, witch doctors, shamans, and perhaps we should allow psychotherapy to be seen for what it is.* It is recognized that trainers depend on trainees for a living, which has financial implications, and *I think that gives a huge potential for distortion.* A trainer acknowledges her own naivety in seeing *devotion and cherishing* as more important than money. As trainers we need to be deeply empathic while maintaining a degree of objectivity and practical common sense.

Professional support for trainers comes in the form of personal therapy, clinical supervision and peer discussions. When invited to comment on containment, one trainer focuses heavily on both supervision and personal therapy, believing that personal therapy *is a lifelong thing.* He points out that this may not be constant, but states that we have a responsibility to take advice of supervisors when they recommend a period of therapy, and he continues to note that we need to be open to the willingness to experience personal therapy when needed, at any time in our professional life. With regard to supervision, he states, *I think supervision is good. I think there's always some client who'll push your buttons . . . where you lose your thinking and arrive in projective identification. Not that that's a bad thing, but if you don't use it constructively and act it out, it can be.*

And with the experience of therapy, in relation to shadow, we are told: *I find in therapy I can take the opportunity to experience the rage, the envy, the jealousy, the stuckness, as well as all the more kindly feelings. I'm not averse to putting someone on a cushion and beating the f— out of them, and in fantasy taking away, peeling their skin off or chopping their heads off and thoroughly humiliating them, because I know that I'd rather do it in the therapy situation than do it in reality.*

While this trainer sees therapy as a means of honouring his own integrity, a moral duty, so to speak, he also believes there should be an ethical requirement for this for psychotherapists, and even more so for a trainer of psychotherapy.

So I think personal therapy, for a therapist, should be an ethical requirement like supervision is. I think for someone who's in the role of a supervisor or trainer, they have a responsibility for developing their professional and personal skills, to be perhaps more conscientious about therapy as a means of dealing with the shadow.

He also comments on the need for our confidence in the skills of our therapist. *As long as we find a therapist who we're confident in and who we can trust enough, and is big enough and strong enough to take all our shit, basically.* We need a therapist sufficiently powerful to contain whatever degree of "shit" each of us carries. Owning our own shadow in therapy is in itself empowering. While another trainer values the support of her supervision, she has taken less of her training group to supervision than she has to therapy. She states, *So, my inclination is to stay more with clearing oneself when working with trainees and students. My commitment has been more to therapy with regard to my trainee work than supervision. And I can't imagine it to be better.*

She suggests that part of the challenge of trainees working with their own shadow is that the trainer experiences this first for herself. With reference to her greater awareness of shadow, she shares this: *Obviously, I've been in therapy as a client, . . . so as I'm moving to it* [shadow], *it loosens something in the trainees.*

The interview process for this study, between myself and a trainer, was in itself a loosening experience, as he reconnected with his awareness of his shadow side and some training experiences in relation to this. *Now I'm on a roll, I can see . . . sometimes what happens in training centres.* The experience was emotionally supportive to him as he says, *I didn't realize all this was around. It's a very cathartic experience getting in touch with this. I'm just aware of how these things are rolling off my tongue. They've been stored up for years.* And the usefulness of thinking is validated with his suggestion that *I'd find it really interesting to bounce these things off other people.*

He acknowledges that in not being in denial, in knowing our own shadow, we can choose not to utilize it, with *I am aware of my own shadow also . . . I tend towards the rescuer rather than the persecutor, kindly and compassionate rather than distant and austere.*

It is recognized that *People need to teach it; teach the energy they invest, the energy in being there, a . . . winging it,* and this is made possible by a more open culture, where the institute's strength is in the fact that it is able to contain and maintain considerable diversity within it, where routine grouses and wrestlings are healthy, where there is a possibility of mediation, where there is understanding of the positions of people with opposing views, where students have a considerable degree of freedom of speech and are offered alternative ways of doing things. The freedom of speech approach to training is valuable as an accompaniment to the more structured teaching and assessing methods. It is useful in the building of the trainees' own sense of integrity and responsibility from within. And one polarity alone is not enough. It is noted that *I know of other trainings where they simply discuss things and don't do assessments. They're in a different position. They have a place for discussing things so that the student comes to realize what they should do. And there's part of me wonders whether this isn't being irresponsible.*

Perhaps what is irresponsible is for the trainer to offer this discussion time without any guidance at all. There is a stage of inexperience where trainees do not know what they do not know. And the most containing teaching stance is to give the information, with a rationale that is open to challenge and critique in a healthy discussion.

Another trainer affirms the normal strategy adopted for healthy getting together with colleagues as being able to get through the resolution of differences. He tells of a situation where this was not possible, and reflects also upon a healthy relationship with another trainer, where they worked together very well indeed. The difference between these two situations was that, in the latter, the shadow side was discussed, dealt with, as they talked about it. He values the need to ensure a culture of competition and openness, and showing people ways forward. This might be done, he suggests, by allowing a space in which all the negative things that are going on could be discussed, and what people felt about them. The subject found this a much healthier approach than its alternative, in which *tactics of manipulation* were used.

Containment is enhanced with written guidelines and agreements. The process stemming from the lack of a written contract between trainee and therapist, following a complaint of ethical breach of confidentiality, brought pain. We are told, *the experience of the therapist was of being quite devastated because the process was very persecutory and highly critical and he touched shame* as *the adjudication panel, in the lack of a written contract, had to conclude that confidentiality had been broken*. This was also sound learning for the therapist, in that *He did learn from it in terms of his professional practice*, as did the training institute. *Now at that time the institute did not have a written policy on what happens in situations like this. As a result of this particular case, the institute now does have a written policy, which is made explicit to all trainees.*

Structure, then, in the form of written guidelines, offers clarity and is containing in training settings, remembering, of course, that guidelines involve some degree of negotiation in their being formed and in their interpretation in order to prevent them becoming toxic introjects.

We have here an implied recognition of the importance of professional codes of practice and to what degree they may need to be imposed upon students. The experience of seeking accreditation from governing bodies, for psychotherapy trainings, brings field dynamics into the training setting.

One trainer attended a workshop on power. She had hoped that this workshop would inform her about institutional power and this did not transpire. Wisdom as a trainer is not something that structured teaching alone can give us. She recollects her early training days, when boundaries between roles were more fluid, and this is not necessarily always a good thing, but, nevertheless, she appreciates the stance of people training alongside trainers, as a way of learning, with, *In the old days it would have been called an apprenticeship.*

The level of experience as a psychotherapy trainer is also recognized as influencing shadow behaviour: *possibly getting into the position of being a trainer too quickly, without going through the process of*

*apprenticeship and learning the ropes . . . practising pseudo-confidently
. . . under that kind of pressure, he* [a trainer] *couldn't contain the shadow
in his bag and he was extremely persecutory.*

Shadow in training is mentioned with *Yes, there are certain things
that are particularly wicked.* It is recognized that missing too much
training time can mean that students are not put forward for their
finals. Shadow needs addressing on the course in order for it not to
be acted out in behaviour such as the students' shadow of not
attending, or the trainer's shadow of not putting trainees forward
for examination. It seems unfair to me that a trainee's progress
should be at the discretion of only one trainer. Trainers' shadow can
be much more easily uncovered and addressed when team discussions and decisions are made in training environments.

Another trainer shares this: *And I think the way my shadow has
been caught in that is, the difficult part of my shadow is naïve. I came into
the business of being a trainer prematurely. So, I think I can get caught by
other people's tides.*

As a trainer herself, the subject values the usefulness of having
peer supervision, a supervisor who is also a trainer, and she recognizes that talking with other trainers is particularly useful. She also
enjoys the *tea and biscuits* element of supervision, *the social part of
supervision.*

Another trainer values the experience of prior learning and
acknowledges that, had she had more experience of therapeutic
ruptures in group process, she might have handled a particularly
difficult situation differently, saying, *I would like to have had some
kind of experience and learning before this happened, so I was prepared.* I
have seen newly qualified psychotherapists go very quickly into
becoming a trainer, with just one year's experiential training practice and a minimal amount of theoretical teaching of learning styles
and teaching methods. In my experience, what has been missing in
their preparation is an in-depth training on group process dynamics, linking theory to practice. I believe it is the group process
dynamics where most therapeutic ruptures take place and I would
welcome psychotherapy trainers being required to undergo at least
one year's training specifically in group-work models before being
expected to contain group dynamics. Sadly, I have witnessed trainers too readily investing in shadow behaviours themselves in
response to the emerging shadows of trainees.

In reference to her own shadow side, in relation to her trainees, a trainer bravely owns that her *Major motivation for setting up a training group was to get through my exams. I didn't focus on them getting through their exams as much as I should have done. I was very interested in producing good therapists, highly motivated to do that. But I wasn't highly motivated to prepare them for the exam. I think that was the one big flaw when I trained.*

I wonder now, who was containing this trainer's own examination process, in order for her to be able to contain that of her trainees?

Containment outside of training settings is important too. We are told, *If I can keep a little more clarity on my personal life, my work outside of therapy, I can handle it* [shadow] *better*. This trainer appreciates spending time with her colleagues, talking through difficult issues and knowing there is mutual support.

Another trainer shares that the strategy she uses to look after herself in the face of shadow experience is to always make sure she has friends; she has a partner and she sees herself as good at creating networks for herself. She maximizes her relaxation time with relaxation on trains. And although she feels she has no trouble now in creating supportive networks, there was a time when there just was not enough in her life. She engaged in therapy for herself and, at the time of needing more support, she went for supervision. However, she says that she had no supervision for a period of two years prior to this, because she felt that she simply did not have the time, although she now, on reflection, supports her own decision to seek supervision.

Meditation and spirituality are important factors in one trainer's life. He states *Spiritual discipline does help to contain the more shadow side of me*. If we see humanism, one of the philosophical bases of integrative psychotherapy, as a spiritual pursuit, then we could consider the humanistic philosophy, which supports the belief in the potential growth inherent in each individual, given the "suitable psychological climate" (Rogers, 1980, p. 20), as a containing factor in our work as psychotherapists. Buber (1923) supports this philosophy, seeing the understanding of another human heart as the ultimate spiritual experience.

Another way of containing shadow, we are told, is to accept our own humanness and have some place in our lives where we do not have to take the care in relationships that the role of psychotherapy trainer necessitates. *There is a side to me that's still that kind of cowboy, rough and ready, macho person. I do need to give vent to that and I don't, I feel, give vent to it as a trainer, because I think one should be gentle and clear, because it's far more challenging than being bombastic at the end of the day.*

This trainer goes on to say how he gets into environments where he can stop being a professional trainer and just be a *bit of a lad.* So, containment is seen here as honouring the professionalism of our work and, alongside this, enjoying being human in a different way, outside of the professional arena. While I hold this belief, and teach my trainees that however passionately we pursue psychotherapy we must have something else in life that we love just as passionately, I have not yet discovered literature supporting this view.

All trainers welcomed the strategy of *Getting people to be their own witness,* and this is the highly valued ultimate goal of containment in our profession. Mirroring is itself containing, and trainer support enables this.

It's so easy, as a trainer, if you get into a scared place, just to go inside yourself and then what happens is, there's a general feeling of "we're all scared". There's nobody who is scared and OK. So, it's really important to be OK, whatever the experience is; not to blot it out. But be a mirror. That's what containment is, to be able to feel this scare and be OK.

CHAPTER SEVEN

Be calmed

"The madman is not the man who has lost his reason. The madman is the man who has lost everything except his reason"

(Chesterton, quoted in Phillips, 1995, p. 15)

Creative synthesis

The calming of the waters, in a journey at sea, follows the weathering of the storm. I hope in this chapter to integrate the whole; to fruitfully consider shadow as just as necessary a part of our experience as any other aspect of being human. I seek to discover themes from all of the research and theoretical data; in particular, what specifically resonates in my own experience to that being described by others who pursue the pathway of shadow. Information directly given by trainers is in italics.

In this final phase of understanding

the researcher must move beyond any confined or constricted attention to the data and permit an inward life on the question to grow, in such a way that a comprehensive expression of the essences of the phenomenon investigated is realized. [Moustakas, 1990, p. 27]

I hope here to free myself sufficiently to allow discussion to emerge spontaneously. My inner sense of calm, results, I think, from my realization that I have engaged at a deep and painful level with my own shadow and I have emerged from this process feeling stronger, more grounded and complete. I feel nourished for having addressed the shadow experience.

I begin with awareness of a metaphor, from a morning's televised weather bulletin that predicted dense fog, which takes some time to lift. The sun breaks through in some areas, with the fog drying up and brightness streaming forth, while in other areas the fog is not budging and will linger for quite a while, taking time to clear. My phenomenological experience is of being engrossed in shadow, lost in this fog, rather than engaged with it, and through this immersion into the process, I trust that insights will potentially become illuminated. It is 1.53 a.m. and I write through broken sleep, as thoughts emerge.

It is nothing new to note that life itself holds many polarities, inconsistencies, and confusions. The anxieties and fears brought about by the unsettled field, the lack of sameness and stability, or the lack of difference and spontaneity, or in the efforts we make to hold a healthy balance between these two aspects of experience are held in check in the containment of the tensions in the in-between. It is the tensions within this process that are considered here, and I support my considerations with experiences shared by the senior trainers who participated in my original research study.

The major themes so far are:

- consideration of what shadow actually is: its differing forms, its depth, breadth, levels of intensity, how it shows itself in human relationships; is it possible to grasp this tenuous experience?;
- shadow in relation to the group component of training, how interpersonal dynamics are coloured by group participation, how shadow and the collective might be mutually influential;
- transference dynamics evident in any group process, and in the power imbalance of training roles and the influence of personality traits upon this. Where is shadow in the transference?;

- field dynamics and the influence of religion, culture, politics, finance, and the integration in training of situations of all current and past experiences. How do field situations influence shadow behaviours?;
- the value and restrictions of shadow to human growth and learning, and to the philosophical underpinnings of the psychotherapy profession as change agent, in an ever fast-changing society;
- the complexity and tensions to be contained personally and professionally in relation to shadow becoming healthily utilized in the psychotherapy profession. Can containment be taught?
- what actual use is this notion of shadow to any of us?

Consideration of what shadow actually is: its differing forms, its depth, breadth, levels of intensity; how it shows itself in human relationships; is it possible to grasp this tenuous experience?

The natural evil–human evil tension

Waller defines evil as follows: "Most would agree that—in its broadest sense—evil is anything detrimental to the well being of living things (2002, p. 12), and "I define human evil as the deliberate harming of humans by other humans" (*ibid.*).

He continues to distinguish between natural evil and human, "moral" evil, saying that natural evil is a function of natural processes of change, originating independently of human actions, such as earthquakes, floods, disease, and then seeing moral evil as referring to the destructive things that human beings do to each other and ourselves. He notes, of course, that, given that human behaviour is subject to genetic influences, a distinction between the two kinds of evil is very often almost impossible to make. I question how one would define "deliberate".

In training situations, there are times when the environment intervenes in the steady processing of institute dynamics; for example, in needing local Borough Council planning permission for the use of a premises, or when the UKCP raises standards and the examination procedure for trainees suddenly results in an extra five thousand words in the final written paper, or a senior member of an institute becomes seriously ill. Some goalposts are changed with-out our expressed consent, and we must learn to adapt in an adult way to these changes.

Moral evil shows in the hostility that is part of every interper-sonal process and covers the kind of circumstances that, with intro-spection, awareness, and courage, it is within our power to change. It could be mooted that moral evil may be in response to environ-mental factors and is not environmental factors themselves. Our unique response to our environment is always potentially involves choice.

The unconscious–conscious tension

This distinction between what is nature and what is humanly induced is struggled with in all walks of life. I think here of my time working in a forensic unit, where one psychotic patient, who was deluded into believing that her family were terminally ill and in great pain, actually suffocated her mother and two young children. When her psychosis lifted, she lived her days in turmoil and despair at what she had done.

Is it humanly possible to allocate illness to someone who rapes one of our children? When is someone ill and when are they simply "bad"? How much of human evil can we be responsible for? And, I would question, is it part of nature's evolutionary way of survival that human beings cause suffering to self and other in certain field conditions? To what degree are we pre-programmed to our way of being in the world (nature) and how much liberty do we have to influence that (nurture)? And is it important to have answers to these questions, or is it more important that we continue to ask the questions?

This issue is considered by colleagues supporting the view that shadow might emerge from the natural process of *people who get caught up in their own unconscious processes* or also may emerge from *people who knowingly and deliberately do evil things*. Shadow is seen as *possibly the greatest characteristic of human nature that we know*. A moot point might be that it could be human nature to deliberately do evil things, deliberation of evil being part of life's natural process of change. One thing is absolutely certain: without awareness we cannot take responsibility.

The moral– immoral tension

Waller (2002) points out that there is a moral difference between deliberate harm inflicted against an acknowledged enemy and deliberate harm inflicted against someone defenceless. And I would ask who makes such judgements as to who fits under the headings of "enemy" and "defenceless". For example, a trainer might consider a trainee's reaction to her as *completely irrational*, indicating a difference of perception. What one trainee *perceived as sexual comments towards her* from a trainer, did not fit with the view of her colleagues. We might stereotype in training groups: *themes of gender bias play out in psychotherapy* and students each have their impressions of trainers (and vice versa) that might be transferential and illusory.

There are suggestions here of misperceptions and differences in interpretation that can render black-and-white qualification of terms such as "enemy" and "defenceless" impossible. What is intended is not always what is perceived. In field theory terms, in seeking to complete gestalten, we perceive what we already know. So, here we clearly have the extremely difficult task of attempting to unravel conscious from unconscious experience in determining the level of intention. One might even suggest that a person chooses to be sufficiently defended to suppress experience to the unconscious realm, whereas repression happens more subtly and spontaneously. How much of the process of rendering unconscious is unconscious, and how much a matter of choice? And even when an act is carried out consciously against an enemy, what right do we have to behave towards another person in a similar way to that which we criticize in them, in naming them enemy? In institute disputes, revenge and retaliation serves only to increase shadow, whereas reconciliation seeks healing.

Much of what is today considered as immoral behaviour stems from a very long history of religious ideals: the divorce law in this country has aspects based on the ten commandments (for example, "Thou shalt not commit adultery"), as have the marriage vows. When the marriage vow of "'til death us do part" came into play, the average marriage lasted eight years, because life expectancy then was very much lower.

In training situations, it is very easy to account for our behaviour by assuming that someone "deserved it". As we deny our own shadow, we can assume a stance of self-righteousness and morally assume a right to blame others. The core conditions of a psychotherapy relationship, as they are mostly taught today, sadly, support this process. Human fear of judgement, criticism, being seen to be wrong, with our perceived consequences of that, can all lead to falsely hiding behind moral reasoning and unhealthy rationalization.

The ideal–real situation tension

One colleague struggles with tension between her wishes to become a trainer and the external need for setting up a training programme alone, which she really did not choose.

I would much rather have worked in an existing training group or set the whole thing up from the beginning with a colleague . . . to get the experience I wanted in order to qualify as a trainer, I had to set up a programme myself. I . . . a big part of me hated doing it.

She refers to the shadow part of herself that was *deeply, deeply reluctant to do it*; an example of how a wish to pursue one's own professional growth, accompanied by a lack of choice as to *how* this is brought about, invites shadow. This lack of choice in the training milieu has an impact on another colleague, who reacted to her tutor's instructions of *You must . . . you must . . . without negotiation* with a response that was to become a *sort of rebel, foot stamping*. In the real world we cannot always have things the way would like them to be, or even the way in which they might better be. Our training encourages us to develop a strong sense of "I" in the world and to make our wishes known. It sometimes provides little in the way of learning the tolerance of frustration.

Shadow emerges both in the form of, and as a defensive result of, personal and environmental impositions on the other in which lack of negotiation and choice are dictated. The absence of negotiation then may be shadow in itself, or trigger a secondary shadow reaction in others. At one end of the spectrum, shadow is seen as the *pain in the butt aspects of human resistance*. At the polarity we have the intensity of shadow as *persecutory, highly critical, malicious, vicious, wanting to destroy* and such experience is both intense and leaves its mark for periods of long duration, the pain of some experience lasting for years. This latter example supports the theory offered by Perls (1947), who discusses annihilation of the other; the desire to render the (offending) other non-existent, as a defence against one's own pain. In destroying the other, we destroy the relationship between self and other and avoid the pain that we must face inside ourselves if we were to uphold the relationship. The shadow, which seeks to destroy others, although bringing relief in the short term, actually denies an aspect of self, albeit a painful aspect, and this is diminishing of the self. Hence, shadow, which on the surface appears supportive, can be profoundly unhealthy.

If we employ this defence as psychotherapists, we hinder the growth of our clients. Guggenbuhl-Craig (1971) believes that our clients, under such circumstances, learn from us only how to fool themselves and the world. And this imposition on our trainees and our self is again our own shadow at work. Paradoxically, the avoidance of shadow *is* shadow.

The projection–ownership of power tension

I recollect feeling narcissistically wounded in training by a shaming guest trainer. Only through a year of therapy, which brought me understanding and allowed me to re-experience early emotions and memories in a contained relationship, was I able to challenge my interaction with this guest trainer when she returned to teach us the following year. Sadly, her therapeutic stance had not changed, but my own work had rendered me sufficiently empowered not to feel annihilated again. As I write, I can remember the wave of pain and sudden draining of energy resulting from being on the receiving end of profound criticism from an eminent trainer. The support from my own therapist made it possible for me to choose to re-experience my original trauma in a contained way, and this is markedly phenomenologically different from being re-traumatized, the difference being the degree to which I was able to retain my own power.

Colleagues clearly illustrate the influence of power imbalance on shadow experience. *What I think about power is that we don't see it when we've got it,* and my own dream process (see dream one) portrays my struggle with owning my own power. One colleague tells of a very conflictual training relationship where healing was not possible because, at that time, he was not sufficiently in touch with his own strength or authority. He believes *there's always a power aspect to any training process . . . and some of that comes out as shadow.*

A trainee, in wanting something from a trainer, may automatically allocate power to the trainer, who is already, by the nature of the relationship, in a powerful position. This can go both ways, as when, for example, a trainer needs numbers of trainees to make a course viable. I know of a training situation where a person was accepted on to the course for the sole reason of their skin colour. It was in the university's interest to be seen to have an African trainee in training, when multicultural interests were part of the education system's growing edge. This trainee was unprepared and out of her depth in an intensively emotional arena, and she suffered profoundly before withdrawing from the course.

Power dynamics invite either compliance or rejection. Just as there is sibling rivalry among trainees, there can be sibling rivalry among trainers of the same institute, with jealousies and resentments needing addressing. Many forward-thinking organizations in our country are bringing in external organizational consultants as a matter of routine, to provide an objective view of the dynamics within the team. Might not psychotherapy training organizations need such a support even more than any other organization, given that the very nature of our work is relationship dynamics, dealing with depth and intensity of emotion within a hierarchical system? However hard we all work to promote democracy, with committees for joint decision-making, the transferential relationships within a training environment, with inequalities and power struggles, will always be evident. A colleague wisely tells us that there comes a time when the older, more experienced trainers must retire, withdraw their power, and make way for the younger, more energized and innovative trainers to take over. One might question the motives of a senior trainer who has an investment in always being the person who knows best.

As students progress and mature thorough the training process, it is the trainer's responsibility to gradually devolve the power back to them, moving from the transferential relationship to an I–thou stance. How much power does each person need in order to be able to act responsibly and accountably?

One of the most difficult aspects of the training and supervision process is when the trainer and supervisor have to determine how much risk they are willing to take with a trainee's client work. How is a trainee to learn how to work with a specific client group, say psychotic clients, without having the experience of doing so? What degree of risk to the client is allowable in the name of the trainee's growth as a therapist? And from where do trainers and supervisors seek their support in containing the anxiety of such risk-taking? One would hope that they, too, have good clinical supervision, but I know that this is not always the case.

Whatever stance a trainer might adopt in relation to the trainer–trainee power dynamic, this might easily be, through a parallel process, re-enacted between trainee and client. And what is needed is a stance of openness and exploration, which, in itself, promotes power and responsibility. The more closed we become, the more, paradoxically, we disempower ourselves in inviting the projections of others.

The defended–openness tension

My own experience, across the board, highlights for me the positive effects of the willingness to endure my own pain, especially that which is brought about by shadow experience of training processes. For example, in every training group I have run, there has been at least one trainee angrily blaming me for their perception of my not supporting them, when my support has been to challenge their time boundary for handing in written work. They have threatened to leave training (a projective identification). Each time this experience occurs for me, the effect of allowing myself to feel the threatened rupture in relationship becomes more tolerable and I feel stronger. So, just as the avoidance of shadow paradoxically intensifies the painful experience when it finally emerges, similarly, the welcoming of shadow dynamics reduces the intensity of pain. Maya Angelou (1994) tells how we can hide ourselves away from the suffering of the world, but perhaps the hiding away is the only suffering we can choose to avoid.

The pertinent question here might be, what internal or environmental conditions determine the individual's potential to choose a willingness to remain open, and is this discussion for consideration under "containment"? It is worth noting, however, that a stance of openness is enhanced through ongoing questioning and not being driven to conclusions; that is, a willingness to engage with the tensions in the struggles, with uncertainty. This quality of personal engagement supports the chosen methodology of phenomenological enquiry and heuristic process for integrative psychotherapy practice, teaching, and psychotherapy research. Through heuristic experience I have learned to remain open to the essence of shadow effortlessly emerging. The attempt to capture ideas detracts from the essence, and provides evidence in itself of the elusory nature of shadow.

Shadow in relation to the group component of training; how interpersonal dynamics are coloured by group participation; how shadow and the collective might be mutually influential.

Waller (2002, p. 20) posits that a "culture of cruelty" can emerge in groups, where the role of professional socialization, with escalating commitments, ritual conduct, and repression of conscience can change people's behaviour. He believes that the factors that bind the individual to a group might include diffusion of responsibility, de-individuation and conformity to peer pressure. While Waller relates his theory to extreme situations, there is much evidence to show how group process occurs in all manner and levels of groups. The de-individuation and conformity to peer pressure, in my experience of psychotherapy training environments, conflict with the individual's capacity to think for themselves and make individual decisions. A colleague notes of her training group members, *It never went through their brains to any part of their behaviour* and *They'd absolutely no understanding.*

An acknowledgement of the power of group/collective dynamics is made by another colleague, as she states that she *tried to find out the kind of things that are in groups, basically and are not my fault.* Group process has a life/power of its own. *Adult people in training groups. When this venom shows itself, the tendency to wipe out, the hostility shows itself and then the terror they feel is enormous. They feel terror;* and another reference is made to the *recognition that people lynch other people in groups and institutions.* More is evidenced with *a part of the shadow side is that as soon as people get into a training group they start to regress to about eight years old. Their behaviour is as if they're back at school with a teacher, which I think is the shadow side*, continued with *very much passive aggressive behaviour*. Group processes occur as a natural phenomenon and we cannot avoid that. We can, however, with awareness, choose how we respond to any patterns emerging. How many psychotherapy trainers have undergone a specific, in-depth, taught programme in group dynamics, I wonder?

Waller notes how

> Laboratory studies indicate that in groups, we become more aroused, more stressed, and more error-prone on complex tasks. Groups tend to be more antagonistic, competitive, and mutually exploitative than individuals. [Waller, 2002, p. 34]

He also explains that

> On a positive level, groups can develop values, institutions, and practices that promote humanitarian caring and connection [and] being in a group reveals who individuals are just as much as . . . being in a group alters who they are. [*ibid.*]

This would support the idea that each of us has innate potential to behave, in our training groups, in ways "either heroic or barbaric" (*ibid.*, p. 35), and in the psychotherapy profession our ethical codes and *raison d'être* are to work towards making the world a healthier place; splitting the heroic/barbaric stances. I believe that this need not discount the tension of polarities of human existence, good and bad, but can, rather, escalate them into our awareness to utilize healthily. Psychotherapy theory shows how what we are aware of we can address, and this reduces the splitting process and acting out behaviours. Again, this is a rationale for trainers to have a sound taught understanding of group-work.

Another colleague offers another perspective on this view and considers a professional tension encouraging splitting, which we ourselves introduce as we request confidentiality from trainees in training group settings. *I think holding confidentiality is a really false kind of situation. It's splitting. We talk about integration and encourage integration in others and then in the profession, we have to split. It's a kind of knife edge that we're giving ourselves.*

The suggestion that splitting is a *false kind of situation* is not supported by the view of Whittaker (1985), who suggests that splitting dynamics arising from the anxiety of human conflict situations are a naturally evolving aspect of any group process. Given that groups are fertile ground for turning "antagonism between neurosis and group formation to therapeutic account" (Freud, 1921c), and that Kernberg (1984) tells us that splitting is a part of every person's developmental process, then this dynamic cannot not occur in healthy training group settings.

My colleague seems to be saying, however, that splitting as a dynamic should not be knowingly introduced into training groups. In support of her trainees, she suggests that we ask for openness and transparency from our trainees in group process and, at the same time, we expect them to hold information. We encourage the very thing that we hope to use group-work to dissolve. Angrily she relates, *Except if you're a trainee! Let's not integrate the whole thing. Let's not integrate the part of you that talks to your clients. . . . Well, there's a shadow in the training!*

She says here that as trainers we do not always use groups as effectively as we might, although, of course, this is constrained by ethical guidelines. Given that supervisors hear of client work, and fellow trainees practise under the same ethical code as supervisors, one might question whether codes of confidentiality might need to be more flexibly applied with regard to client material in training groups?

And I wonder whether, as trainers, it might be healthy and growth enhancing to encourage trainees to hold boundaries themselves internally, in relation to their own professional experience and making their own choices around levels of disclosure, rather than imposing ethical codes. Ethical codes then become useful as guidelines only. Integrity and genuine openness comes, I think, with the personalization of standards and values. It is the working through of shadow in group, collective, dynamics and finding our individuality through this process, which builds integrity and supports trainees to hold the tension between ethical codes and their personal moral beliefs without employing defensive shadow tactics.

A colleague supports trainers holding the splitting processes pertaining to shadow, in a way that *is not utopian or naïvely optimistic or pretends away the savagery and brutality of human nature; that enables us to work with it, assimilate it, transform it, to be more creative, and that's the endless struggle, I think.*

Schmukler (1998) defines the purpose of group process as that which makes the unconscious conscious. And, as such, the training group becomes a growth medium for shadow. How we use this potential in relation to shadow experience is open to differing training stances and philosophical underpinnings.

I am told that there is *the shadow aspect of group process, the lynch mob, and the polarization that takes place in groups, particularly when they're in fight/flight mode.* This colleague suggests that an analytic training stance enhances this process negatively, with *I suspect the scale and degree of lynch mob happens in psychoanalytic groups.* This would support the view of Lake (1987) that what is needed in adulthood is "companionable interaction" rather than the therapeutic abstinence of analytic work. My experience is that, paradoxically, a degree of abstinence as a training group facilitator does prove useful in encouraging unconscious dynamics to become figural. Then, what is of paramount importance is the containment, at the same time, offered by the trainer, so that re-experiencing does not become re-traumatization. Phillips (1995, p. 3) considers therapeutic abstinence, believing that "at its worst, and it is often at its worst in analysis, it merely repeats the childhood trauma of the inaccessible parent". McClusky (1989) tells how, with the inaccessible parent, *the sense of self is eroded.*

The therapeutically abstinent stance of the trainer might be perceived, by trainees with a history of an emotionally missing parent, as one of inaccessibility, as transferential processes emerge in training situations. One colleague *couldn't continue running the course. I wasn't feeling well, and knew I had to pull out. They were all so angry with me, they went to another training institute.* Her inaccessibility (sick leave) preceded trainees' leave-taking.

The tension with which every trainer struggles, in the development of the group life, incorporates the following questions.

- How much therapeutic abstinence do I need to use in order to allow transferential dynamics to emerge in the group while taking care not to "abandon" anyone?
- How contactful can I be in the working through of the transferential components?
- How do I balance the transferential needs of each individual trainee when they are each at a different stage of personal and

professional development in their training, with differing needs from myself?

These questions determine the level of self-disclosure of the trainer, as well as the nature, timing, and frequency of intervention. In the end, it is important to remember that, as trainers, although we have group dynamics to contain, we are not therapists for our trainees and each trainee has a therapist of their own for personal support. Not to take heed of this serves only to enhance a trainee splitting process between trainer and therapist, idealizing one and belittling the other.

Transference dynamics evident in group process and in the power imbalance of training roles, and the influence of personality traits upon this. Where is shadow in the transference?

What is inescapable in the integrative psychotherapy profession is that, because of the very nature of the beast, that is, to explore childhood influence on adult experience, there must be a power imbalance in relationships. That is not to say that one cannot explore and understand childhood experience from an adult perspective. Of course this can be done cognitively. However, the quality, depth, and intensity of awareness that arises in phenomenological inquiry brings the past into the present in such a way as to emotionally feel that the past is being re-experienced as if it were still happening in the present moment. In adulthood, we can feel like a child. Some theorists might refer to this experience as regression, as a going back to an earlier feeling state. I think that this understanding of such experience is slightly misleading. We do not so much regress as move forward, to make it possible for something that is always with us to become more accessible to our awareness in the current field conditions. Ideally, the training milieu creates the appropriate field conditions.

The reality factor is that trainees relate to trainers because the trainers have something they need; training organizations relate to governing bodies because they have something they need; governing bodies relate to government officials because they have something they need; and so it goes. Wherever one person has a need for something from another, vulnerability *vs.* power dynamics is fuelled.

A colleague believes that *there's always a power aspect to any psychotherapy training process that people chafe with, both at the level of students, and at the level of people running the training and at every level of that, some of it comes out as shadow.* He relates incidences of cruelty in his *fair amount of experience* as a trainer at both wider institutional and political level to people who are *quite totalitarian in how they go about managing power.* For example, *adhering to the party line, pure and simple.* The potential transferential component to these dynamics are acknowledged with *I'm very familiar with this particular historical sequence, where I'm dealing with a person who overrides all considerations of fairness in pursuit of her own power, and scapegoats people who don't conform. That pattern goes back to my experience of prep. school,* and he takes care transferentially *lest I, in my turn, am projecting my own totalitarianism on to this person.* The positive aspect of transference is valued with *it gave me radar for these kinds of people.*

The issue of being the recipient of trainees' projections, and also the projector, is addressed by another colleague with *One of the problems I've found really difficult, struggled with as a trainer, was other people's projections on to me and sometimes my reciprocal ones on to them.* The two-way nature of transferential phenomena such as projection is accepted by Guggenbuhl-Craig (1971), while in my personal experience I have often found transferential dynamics defensively and unhealthily attributed by trainers to only the trainee's process; this is shadow at work, I think. One profound learning experience for me, from the beginning of my thoughts on shadow, is the ownership of my own projections in imagining that it was my role as a trainer to contain alone the shadow processes of trainees. This, I think, is only part of the interactive process. What I had split off from my awareness at that time was the impact of my own shadow upon the training process and group dynamics, and also the trainees varying levels of responsibility (according to their stage in training) for their own self-containment. Paradoxically, the stance of trainer taking full responsibility in this area may well be an example of female shadow at work in infantilizing trainees. This aspect of shadow allocated to female trainers is recognized as *women's shadow is to keep clients dependent.* I am acknowledging here that to attribute all trainees' behaviour to transferential process is unhealthy, and yet, when the transferential aspect of a trainer–trainee relationship is threatened inappropriately, shadow behaviours can emerge. Holmes (1993) recognizes that "bad behaviour is the normal response to the threat to an attachment bond". Transference is symbolic attachment.

In her relationship with a trainee, a colleague refers to *all of the sort of transferential possibilities I'd expect would emerge with a male client* [trainee] *and a female therapist* [trainer]. She continues to share her own experience as a trainee in working with a trainer who *was all over himself in terms of sexual orientation*, and she attributes the leaning in today's society towards political correctness as contributing to trainers' avoidance in addressing those issues *which might be bodily references and relate to sexual preferences*. What remains unaddressed openly is particularly likely to colour transferential process if it becomes relegated to unconscious experience. Sexual feelings and experiences inform our identity and sense of self, which is the very material invited in psychotherapy trainings. The pertinence of sexual experience to psychotherapy training is acknowledged with *power and sex. They're the two aspects of shadow . . . because power is very sexy*. Power and sex are two of the experiences underpinning the process of projective identification occurring in the transference, as discussed by Cashdan (1988) and the power of the sexual transference cannot be underestimated, given the incidences of trainer–trainee boundary breaches in this area, despite very clear teaching and ethical codes which firmly deny this abusive behaviour. A colleague reminds us that *Training's intimate*, and in adulthood, intimacy is often expressed sexually. This data is supportive of Mathes' (2001) understanding of one aspect of the erotic transference.

There is evidence that personality traits of schizoid, borderline, and narcissistic process seem most likely to carry the potential to shadow behaviours. These traits are those that Greenberg (1998) would attribute to identity and the formation of the sense of self. All who have trained as integrative psychotherapists must surely recognize the destructive dynamics of varying degree that are exercised when someone believes his or her own sense of self to be under threat; for example, *there was a huge narcissistic wound and they lashed out towards us*, and *pretty powerful hostility and a total wiping out of the other person, usually it's from a transferential place*. Paradoxically, it seems to be the case that the more grandiose are the illusions of the trainer, the more the trainer needs them. This process, which precipitates toxicity, is referred to as the *malicious, vicious, wanting to destroy* behaviour of someone who *was presenting as someone narcissistic.* Another belief is that a fellow trainer, *in his narcissistic process, had got caught up in the grandiosity and the idealization* and had resorted to diminishing a co-trainer.

Our sense of who we are in the world is always reworked through in group dynamics; that is "Who am I?", "Who are you?", and "How are we going to be together?" This process invites power issues, sexual awareness, and sometimes very entrenched transferential positions of trainees and trainers alike.

Winnicott (1947) discusses hate as part of countertransference phenomena. He sees this not simply as a reaction to trainees' behaviour, which it might be, but as a natural occurrence regardless of the nature of the behaviour of the trainee. My own countertransferential hate is evidenced in dream two of dream analysis. My colleague shares, *A big part of me hated doing it* and *I felt very, very resentful of the amount of work.* The enormity of the workload in being a psychotherapy trainer, with its many layered responsibilities to trainees, to committees, to institute members, to the public relations work across fellow professions, to UKCP, and to the overall group process in the development of an institute is almost beyond belief until one has personally undergone such a mammoth task.

It is interesting, and, on reflection, not surprising, that a colleague believes that to run a psychotherapy training institute it is an advantage to have some degree of charisma, with an air of confidence that enhances the belief that one deserves an institute. How else might one tolerate the enormity of the task? However, this element of narcissism is often accompanied by the trainer taking all of the authority, resulting in those around them giving up their power, in feeling beholden to them. Quite serious loss of skill emanates from this dynamic. Having personally set up and run a training institute, I can understand the need for perseverance and a sheer determination to survive against all odds, given the shadow experiences one encounters, as discussed in the rationale for this book, and I also appreciate the need for an optimum degree of promotion of democracy in any training culture. A colleague tells how he believes in *maintaining, in my training with my students, a considerable degree of freedom of speech.*

Sadly, hidden somewhere beneath the sheer determination of the controlling, grandiose narcissist is the toxic character that can annihilate, or can diminish, another in the most subtle, almost undetectable ways. It is at the level of personality trait formation, as in the emergence of schizoid, borderline, and narcissistic process, that most ruptures in the transference occur.

Field dynamics and the influence of religion, culture, politics, finance, and the integration in training situations of all current and past experiences. How do field situations influence shadow behaviours?

The influencing field dynamics, in all of their forms, are sufficiently expansive to deserve a book in their own right. Here, however, it must suffice for me to generalize the information, which is more detailed and referenced elsewhere throughout the book. When addressing shadow, we are obliged to consider the following.

- The impact of childhood experiences and the personality patterns resulting from those early life interactions: the underlying dynamics of the personality traits of schizoid, borderline, and narcissistic processes and the predisposition to the acting out of shadow experience, in differing forms, are evidenced in all trainings. This acting out occurs in interactions among professionals at individual, group, and inter-group levels.
- Religion and the effect of religious values on moral judgements: there are idealizations and splitting processes inherent in most religions, and psychotherapy may well fall into the trap of becoming a replacement for failing religious ideologies in today's society. Do people turn to therapy as panacea for making their world right? When one way of being in the world becomes idealized, as can happen in religious cultures, then the polarity becomes acted out in shadow form. With this dynamic apparent in the psychotherapy profession, shadow is relegated to the unconscious, and potentially dangerous energy is fostered.
- Cultural norms and ways of being socialized into one's identificatory groupings, including one's training group: much is

addressed in the field on the effects of group process on individual behaviour and the enhanced predisposition to shadow in group experience. It is suggested that choice of behaviour is less available to people who engage at a group process level than it is in one-to-one interactions. Paradoxically, this situation can be turned around.

My initial engagement with the caring professions I know now to be in part a displacement of my pseudo-attachment to my mother, in my identification with her religious pursuits. I was seeking a place to belong by becoming a carer of others. Paradoxically, my resistance to becoming socialized into training groups has been resistance to my father's lack of democracy and his need for control. The way for me to belong in a family (group) was to both conform and identify with my mother (do not have a shadow?) and also my father (I know what is best for you?). In shadow dynamic terms, my process of identifying with an idealized other rendered me vulnerable to criticizing those whose standards I perceived to be lower than my own, and to desensitization towards the dangerousness of others (and myself). This led to frequent challenge from my colleagues in forensic work that I was "too soft" and that I placed myself in potentially dangerous situations.

- The theoretical orientation and philosophical beliefs underpinning our profession: the range of psychotherapy cultures across the board carry a diversity of differing ideologies and relational stances taken, both in integrative and other psychotherapy trainings. A difference is perceived in relation to shadow in differing psychotherapeutic orientations, in that integrative psychotherapy practice is regarded as more containing of shadow behaviours than, for example, some analytic trainings. Cognitive–behavioural therapy may attempt to reframe negative experiences into positive experiences, though without actually experiencing either phenomenologically. What happens then to what gets missed?

- The teaching style and patterns of power dynamics within a training institute and between training institutes: interviews explore transferential phenomena and forms of abuse of power. Parallels can be drawn between teaching stances and personality traits of trainers. The toxicity of shadow can be seen as emerging in response to the trainers' perception of their sense of self being threatened.

I currently communicate painfully with a colleague with whom I have differences in theoretical understanding, leading to our different ways of addressing situations with trainees common to us both. The containment is for we two to struggle ourselves, through dialogue, to model to trainees that difference can be open to contact. Working with my own shadow has given me strength to engage with this struggle.

● The current political positions in relation to psychotherapy: here, we must acknowledge the current proneness to litigation, society's attitude towards political correctness and its effects on professionals, in that they experience a need to be more guarded and less open about shadow phenomena. Afternoon television carries advertising from firms of lawyers inviting and suggesting that people make claims for accidents, for being mis-sold policies, etc. And the attitude of gaining money through litigation is encouraged.

It is also the time of government legislation for the psychotherapy profession, through which some people/trainings will be acceptable and some not. This induces sibling rivalry among approaches, training organizations, and governing bodies. While the formalization and accountability of our profession is imperative, the process of attaining appropriate standards leaves some practitioners who have been part of this profession for years concerned that they may find themselves suddenly not belonging in the same way. In field theory terms, the fears of senior and politically involved practitioners influence the experience of junior practitioners. and this carries on down a line to trainees.

● The human predisposition to symbolic understanding as containment of splitting processes: interviews and dream analysis address the profound need for containment of shadow phenomena in relation to the human predispositions for polarization of good and evil. These dynamics are clearly evident in fairy-tales and folk-lore, with acknowledgement of stories and dreams as processes of integration. As political correctness becomes more sought-after in our society, children's fairytales are open to scrutiny and the stark shadow phenomena are being removed; for example, the *Noddy* series, which I loved as a child, is criticized for the story of the ten gollywogs.

So, while older children are becoming more exposed to shadow in destructive science fiction and horror movies, and this may be containing for adults, though not necessarily for the youngsters being given freedom of access to this material in today's society, the smaller children are beginning to be denied a level of symbolism in their formative years, where it is so necessary.

I am surprised as I write, as I never cease to be surprised, by the power of unconscious process. This illuminates for me that, however much personal work we undertake, we never graduate from the impact of our unconscious and transferential issues. As such, learning is a life-long experience, because field dynamics and our sense of self-in-relation are ever changing.

In any field situation we are faced with difference, not least in religious circles. Whole nations make war in relation to differences in religious beliefs. In the psychotherapy profession as a whole, in the philosophies underpinning our practice, we have serious differences between and within groups, as well as differences of religious values within each group. A Sunday radio discussion considered dialogue between the Jewish and Christian faiths. Professor Ahmed shared his belief that the stereotyping that each of the orders employ is the same stereotyping; the same myth that each group creates in their own mind, rather than engage in the scary place of dialogue between difference. This is true of interpersonal dynamics between people in the same group, or between groups in the same profession. Ahmed believes very strongly that this process needs to be broken down, and the way forward is through dialogue between groups and traditions. In positing that violence stems from ignorance, and ignorance stems from lack of communication, he goes on to say, "When we stop talking with each other, about each others pain, we become locked in a cycle of violence" Ahmed (2005).

In this process of government registration for psychotherapy as a profession, where licence to practice is now at stake, each orientation must enter into dialogue with others to discover the common factors contributing to the profession as a whole that bind us together. Shadow shows itself in this process inter-denominationally, with criticism, projections, and dismissal. A colleague highlights the importance of *what we would normally do, which would be to get through the resolution of differences*. The modelling that trainees need at this current time can only come from the senior practitioners with political and group process insights. Again, we are made aware of the importance of acceptance and honouring of difference.

With statutory registration looming large, the UKCP, our lead body, is itself struggling with issues of difference and dialogue between orientations. In field theory terms, this in turn rocks the stability of training organizations when their very existence and licence to train might become threatened. We must professionally respond to the government's request for common guidelines pertaining to psychotherapy registration, and our own need for this, while at the same time acknowledging and respecting our differences between orientations. The insecurity that this process fosters predisposes *rivalry between training organizations* resulting in *venomous letters . . . real paranoia that came from the other person*, and shadow behaviours of *When someone attacks, to want to attack back*. Some headway is being made in working with this, as the profession is in the process of acknowledging difference and diversity, demonstrated by the formation of a new Psychotherapeutic Counselling Section of UKCP. In field theory terms, this will assist the healing of inter-organizational splits, and this has the potential to reduce any subsequent grandiose or paranoid ideations between counselling and psychotherapy training groups. What is needed is to go back to our roots and find what links us, not simply what divides us. The tension between sameness and difference meets us once again.

When, alongside seeking sameness, we acknowledge the importance of addressing difference, this implicitly allows for choice. A colleague refers to her training group experience *It's come to awareness because it's caught their perception strongly enough for them to confront me about it. They confront me as to how I teach, with differences. It's what they haven't confronted me with . . . there's shadow!*

The value and restrictions of shadow to human growth and learning, and to the philosophical underpinnings of the psychotherapy profession as change agent

Waller (2002) makes reference to accidental and unintended harm. And even if we, in the profession of training psychotherapists, were able to make distinction between all conscious or unconscious, accidental and unintended or premeditated, harm, which, of course, we cannot possibly do, given the complexities of human motivation to behaviours, then, I wonder, what right do we have to impose change on others anyway, and might such imposed change in itself be our own shadow behaviour at work? A colleague, when offering discussions to trainees to determine what they *should do*, questions *whether there would be some trainees who wouldn't conform*. Even when we offer freedom of choice through discussion, it is often the case that, perhaps beneath our own levels of awareness, we have our own, subtly imposed value system to which we want trainees to adhere. A colleague believed that shadow is *imposing a theoretical viewpoint* on trainees. Perhaps a trainee enters a training programme to learn alternative ways of practising. Until the customary way is recognized, that is, her starting point, she cannot hope to assimilate new knowledge. So, having a trainer who is too rigid in his own orientation can be restrictive.

However, it is noted that *change in our field and our work is so very difficult to achieve.* Do we, as psychotherapy trainers, have an assumption that shadow behaviours are changeable or can be eradicated? Is it what we are about as psychotherapy trainers, to "socialize" our trainees to behave in a more socially acceptable way, or without shadow? It would seem from available theory and the considerations of my colleagues that this might be the case, given the many references to how making shadow welcome disempowers it. Evidence is given to support two viewpoints. First, that change in shadow behaviour is brought about by challenge, control, and imposing difference, and, second, that shadow energy can be more healthily utilized by welcoming, experiencing, and understanding. I would suggest that we can only truly employ a different way of being if we also have understanding of what it truly is that we are hoping to contain. We can deny negative energy and, with determination, do something else with that energy, or we can feel the negative energy, along with its discomfort and pain, and transform it to new and more fruitful use.

Theory shows that the most profound human abuse is that *the child is left alone at times of suffering* (ISA, 1990). This is true also of adults (Schmukler, 1998); understanding comes with sharing. One colleague advocates supportively challenging her students shadow behaviour with *Stop, and let's talk about what's happening*, which acknowledges the need for challenge to be supported by sharing, understanding, and negotiation. The imposition of difference leaves the trainee alone in their suffering and this fosters the intensity of shadow.

One trainer refers to another with *there were things that she was prone to do that she would need to be headed off from.* He believes it to be his role to *ensure that face to face norms of respectable behaviour are maintained.* Another says of his students, *What they need is a change of thought.* One might assume that a process is expected where shadow behaviour, to some degree at least, will be reduced. Perhaps we do need to address the question of degree of acceptability of the processes that psychotherapists understand as shadow? And acceptable to whom? We have here, again, the tension with which psychotherapists struggle; that between what is expected from one's organization's ethical codes and that which fits with one's own personal moral belief system as a trainer.

In considering the place for shadow, or not, in training, a pertinent point is made by a colleague who refers to the tension between something being sufficiently experienced for it to be worked with, rather than denied or changed, while not causing too much pain to people. That is *if something overspills and needs to overspill, it has opportunity to do so, but nevertheless, that it is not to become the norm.* Negative experience is also perceived as potentially positive to some degree by the subject, who refers to arriving in projective identification with *not that that's a bad thing, but if you don't use it constructively it can be.* The question emerges, *How can we integrate it when we haven't had that part to integrate?* A very valid point is being made that experiences must be welcomed in training for us to choose how we accommodate them into our psyche. Shadow is no exception to this viewpoint.

I am aware here of two things; first, of the ever increasingly complexity of shadow experience, and second, yet again, of the delicate balance and tension between two seemingly opposing stances of being in relationship. I have experience of a trainer challenging persecutory behaviour in a training group situation, with *That behaviour is not permitted here*, with no follow-up working through of its meaning. So, this persecutory energy simply gets blocked, as opposed to my supervisor challenging me with the question, *Why do you have an investment in your trainees not persecuting you?* And I was left to struggle with the issue of how anyone can really become familiar with their desire to persecute, and then transform it, if experiencing this aspect of themselves is denied in the training context.

The optimum process of the degree of welcoming of shadow is seen as one of damage limitation, and this again seems often to be a question of intensity. For example, paradoxically, although attachment is seen as healthy in relationships (Storr, 1997), too much attachment on behalf of the trainer is seen as shadow: *The shadow of attachment—the trainers' attachment.* This tension manifests itself as *My role is to balance offering nourishment without infantilizing.* This is supported theoretically, as Bly posits the importance of "living in the space between" opposites. How can we, as trainers, meet the trainees' need for support and, at the same time, take care not to deny their own independence? The phenomenological process of shadow can be defined in terms of degree and intensity of harm inflicted, be that physical, emotional, or both.

I qualify this belief with experiences of physical harm being, in part, manifested in the retroflections that trainers employ: for example, *a trainer comes to mind who . . . has been a consistent alcoholic as a trainer . . . he just runs from himself in alcohol.* Here we have a question of extremes; a life-threatening retroflection as opposed to the less severe self-limitation of withholding one's energy: *I suppose I think of shadow as so self-limiting. . . . not turning over those sods of earth which are the shadow, so as to actually just capture that energy there.* Another example of somatization of shadow is the physical experience leading to someone becoming so ill that they were obliged to leave their training commitment, with *It was actually quite dehydrating. I wasn't feeling well and I was feeling very tired and I knew I had to pull out.* This resulted in experience of trainees acting out *very much passive–aggressive behaviour* in the training groups. Severe illness lies at one extreme of a continuum, with a stress reaction at the other end; for example, *I felt sick in the room. I was physically shaking.* The latter experience could be seen as a useful somatic prompt of the need for containment, as in *I had to stay in thinking, very powerfully, to hold myself together,* while the former was a dangerous, life-threatening situation.

In speaking with colleagues across the board in the psychotherapy profession, I am struck by my awareness of how many female psychotherapy trainers have undergone gynaecological surgery. While, of course, without a properly researched viewpoint one can only interpret, it seems to me that there might be a correlation between transferential attack on symbolic mothers and the gynaecological difficulties that trainers undergo and that render us unable to "mother" again. In working holistically with our trainees we are naturally prone to respond to negative transference in several ways, including somatically. The physical aspect is also borne out metaphorically, with *I feel kicked if you do that*.

While the damaging effect of shadow is noted, it was also mooted that shadow experience could have positive qualities, with *there's a part of shadow that becomes enjoyable, which is the shadow that's in the light*. In reference to acknowledging our limited abilities of being human, a colleague shares her belief that *With shadow comes something that's fantastic*. In process terms, the benefit of sharing of shadow is experienced with *It's a very cathartic experience* and Evetts-Secker (2003) acknowledges how, sometimes, when we are depleted of energy for change in our lives, we need to resort to the energy of shadow to implement progression forwards. I remember a colleague who acted out her shadow experience in the form of shoplifting, for the first and only time, as a consequence of coming into training. At that time in her life this was her only known way of becoming sufficiently noticed to access the emotional help she needed. This understanding of process might throw some light on the experiences of petty theft in training situations.

According to Yin-Yang philosophy, it is when we go deeper into one polarity that we reach the other polarity. The pathway to the light may well be through the darkness. Coyle shares Yin-Yang understanding in his translation of the Yellow Emperor's work

> Violent anger depletes Yin; violent joy depletes Yang. When rebellious emotions rise . . . when joy and anger are without moderation . . . life is no longer secure. Yin and Yang should be respected to an equal extent. [Ebrey, 1993, trans. Coyle, p. 3]

This supports the view that seeks the optimum balance between good and evil and the formation of an integrated boundary which lies in the between of both qualities of energy.

I know, from my own therapeutic journey, that in allowing myself the fantasies of "over the top" anger at someone, wiping him out, and acknowledging the transferential component, I have returned to the loving place I knew before the incident that triggered the change. I now have the qualitative difference of feeling more grounded than before. I am staying now with my awareness that the form and intensity of shadow experience must be in relation to the individual's field experience, their history story, their personality pattern, their levels of awareness, and, above all, their internal and external support systems.

As I consider the current National Health Service trend to encourage talking therapy interventions to be employed by psychiatric nurses (very basic counselling skills are now part of their training curriculum), I own that I believe that nurses are often insufficiently trained or personally and professionally supported to engage in a counselling relationship with some of the very damaged clients they encounter. This situation is potentially painful for both patients and staff alike. Yet, psychiatric nurses are well equipped to monitor the pharmaceutical needs of their patients. I wonder how much shadow is involved in psychotherapists discouraging clients to seek the medical model help of pharmaceutical interventions? In idealizing our own profession, how much might we discourage a trainee to accept medical help for emotional difficulties?

The complexity and tensions to be contained personally and professionally in relation to shadow becoming healthily utilized

Our primary question as a psychotherapist and/or trainer is "What do I need for myself, in order to be able to do what I do with my clients/trainees?" We can see how containment, in its many forms, is a necessary field condition for shadow to be expressed and experienced, without becoming acted out in a damaging way. Containment may be experienced at any or all levels of human interaction, cognitively, emotionally, somatically, symbolically, consciously, or unconsciously. I am considering now some of the data from my original research study to support my thinking.

One trainer honours the need for explicitly (cognitively) addressing shadow theory and experience, supporting how *this may be explained and addressed*. Regarding containment, she follows on with *We call it talking about it*, and she mentions the importance of *naming*. Another colleague also mentions theory as supportive in diminishing shadow behaviour, as she shares *I used theory to illustrate what they were doing and it stopped*. Here, the trainer is taking responsibility for initiating the containment, and, in this reference, containment follows the intellectual understanding of the behaviour. This data supports Whittaker's (1988) belief that "a practical person cannot do without theory . . . to quickly retrieve errors . . . predicting the likely consequences of particular courses of action". The advantage of essays is also advocated as containing of shadow phenomenon. Trainees gain understanding in the written component of training, and this brings a degree of safety to phenomenological experience. Of course, the opposite might also be true, that a trainer or trainee whose awareness is always primarily cognitive adopts this position so as not to have to feel emotions. Containment is seen to be provided mainly by trainers, but also by therapists and supervisors: *They* [trainees] *also have containment in their own therapy and supervision*. Again, containment here is seen to be the responsibility of the qualified professionals rather than trainees.

The symbolic containment of shadow is referred to in *theories in regard to nursery rhymes*, and is powerfully evident for me throughout the dream analysis. One colleague believes that containment is derived from a specific attitude of welcoming difference and respecting others, even when they are behaving from a shadow side. He states . . . *containment involves maximizing people's freedom to express the diversity of their views, cultural preferences . . . while at the same time ensuring that face-to-face norms of respectful behaviour are maintained*. He seems, as he continues to differentiate levels of containment, to be implying that the primary responsibility for this lies with the trainer, in that he sees the more extreme lack of containment stemming from *situations where the facilitator colludes with the marginalisation or abusive treatment*. He continues, *reasonable containment is about time boundaries* and *modelling*. Another colleague refers to his *sense of working below boundary level* at times when he has *noticed the shadow coming out*. Boundaries themselves are containing.

The avoidance factor in deflection into humour is recognized, while, at the other end of the spectrum, humour is seen as *permitting a great deal of free expression to happen in a good natured way, that doesn't evoke lynch mob in groups.* So, humour that is not so extreme as to constitute deflection is valued here as a containing factor in itself. To address shadow directed against the self, humour is valued in working with superego; that is, *In a group, I mean just in a simple playful way and the laughter comes with it.*

The lack of containment is enhanced when too many trainees are training together with one trainer. We are told, regarding a training group of twenty-five, *We were just too big for me to manage.* Again, this trainer informs us of the containing factor in both theory and good boundaries with *As a trainer . . . you are responsible for teaching them things . . . responsible for maintaining boundaries.*

It could be argued that the healthy attitude of the trainer, as enhanced through the process of self-searching, means that as trainers we need our own containment, and this is to be found in our own personal therapy and to some extent in clinical supervision, in that we here unpick our own process in relation to our trainees. It is interesting that one trainer, who finds herself so severely physically ill that she needs to withdraw from training, mentions that for a long period of time she had no clinical supervision for her work. The process of somatization, as a form of containment, is experienced alongside the use of imagery and the dream process to bring training group dynamics into awareness. However, in this example, somatization became the unhealthy containment of retroflection. We return again to the realization that most human experiences that we use to self-support can become disadvantageous when used to extreme.

Writing about this now invites my memories of when I have allowed myself the luxury of emotionally wailing in becoming the vessel (container) for training group despair. And in considering a deep empathic response to any trainee with a history of being physically abused, how can a trainer not experience this attunement at a physical level? For myself, emotional and somatic awareness play a huge part in the containment of my work with my training group, in that the metaphor, "I stood my ground" involved the healthy deliberate upright positioning of my body and focusing my awareness on breathing and body tensions as self-support. On reflection, I see my own need for three major operations as a result, in part, of my unhealthily retroflecting the shadow of the training groups I was working with at that time.

What is very obvious is that trainers need their own means of support, on all levels, in order to be able to support trainees. Six out of seven colleagues, in consideration of their own support systems, referred to their clinical supervision, and three expressed a belief that personal therapy for psychotherapy trainers should be a life-long process on a pro-rata basis. One colleague tells how she has taken less of her training group to supervision than she has therapy, emphasizing the use of self as the containing factor for shadow: *My inclination is more to stay with clearing oneself when working with trainees and students . . . if I can keep a little clarity on my personal life, I can handle it* [containment] *better . . . my commitment has been more to therapy with regard to my trainee work than supervision.* Here, more evidence of the usefulness of personal therapy to psychotherapy trainers.

While professional support is greatly valued, colleagues also mooted that trainers need something other, outside of therapy circles, by means of support. This was exemplified with enjoyment of *tea and biscuits*; or *I do get into environments where I can stop being a professional trainer and just be a bit of a lad*; or *I maximize my relax-ation time as well; I like travelling on trains.* One colleague shares her instructions to her students to *hang on to the day job*, as a way of having some ordinariness in their lives. Another acknowledges that in psychotherapy we are the modern versions of *clergy, shamans, teachers*, and we need to be *clear about ourselves and commonsensical.* I think that people are honouring the humanness beneath the ther-apist in these statements. First, I am a person, then a psycho-therapist. Schmukler (1998) tells how as human beings we all have sustaining needs. How much more so is this true when we deal with the pain and trauma of others and ourselves in our workplace?

The need for support is greatly acknowledged by my colleague, who highly correlates her isolation in her experience as a trainer with the somatized trauma she has suffered. *There was nobody. I would have much rather have worked in an existing training group or set the whole thing up from the beginning with a colleague.*

She attributes the trainees' *shadow side coming out* as the reason why she is now *very unwilling to ever be a major trainer again.*

We need to acknowledge here the complexity of each act of shadow in relation to the field in which it is executed, the degree of shadow-inflicted damage being, in part, in relation to the trainer's level of support systems. While the psychotherapists' potential to relate in certain ways is innate, factors contributing to the actualization of that potential come from the field, both archaic and current. These factors are so very varied in origin, form, quality, and intensity; they are multi-layered, interrelational, and impossible to grasp in their complexity.

> Last night I dreamed of sitting at a table, shaking dice with a colleague to turn-take in the pulling of soft toy cats from a paper bag, with floppy rope handles. The room surroundings, chairs, table, bag, and cats were all shades of white and silver. My colleague drew from the bag with collapsible handles, a black and brown live cat, which was impossible to hold. The cat ran off around the room and we could not retrieve it. I wake anxious. The value of the tacit knowledge, as evidenced in the dream, is as follows.

"Underlying all other concepts in heuristic research, at the base of all heuristic discovery is the power of revelation in tacit knowing" (Moustakas, 1990, p. 20).

The "subsidiary" (Moustakas, 1994) factors of tacit knowing are those which are figural, visible, and can be described; for example, the constituents of a dream. "Focal" factors (*ibid.*) are those which are implicit or subliminal, such as the meaning of a dream to the dreamer. Psychotherapy has taught me to trust and respect tacit knowledge.

In the above dream, it is the shadow (cat), which emerges unexpectedly, is untenable, pervades all the space, cannot be grasped; and this results in the experience of anxiety. Shadow is not an experience that can be captured, enclosed, rendered unreal, "toyed" with, or nicely sanitized into white, false, immobilized, lifeless form. An existential message from this dream might be that shadow is about "letting the cat out of the bag", or that one "cannot get a handle" on shadow.

In my experience of this study, at best, I think that attempts to "cat"egorize shadow can only be useful in the understanding of the depth and breadth of the phenomena. The more we attempt to grasp our shadow experience, the more it evades us. Shadow is elusive.

I return to the beginning of this creative synthesis, to my experience of shadow as fog; in existence, visible, tactile, all pervading, with no clear boundaries, no certainty of where it begins and ends, something that supports the "hidden", something that can be very beautiful when we rise above it and see it from a distance, or dangerous when we allow it to envelop us.

What actual use is this notion of shadow?

Life is a series of tensions and polarities and much of our energy for change is in the realization, as in the making real, of this experience of staying with the tensions of uncertainty, indecision, and not knowing. The difficulty in struggling with this tension emerges in many forms, emotionally, somatically, cognitively, and behaviourally. From my heuristic engagement with meditation, I learned that it is not possible to be grounded in loving human contact without also having shadow emerge alongside. I attended an early-morning meditation group in France, with the invitation to explore "radiant peace and love", and I experienced finding myself in another era from the past and in environments that are far from peace and love. I imagined myself within a hospital tent in the Crimean war; a sensatory experience. I could hear, smell, feel the cold, and taste the stench of gangrene in the air.

Another meditation brought nothing but blackness. I felt a burning pain in my wrist of being shackled in chains. I have no thoughts accompanying this somatization, but felt imprisoned. My dreams accompanying these five days were of foul stenches and murder through drowning. I was vividly killing some men from previous times in my life. Human horror was much in my field at that time. I am fascinated by how the invitation to intensification of peace and love in my awareness brings alongside it an intensification of the polarity. Guggenbuhl-Craig believes that shadow "is always somewhat destructive, operating negatively on the positive ideals". It is very true for me that positive also brings negative.

However, the gains of engagement with the complexities of any struggle far outweigh the resistances to it, in that, without acknowledgement, awareness and experience of the shadow polarity of humanness, as human beings, we deny ourselves a level and quality of energy for living.

A further gain is that, in owning shadow and claiming choices, we reduce the potentially destructive components that it carries with it, which may be life denying. A colleague shares, *I suppose that everything in there* [shadow] *is potentially valuable if we can harness it and not deny it. If not, it's destructive.*

Perls (1947) believed that individual shadow suppressed becomes collective energy, emerging as a process of executors and victims of collective aggression. This is useful professionally in understanding processes emerging in the collective, group component of training experience. If we believe, as Jung purports, that shadow's origin is often largely unconscious, that is, "not individual but universal; in contrast to the personal psyche", then the closer to the unconscious we become, the more generalizable is the information gleaned.

In the biological field, man can deeply probe into the heart of matter; microscopic studies have become possible with the advancement of aseptic technique, as surgeons "scrub up" before operating. Likewise, psychotherapists need to remove invasive organisms from the psychic temenos to probe into matters of the heart. I wonder how much shadow psychotherapists are expected to tolerate in the upholding of this temenos. Basic human kindness, offering someone a lift, changing an appointment at the last minute, may erode the therapeutic boundary and are not available to the therapist. The tension then is that psychotherapy relies heavily on both the celebration of human contact within session and the denial of human kindness external to the therapeutic frame. Might not the delicate balance of humanness inside and outside of the frame be open to shadow dynamics at work? The question is not whether humanness is welcomed or not in psychotherapy, but how much?

In addressing the struggle, a healthy balance can be found and energy may be utilized fruitfully for the optimum experiencing of life at both individual and collective levels. People, families, training groups, and whole societies alike might well benefit from this awareness.

Concluding thoughts

Shadow is very much evidenced at some level, and to some extent, in all human interaction, whether or not it is acknowledged. The awarenesses to note at this stage are:

- that male and female aspects of shadow inhabit different relational dynamics at the contact boundary, to push and to pull, respectively;

- that the culture of the sacrificial lamb, evident in some psycho-therapy training institutions as grandiosity in the form of martyrdom to a cause, results in the painful disempowerment of trainees;
- that shadow emerges in the differing forms of subtle leakage or of overtly bursting;
- that shadow may emerge transferentially as somatic experi-ence, which can be potentially very destructive or life threaten-ing for the recipients;
- that the kinder human qualities encouraged in psychotherapy training are merely superficial if shadow qualities are not also welcomed and worked with, and that this can overtly or subtly cause harm: to avoid shadow is shadow;
- that there is interorganizational movement among trainees and currently no UKCP guidelines to monitor this process;
- that the age-old professional split between counselling and psychotherapy is in the very new position of engaging in a potentially healing process;
- that the profession as a whole is imbued with paradox and polarities, and people become hurt when the optimum balance between opposites is not held.

Perhaps the most important outcome is the process outcome of the raising of awareness and enhancing of a questioning stance in relation to shadow among all those of us who consider this theme.

This book falls short if it cannot, in some way, make human experience more real and more open to contact. After all, the abil-ity to maintain and sustain contact with others is the ultimate psychotherapeutic aim, and I believe that this is only truly achiev-able when we have learned to endure healing solitude (individua-tion) that emerges through the transformation of the shadow of enforced solitude (ruptures in relationships) as object constancy becomes possible. In reality,

> We are left with the humbling and painful recognition that the persistence of inhumanity on human affairs is incontrovertible. . . . It is only in accepting who we are that we have a legitimate chance to structure a society in which the exercise of human evil is lessened. [Waller, 2002, p. 278]

Reflective activity

Having considered, with awareness, shadow phenomena in reading this book, complete the following experiment as you did at Chapter One. Notice new insights, and any new attitudes you may hold towards your own process and to others.

1. Write a list of words, describing all you aspire to as a psychotherapist: your positive attributes, beliefs and values about yourself, your character, and your behaviour.
2. Now, alongside these words, write down their opposite qualities.
3. Slowly, with awareness, read out aloud your second list, owning theses qualities as your own, beginning with "I am—".
4. Allow yourself to notice what this experience was like for you. What did you feel? What did you think? What did you experience in your body? What images came up for you?
5. Spend some time reflecting upon:
    whom you dislike;
    what qualities you despise in others;
    what it is like for you to own these qualities in yourself.
6. Consider the situations where, and how, these shadow qualities in *others* may have shown themselves in your relationships. What was your part in that? Consider the situations where, and how, these shadow qualities in *yourself.* may have shown themselves in your relationships.
7. Write a sentence about your own shadow, from a place of continued reflexive practice.

CHAPTER EIGHT

The journey ends; the journey begins

"Go afield and dream and forget;
And you will see that you are changed when you return and
the lights of the city gleam in the twilight"

(Ehrmann, 1948, p. 61)

I t is time now to reflect upon this journey into shadow phenomena and look at what insights might have become apparent that could throw light upon both human relationships across the board and psychotherapy professional practice.

What implications are relevant to the profession?

I recall in my work with clients who have suffered abuse at the hands of their fathers that their anger towards their mothers for not protecting them is always more intense than that towards the male abuser. Are there correlations with this in psychotherapy training organizations and transferential aggression directed towards male and female trainers? When a male trainer made his decision to leave the training institute where I also taught, it was me who was the target of transferential aggression. Was this because I was the trainer left to contain the dynamics? Or was it deeper than that, in that male and female trainers invite different transferential processes? Is a mother's emotional abandonment more shocking to the recipient and to society than a father's?

It has been mooted in this book that male and female shadows show themselves differently at the contact boundary. This leaves much room for further inquiry, pertinent to psychotherapy training, in that shadow could be studied from a more personal perspective of psychotherapy trainers of both sexes, or psychotherapy trainees of both sexes. It might also be useful to embark on such a study in the wider field of society. Are mothers more likely to overwhelm their children through suffocation and clinging, and fathers through control and distancing, as this study might suggest happens in psychotherapeutic relationships? And if there is a difference between what happens in reality, in society, and what happens symbolically in psychotherapy training, then what is it that makes the difference?

Any specific aspect of shadow experience might be studied as carrying weight in its own right, to bring more specific detail, the two prime areas being power and sexuality. Trainees may be asked to share their experience of power dynamics over the duration of their training; or of sexual issues; or of political awareness; or of religious influences; or of the relevance of the financial implications of training; or, more generally, of the interdisciplinary processes and dynamics evident across the caring professions. Each generalized theme of environmental influence on interpersonal shadow could be studied in more depth. By the same token, each aspect of individual shadow experience (cognitive, affective, behavioural, somatic, and spiritual) might also be studied more specifically, with considerations made for the mutually influential dynamics between them.

I am reminded here of the difference between research and professional/industrial application. I remember the French farmhouse, which boasts time and space for introspection, as befits heuristic methodology, considering both the grape-growers, as researchers of best stock, and also the wine-makers, as those who make practical use of the grapes. How do we, as we are increasingly employing research in our profession, ensure that the research guides our practice? Who does our research reach, and how?

I would hope that the very consideration of shadow experience, the purpose and practice of this book, becomes a sound model for therapeutic practice for myself and others in and of itself, in that it will, ideally, inspire those who read it to pursue their own interest in the shadow side of human experience in an ongoing way. The process then becomes the goal.

Ultimately then, researcher and practitioner become one and the same, and shadow is given an invitation into our awareness. Of course, our own shadow is a vital part of this picture, and in this light, personal therapy itself is a research process. Might it be a future professional requirement that personal therapy becomes an ongoing, life-long journey for those professionals practising integrative psychotherapy? Certainly, self-reflection is a very necessary part of what integrative psychotherapists do.

What we must ask ourselves in relation to shadow is "How can we become more aware, more empathic and understanding, without this deterring us from the task in hand of challenging inappropriate behaviours?" If, indeed, this is the task that we are about.

Bettelheim (1992) shared his fear of understanding the atrocities in life, stemming from his concern that such understanding might bring forgiveness and acknowledging that some acts of human violence are unforgivable. I have personally worked with adult survivors of childhood sexual abuse whose psychological symptoms pervade their lives, despite years of encouragement from well-meaning professionals to learn to forgive. Clarkson (1995) has a powerful contribution to make to this theme in her work with abuse victims, expressed in her quotation in the rationale for this book.

I believe that some human deeds are unforgivable and that, in relation to what has already happened, what we cannot enjoy or change in this life we must learn to endure and live alongside. While psychotherapy is intended to lead to empowerment and enabling the choice of embarking on our future lives in a healthier way, perhaps some things inherent in human nature are beyond the scope of our changes. I differentiate in this view between forgiveness and compassion. The compassion that comes with understanding does not necessarily mean forgiveness.

I believe that some human deeds need both understanding and rejection. Waller posits that the understanding of any behaviour may lead to justification of that behaviour. He suggests that "Explanation inevitably leads to condoning, pardoning, and forgiving, or—at the very least—a shift in the direction of a more favourable attitude towards the perpetrator" (Waller, 2002, p. 15).

Having worked in forensic psychiatry for two years, I was obliged to struggle with this moral dilemma, and learn to separate the deed from the person. Without a "more favourable attitude towards the perpetrator" nothing of value will be gained in our society. I would argue that the psychotherapist who refuses to work with perpetrators of abuse, on grounds of morality rather than skills ability, may well be coming from their own shadow experience.

I would hope, too, that reading this study might well encourage psychotherapists to rethink their own philosophical bases for their work. Humanism proposes that people are basically good. Freud recognizes both the drive for life and also the instinctual drive towards death. Jewish tradition speaks of *yetzer ha-tov*, the good inclination and *yetzer ha-ar*, the bad inclination. In the psychotherapy profession our basic predisposition is towards goodness; all ethical codes support this aim. I would suggest that we are more likely to achieve that aim when we face up to the reality of human destructiveness. Waller supports this with

> Man is neither good nor evil. If one believes in the goodness of man as the only potentiality, one will be forced into rosy falsifications of the facts, or end up in bitter disillusionment. [*ibid.*, p. 137]

In the psychotherapy profession today, a shift is happening as our profession matures to a position where trainers are no longer seen as the gurus and charismatic leaders. This is useful in fostering democratic training cultures where "trainers are seen more as sisters and brothers than mothers and fathers" (Evans, 2005). The tension, of course, is what happens to the invaluable learning inherent in transferential process.

Above all, I am profoundly grateful to the work of Jung and the insights that his understanding have contributed to my own work of integrative psychotherapy. Perhaps more discussions and openness across differing training orientations would be useful.

What implications are relevant to society?

Waller addresses the one-sidedness of attitude towards society's carers and tells us that, until recently,

> The prevailing normative picture held up by the social sciences still portrayed, for the most part, rational creatures who could be expected to relate to and treat fellow humans with basic empathy, kindness, respect and decency. [Waller, 2002, p. 10]

This denies the shadow of carers. Waller continues to note, however, that this picture is slowly beginning to change and the social scientific neglect of evil is being rectified. A televised news bulletin recently featured how the government is launching a concentrated campaign to reduce bullying in schools. Emiley (2005) believes the increase in bullying to be because we live in a violent society with no healthy outlet for the expression of our instinct towards destruction. One almost expects to find vandalism and attacks on passers-by at night, often linked with overuse of alcohol, in overcrowded inner city areas. However, it is happening now that youngsters and elderly folk alike are suffering abuse and violence from gangs of frustrated teenagers, and in daylight hours. Is society splitting good from bad, as in social care, working towards what Waller understands as "the prevailing normative picture", which results in the increase of shadow in society? And how, if at all, might we as psychotherapists be reinforcing this split?

The moral dilemma of to work or not to work with the more dangerous, troubled individuals in our prisons (and I choose this terminology purposefully, because I believe that English prisons are full of very emotionally damaged and neglected people) leads me to question the role of psychotherapy in the maintenance of society's values and well-being. And this has repercussions for psychotherapy training organizations and the caring professions across the board. How might it come about that some psychotherapists choose not to work with perpetrators of crime? We are not taught in our training programmes how to work with sociopathic personality traits, yet this pattern shows itself in people at all levels of experience, not only in the criminal world, but, for example, in politics, in psychiatry, in high-powered sales positions. Does the psychotherapist's shadow show itself in our exclusion of some people from therapeutic support?

Evetts-Secker (2003) tells how society's idealization of ministers and religious values and beliefs makes no room for the shadow side of humanity, and such members of the clergy can, as can the general public, easily resort to inflicting the shadow on their children. The son of one such "pillar of society", who was publicly respected and revered, cowered in his childhood until the next beating came from his father. To explore this theme further, please read *Kathy's Story* (O'Beirne, 2005), which tells of the Magdalen Laundries in which children and young women led tortured lives in the name of Christianity: the taller the pillar, the longer the shadow (Evetts-Secker, 2003).

We need to guard against the dangers of psychotherapy falling into that similar dynamic of idealization, with a failing Christian ideology in society that is perceived to have let people down. It would be dangerous to replace society's need for idealization with psychotherapy. A colleague shares her concern of how *that will mean certain trainers become the High Priests and Priestesses*. She notes that we need to *resist that systemic force that is there and very much in the field*. With such potential splitting being out there in the wider field, in society in general, we in the psychotherapy profession need even more to address shadow.

At a recent psychotherapy conference in Prague, a task of the participants was to decide on whether or not to hold the next conference in Israel. A debate emerged, questioning the safety of this proposed venue, and discussing the role of the psychotherapist in today's society. Do we have a social responsibility to attempt to heal society's interrelational splits? One delegate asked, "Are we psychotherapists or politicians?" Another argued vehemently that, "We cannot not go to Israel". Yet another questioned where his first loyalties lie, with, "I have a responsibility to stay safe for my family and my clients". With what level of dangerousness is each of us willing to engage, in others or in ourselves, to uphold our own beliefs and values?

This conference closed with an experiential exercise between four hundred and fifty people, progressively in pairs, in groups of four, and in general discussion of the whole floor. We learned how the contact between two people can bring about change in each of them. Each one of four hundred and fifty therapists has family, clients, friends, and colleagues, amounting to, from conference examples, between seventy and two hundred others per therapist. If we take the average of one hundred and thirty people each, this is six thousand, seven hundred and fifty people, all potentially affected and changed towards a healthier community. This begins not with denial of evil, but with awareness, acceptance, and understanding of it and, subsequently, choice.

Each conference participant was encouraged to take their particular line of work one step further into the field: if we work with individuals, then begin to work with couples; if we work with couples, then begin to work with families; if we work with families, then begin to work with groups, and so on. In this way, such studies as this one might well, like a pebble thrown into a lake, send ripples out into the field of the psychotherapy profession and of society.

One dynamic responsible for the lack of addressing shadow in others is very probably the unconscious realization that actually we each have potential to this experience. Fear of contagion is rife in our psychiatric systems, with staff resistance to exploring their own process, ranging from emotional awareness to their own shadow emerging. I think, this is primarily due to the profound lack of support offered to those staff who deal with the most entrenched of painful human emotions. Today's medical model of emotional difficulties leaves no room for the phenomenological experience of staff working in psychiatry.

I have recently heard it celebrated by a group of nurses that people are living longer. My daughter, like myself, works in psychiatry, and feels relief that, over the years, medication has taken the place of stigmatization and locked units for the sufferers of mental disturbance. Technology and research have improved for the most part, the longevity and the quality of human life and people's expectations. Society has rightly closed down the large Dickensian psychiatric hospitals in the hope of integration into society and normalization. However, it is also true that technology and research have made it possible to wipe out whole societies with chemical warfare and imposed famine. It seems very much within the realm of human nature to both maintain and destroy life. While the conference delegate pointed out to us that we are not politicians, we are human beings privileged with insights and understandings that I think we have a responsibility to put to good use in any way that we might, each of us using the opportunities with which life presents us.

I am fortunate enough to realize that, at a fundamental level, the question of shadow dynamics in any walk of life is also about my own human nature. I cannot distance or objectify what has emerged in this book. I am what I am, as is everyone else, and each of us has a responsibility to address this in relation to our own social circles.

What implications are relevant to me as a psychotherapist and as a person?

As a psychotherapy trainer I am in a position of authority, that of the reality of having power of assessment over my trainees and at the level of illusion, potentially becoming a transferential figure in their lives. I have, in my work in psychiatry, seen how easily staff resort to the dehumanizing of those in the more vulnerable positions. Waller (2002, p. 20) understands one aspect of relating to our own authority in relationships as resulting in "social-death" thinking and the dehumanizing of others, rendering them victims. I have difficulty in owning this dynamic in my relationships with my trainees, although I know, as the daughter of a controlling and bullying father, that I might well be vulnerable to its occurrence. In owning the impact of shadow of the training situation on myself, *the impact was enormous, in my personal life and in the training group,* I hope to remain sufficiently open to this potential, for it not to happen.

I am also aware of my compensatory predisposition to be too nurturing and insufficiently challenging. *Women's shadow is to keep clients dependent.* Perhaps this is enhanced by the *addictive, seductive qualities* of *attunement into profound feelings.* I hope that I never cease to work at balancing the tension between these two aspects of the authority inherent in my role as a trainer and as a therapist with my clients.

Linked with my tendency to over-nurture has been the retroflection of my shadow energy and the somatization into physical illness. In personally owning my resentment of the trainee dependency, which at some level I have invited, I am able to free myself to become more empowering of myself and, subsequently, of my trainees. Throughout this study I have known and worked with my own narcissistic needs and defences in a way more painful and growth-promoting than through nine years of therapy. This journey has been integrated in that all aspects of humanness, including animal forces, have constituted shadow for me. Stein (1998, cover) states, "No healing of the conflict between the spirit and the flesh is possible, so long as our animal–instinctual nature is considered inferior to the mind and psyche". And this is supported with "Everything that man has achieved in the world somehow is surpassed by nature" (Equire, 2005).

Nature supports humankind with the gift of a potential bravery and courage to survive. When love is in our world alongside shadow, then, for most of us, endurance can become transformed. Hayden posits (1980, p. 2), "Belief in the human soul escapes all reason and flies beyond the frail fingers of our knowledge". Buber (1923) supports this belief as he tells us that the understanding of another human heart is the ultimate spiritual experience.

One of the most supportive experiences for me throughout this work has been my dream analysis, my heuristically explored inner domain of my unconscious. I have known the pain of my own shadow, split, and projections, and seen through my feelings of isolation, transforming them into a replenishing solitude.

I am now in the fortunate position, in my trainee and client relationships, of feeling solidly able to address my own shadow and theirs. This adds a greater degree of satisfaction and contentment for me in my work, alongside a deeper ability to tolerate and contain dark emotional pain, mine and others, in all walks of my life. I am privileged that this brings with it for me an inner peace and gratitude, with respect, acceptance, and joy for the human condition. West (1988, p. 64) tells us that "There is another level to the demands that heuristic research makes on the researcher. Deeply engaging in these tacit processes changes the researcher".

At a personal level, my learning from this study has been immense. I have struggled with and relished the experience of not-knowing. I have matured from two profoundly important transferential relationships in my life, learned to love my own soul-searching and be nourished by this, and forgiven some of my own deeds that I now regret, from a time in my life when I was less aware than I now can be. I have lived my experience of shadow to release me to engage lovingly with those in my past with whom I have had differences. I feel prepared for what life brings me. This is a remarkably valuable reward in itself for these years of study.

My shadow serves me well.

Shadow

> I stand alone on this beach as day draws to a close and I am nourished by the sea.
>
> This is my sea; my beach shadows; my darkness; my waters streamed with slivers of moon-beam silver.
>
> The eventide of my immersion into shadow is drawing nigh. It is captured in the eventide of this day, reaching its completion. I reach my own completion of my being, in engagement with my life and this world that bathes me with the influence of love and pain, the passionate and anguishing reality of my existence.
>
> It is time to let go. I cannot hold on to my memories still to keep them. Souvenirs will remain beside me only if I ask nothing of them, save to come to my awareness from time to time, to soothe and guide and replenish me for each new moment.
>
> The light looks brighter through the darkness. My life is deepened and empassioned with my pain. Let me never cease to love whole-heartedly, or to know the unloving that makes my loving dearer.

"With all its sham, drudgery and broken dreams, it is still a beautiful world" (Ehrmann, 1948, p. 11).

GLOSSARY OF PSYCHOTHERAPEUTIC TERMS

Acting-out: the behaviour that the client exhibits (in response to emotions) outside of the therapeutic relationship and that would be better addressed by bringing those emotions into the therapy session. This is a very limited "psychotherapeutic" view. In the wider frame, acting-out is the enactment of subconscious impulses, often emotionally driven and relating to a person's more pathological aspects of self, which escape ego control to manifest in impulsive behaviour.

Adult ego-state: the aspect of personality that discriminates between what is and is not right for the individual. A state of observation, thinking, storing and retrieving data, reality testing, and acting upon that data; the ability to make decisions, judgements, and choices.

Archetype: an unconscious, universal, innate predisposition to specific life situations and experiences. Archetypes are seen to bridge the conscious and unconscious, the symbolic and what is actual; they enliven imagination and tend to relate to core processes such as the rites of passage of birth and death, and to such meaningful and important others as father, mother, heroic and death-dealing entities.

Borderline: a stage in early infancy before there is recognition that experiences can be retained healthily in memory form. Anger is experienced in the form of destructive behaviours towards the self or to the environment/another person.

Child ego-state: the balance of response to one's own desires and the satisfaction of others. This is the source, the wellspring of feelings that contribute to the aspect of the grown person who behaves as the person did in the past. Ever growing and developing, the experiencing, copying, and incorporating process of childhood is continued in adulthood.

Containment: the acknowledgement by the therapist of the client's anxieties, exuberance, rage, despair, which are intolerable for the client. The therapist tolerates these emotions and, through this process, the client learns to tolerate these experiences for himself.

Countertransference: the therapist's reaction to the transferential position of the client.

Group process: developmental dynamics between group members, occurring as a natural part of any evolving group situation.

Introjection: taking on board as our own all societal and parental instructions without consideration and assimilation or rejection. For example, "I should do . . .", rather than "I choose to do . . .".

Narcissism: a stage in early infancy before there is recognition of other, and when the infant's love is directed at the self. Anger is experienced in the form of persecutory thoughts, and ridicule or avoidance of another person.

Parent ego-state: the childhood incorporation of people around in the environment. It is made up of critical and nurturing aspects from both actual parents and society, as well as our assumptions and messages to the self in relation to behaviours of authority figures in our lives. It is also the sum total of the beliefs, emotions, and behaviours that the person chooses to incorporate on a remembered verbal level.

Passive–aggressive: a personality type in which blame is projected and little responsibility taken for one's influence on the environment.

Proflection: projection of one's own need on to another and then behaving in a way to satisfy that need. For example, "You are vulnerable, so I'll look after you, so I don't have to be vulnerable".

Projection: attribution to someone else of one's own feelings which are too painful to tolerate. For example, "I am angry with him", becomes "He is angry with me", and can lead to paranoia.

Poisonous pedagogy: the child-rearing practice whereby children can be

> molded, dominated, taught good habits, scolded and punished. The child will overcome the serious consequences of the injustice he has suffered . . . if he is allowed to express his pain and anger. If his parents . . . forbid this . . . then the child will learn to be silent. This silence is a sign of the effectiveness of the pedagogical principles applied, but at the same time, it is a danger signal pointing to future pathological development. [Miller, 1987, p. 7]

Projective identification: a fantasy, remote from consciousness, that entails a belief in certain aspects (qualities) of the self being located elsewhere, with a consequent depletion and weakened sense of self. Behaviour supports the fantasy, for example, leaving the training environment in a mess so that the trainer will be angry with you, so that you do not have to own your own anger.

Retroflection: turning back on the self the energy which would be more healthily directed into the environment, for example, physical symptoms instead of being angry, suicide.

Scapegoating: the process whereby one person is blamed for more than that which is their responsibility. In Leviticus, put all the sins on the goat, and then sacrifice the goat to rid oneself of guilt.

Schizoid: the primary stage in early infancy before there is recognition that the self exists independently of others. Awareness of one's somatic self is limited.

Splitting: the adoption by the mind of two or more separate points of view, in which a person is seen as having only one of their qualities: for example, as being either all good or all bad. Hence, some personality aspects are denied or projected. The integration of such splits into realistic forms of discrimination was seen by Klein (1946) as the key feature of child development.

Temenos: the sacred, spiritual space encompassing the experience of the client–therapist relationship; the safe ground, upon which containment allows spontaneity and creativity to emerge. A healthy temenos is created as the therapist provides sufficient, though not too much, stability and consistency for creativity and spontaneity to become possible for the client.

Transference: the illusory process whereby the client (trainee) can re-enact the early childhood situation, or their fantasy of their early childhood, in the relationship with the therapist. This often occurs in the earlier stages of therapy, with a developmental process of its own, in preparation for the later, more dialogic relationship between client and therapist, which promotes contact.

REFERENCES

Ahmed, A. (2005). Address: *Good Morning Sunday*. British Broadcasting Corporation, Radio 2.

American Psychiatric Association. (1997). *Diagnostic and Statistical Manual of Mental Disorders (DSM-IV)*. Washington, D.C.: American Psychiatric Association.

Angelou, M. (1994). *The Complete Collected Poems*. London: Virago.

Berne, E. (1964). *Games People Play*. London: Penguin.

Bettelheim, B. (1992). The man who cared for children. British Broadcasting Corporation: TV2, *Horizon*.

Bion, W. R. (1961). *Experiences in Groups*. London: Tavistock.

Bly, R. (1990). *Iron John*. Shaftesbury: Element.

Bollas, C. (1987). *The Shadow of the Object*. London: Free Association.

Bowlby, J. (1953). *Child Care and the Growth of Maternal Love*. Abridged version of *Maternal Care and Mental Health* (1951) London: Penguin. New edition, 1965.

Bowlby, J. (1979). *The Making and Breaking of Affectional Bonds*. London: Routledge.

Bowlby, J., & Robertson, J. (1952). A two-year-old goes to hospital: a scientific film. *Proceedings of the Royal Society of Medicine, 46*: 425–427.

British Association for Counselling and Psychotherapy (2002). *Ethical Framework for Good Practice in Counselling and Psychotherapy*. Rugby: BACP.

Buber, M. (1970). *I and Thou*. R. G. Smith (Trans.). Edinburgh: T & T Clark.

Carkhoff, R. (1969). *Helping and Human Relations. Practice and Research.* New York: Holt, Rinehart & Winston.

Cashdan, S. (1988). *Object Relations Therapy.* New York: W. W. Norton.

Clarkson, P. (1989). *Gestalt Counselling in Action.* London: Whurr.

Clarkson, P. (1995). *The Therapeutic Relationship.* London: Whurr.

Dollard, J., & Miller, N. E. (1950). *Personality and Psychotherapy.* New York: McGraw-Hill.

Ebrey, P. (1993). *The Yellow Emperor, A Classic of Medicine*, in *Chinese Civilization: A Sourcebook* (2nd edn). M. Coyle (Trans.). New York; Free Press, 2004.

Ehrmann, M. (1948). *The Desiderata of Happiness.* London: Souvenir.

Emiley, Dr (2005). *Good Morning Sunday.* British Broadcasting Corporation. Radio 2.

Equire, N. (2005). *Holiday.* British Broadcasting Corporation. Television programme, 6 March.

Erikson, E. H. (1959). Identity and the life cycle. *Psychological Issues, 1*(1). Monograph. New York: International Universities Press.

Erskine, R. (1991). Inquiry, attunement and involvement in the psychotherapy of dissociation. 29th International Transactional Analysis Association Conference, Stamford, CT, USA. *Transactional Analysis, 23*(4), 1993.

Erskine, R. (1996). Personal communication. Training workshop, Sherwood Psychotherapy Training Institute.

Erskine, R. (2003). Personal communication. Training workshop, Scarborough Psychotherapy Training Institute.

Erskine, R., & Moursund, J. P. (1998). *Integrative Psychotherapy in Action.* Highland, NY: Gestalt Journal Press.

Erskine, R., Moursund, J. P., & Trautman, R. (1999). *Beyond Empathy: a Therapy of Contact-In-Relationship.* Philadelphia, PA: Brunner/Mazel.

Evans, K. (1998). Personal communication.

Evetts-Secker, J. (2003). Personal communication. Scarborough.

Evetts-Secker, J. (2004). Personal communication. Scarborough.

Foulkes, D. (1966). *The Psychology of Sleep.* New York: Scribner.

Foulkes, S. H., & Anthony, E. J. (1971). *Group Psychotherapy.* London: Penguin.

Fox, M. (1991). *Creation Spirituality: Liberating Gifts for the Peoples of the Earth.* New York: HarperCollins.

Freud, A. (1936). *The Ego and the Mechanisms of Defence.* London: Hogarth.

Freud, A. (1946). The psychoanalytic study of infantile feeding disturbances. *Psychoanalytic Study of the Child*, 2: 119–132.

Freud, S. (1985). Letter to Martha Bernays. 21 October 1885. www. freud.org.uk/fmfaq.htm.

Freud, S. (1912b). The dynamics of transference. *S.E.*, 12: 97–108. London: Hogarth.

Freud, S. (1921c). *Group Psychology and the Analysis of the Ego. S.E.*, 18: 67–144. London: Hogarth.

Freud, S. (1930a). *Civilisation and Its Discontents. S.E.*, 21: 59–145. London: Hogarth.

Fromm, E. (1974). *The Anatomy of Human Destructiveness*. London: Cape.

Gallman, K. (1991). *I Dreamed of Africa*. London: Penguin.

Geertz, C. (1993). *The Interpretation of Cultures*. First published 1993, London: Fontana In: C. Seale (1999). *The Quality of Qualitative Research*. London Sage.

Gilbert, M. (1999). Personal communication. Sherwood Psychotherapy Training Institute.

Glover, E. (1937). The theory of the therapeutic results of psychoanalysis. *International Journal of Psychoanalysis*, 18: 125–189.

Greenberg, E. (1998). A brief guide to borderline, narcissistic and schizoid disorders. Unpublished paper.

Greenberg, L. S., & Pinsof, W. M. (1986). *The Psychotherapeutic Process: A Research Handbook*. New York: Guilford.

Greenson, R. R. (1965). The working alliance and the transference neurosis. *Psychoanalytic Quarterly*, 34: 155–181.

Grove, D. (1989). *Resolving Feelings of Anger, Guilt and Shame*. David Grove Seminars.

Guggenbuhl-Craig, A. (1971). *Power in the Helping Professions*. Woodstock, CT: Spring.

Hadfield, J. A. (1954). *Dreams and Nightmares*. London: Penguin.

Haule, J. R. (1971). Foreword. In: A. Guggenbuhl-Craig (Ed.), *Power in the Helping Professions*. Woodstock, CT: Spring.

Hayden, T. (1980). *One Child*. London: Element.

Heard, D., & Lake, B. (1986). The attachment dynamic in adult life. *British Journal of Psychiatry*, 149(4): 430–438.

Henderson, J. L. (1967). *Thresholds of Initiation*. Middletown, CT: Wesleyan Universities Press.

Hinshelwood, R. D. (1989). *A Dictionary of Kleinian Thought*. London: Free Association.

Holmes, J. (1993). *John Bowlby and Attachment Theory*. London: Routledge.

Husserl, E. (1975). The Paris Lectures. P.Koestenbaum (Trans.). 2nd edn. The Hague: Martinus Nijhoff.

ISA Editorial Team (1990). An introduction to the Institute and its training. *Journal of the Institute for Self Analysis*, 4(1): 73–75.

Johnson, S. (1991). *The Symbiotic Character*. New York: W. W. Norton.

Johnson, S. (1994). *Character Styles*. New York: W. W. Norton.

Jung, C. G. (1932) [1959]. *The Archetypes and the Collective Unconscious*. *C.W.*, *9(i)*: 42–53. R. F. C. Hull (Trans.). London: Routledge & Kegan Paul.

Jung, C. G. (1952) [1954]. Answer to Job. *C.W.*, *11*: 355–363. R. F. Hull (Trans.). London: Routledge & Kegan Paul.

Kagan, N. L., & Kagan, H. (1990). IPR-validated model for the 1990s and beyond. *Counselling Psychologist*, 18: 436–440.

Kalsched, D. (1996). *The Inner World of Trauma*. London: Brunner-Routledge.

Kepler, J. (1619). *Harmonice Mundi, Book IV*. Linz. Quoted by Pauli (1955) in A. Stevens (1982). *Archetype: A Natural History of the Self*. London: Routledge.

Kepner, J. (1987). *Body Process*. New York: Gardiner.

Kepner, J. (1995). *HealingTasks: Psychotherapy with Adult Survivors of Childhood Abuse*. CA: Gestalt Institute of Cleveland.

Kernberg, O. (1984). *Severe Personality Disorders*. New Haven, CT: Yale University Press.

King, M. L. (1963). *Strength to Love*. Minneapolis, MN: Augsburg Fortress Press.

Klein, M. (1932). *The Psycho-Analysis of Children*. London: Virago.

Klein, M. (1946). Notes on some schizoid mechanisms. *International Journal of Psycho-Analysis*, 27: 111.

Klein, M. (1988). *Envy and Gratitude*. London: Hogarth [reprinted London: Virago, 1989].

Kohut, H. (1992). *The Analysis of Self*. CT: International Universities Press.

Lacan, J. (1954). *The Seminars of Jacques Lacan, Book II*. Cambridge: Cambridge University Press.

Lake, B. (1987). Personal communication. Ripon.

Lee, S. G. M., & Herbert, M. (1951). *Play, Dream and Imitation in Childhood*. London: Routledge & Kegan Paul.

Mahler, M., Pine, R., & Bergman, A. (1975). *The Psychological Birth of the Human Infant*. New York: Basic Books.

Maslow, A. H. (1966). *The Psychology of Science*. New York: Harper & Row.

Masterson, J. (1988). *The Search for the Real Self*. London: Collier MacMillan.

Mathes, D. (2001). Issues of attraction. Handout from Post Adoption Centre.

McClusky, U. (1989). In praise of feeling. Theme focused family work. Unpublished paper.

Miller, A. (1987). *For Your Own Good*. London: Virago.

Mills, J. C., Crowley, R. J., & O'Ryan, M. (2001). *Therapeutic Metaphors for Children and the Child Within*. Philadelphia, PA: Brunner-Mazel.

Moursund, J. P., & Erskine, R. G. (2004). *Integrative Psychotherapy. The Art and Science of Relationship*. Pacific Grove, CA: Thomson Brooks Cole.

Moustakas, C. (1990). *Heuristic Research: Design, Methodology and Applications*. London: Sage.

Moustakas, C. (1994). *Phenomenological Research Methods*. London: Sage.

Oaklander, V. (1978). *Windows to Our Children*. New York: Gestalt Journal Press.

Oakley, A. (1981). Interviewing women: a contradiction in terms? In: C. Seale (1999). *The Quality of Qualitative Research*. London: Sage.

O'Beirne, K. (2005). *Kathy's Story*. Edinburgh: Mainstream.

Oppenheim, A. N. (1992). *Questionnaire Design, Interviewing and Attitude Measurement*. London: Pinter.

Oriah Mountain Dreamer (1999). *The Invitation*. London: HarperCollins.

Perls, F. (1947). *Ego, Hunger and Aggression*. New York: Gestalt Journal Press.

Perls, F. (1967). *Gestalt Therapy Verbatim*. Moab, UT: Real People Press.

Perls, F., Hefferline, R., & Goodman, P. (1951). *Gestalt Therapy: Excitement and Growth in the Human Personality*. New York: Gestalt Journal Press.

Phillips, A. (1995). *Terrors and Experts*. London: Faber and Faber.

Philippson, P. (1986). Awareness, the contact boundary and the field. *The Gestalt Journal*, XIII(2): 73–82.

Philippson, P. (1989). Handout. Diploma in Gestalt Psychotherapy. Manchester Gestalt Centre.

Philippson, P. (1990). Personal communication. Manchester Gestalt Centre.

Post Adoption Centre. (2002). Information handout. Post Adoption Centre.

Price, H. H. (1953). *Thinking and Experience*. London: Hutchinson University.

Rogers, C. R. (1980). *A Way of Being*. Boston, MA: Houghton Mifflin.

Schmidt, L. (1992). The shadow as a Jungian archetype, Unpublished doctoral dissertation, Union Institute, Cincinnati. In: C. Moustakas (1994). *Phenomenological Research Methods*. London: Sage.

Schmukler, D. (1998). Personal communication. MA, Integrative Psychotherapy. Sherwood Psychotherapy Training Institute.

Seale, C. (1999). *The Quality of Qualitative Research*. London: Sage.

Segal, H. (1978). On symbolism. *International Journal of Psychoanalysis*, 55: 315–319.

Silverman, D. (1993). *Interpreting Qualitative Data*. London: Sage.

Spinelli, E. (1997). *Tales of Un-knowing. Therapeutic Encounters from an Existential Perspective*. London: Duckworth.

Stein, R. (1998). *The Betrayal of the Soul in Psychotherapy*. Dallas, TX: Spring.

Stern, D. N. (1985). *The Interpersonal World of the Infant*. New York: Basic Books.

Stern, D. N. (1996). Taped lectures from the World Congress of Psychotherapy, Vienna.

Stevens, A. (1982). *Archetype: A Natural History of the Self*. London: Routledge.

Storr, A. (1968). *Human Aggression*. London: Allen Lane.

Storr, A. (1997). *Solitude*. London: HarperCollins.

Strauss, A. (1987). *Qualitative Analysis for Social Scientists*. Cambridge: Cambridge University Press.

Strauss, A., & Corbin, J. (1990). *Basics of Qualitative Research: Techniques and Procedures for Developing Grounded Theory*. Thousand Oaks, CA: Sage.

Strupp, H., Hadley, S., & Gomez-Schwartz, B. (1977). *Psychotherapy for Better or Worse: An Analysis of the Negative Effects*. New York: Jason Aronson.

United Kingdom Council for Psychotherapy (2004). *Continued Professional Development Policy*. London: UKCP.

Waelder, R. (1956). Introduction to the discussion on the problems of transference. *International Journal of Psychoanalysis*, 37: 367–368.

Walker, M. (2002). Assessing trainees in a psychodynamic context. *Counselling Psychology Journal*, 13: 42–43.

Waller, J. (2002). *Becoming Evil*. Oxford: Oxford University Press.

West, W. (1988). Passionate research: heuristics and the use of self in counselling research. *Changes*, 16(1): 60–66.

Whittaker, D. S. (1985). *Using Groups to Help People*. London: Routledge & Kegan Paul.

Whittaker, D. S. (1988). Personal communication. Therapeutic Group-work Training, University of York.

Wilkinson, H. (1998). The total transference situation. Unpublished paper.

Winnicott, D. W. (1947). Hate in the countertransference. In: D. W. Winnicott, *Collected Papers: Through Paediatrics to Psycho-Analysis*. London: Tavistock.

Winnicott, D. W. (1965). *The Family and Individual Development*. London: Tavistock.

Winnicott, D. W. (1969). *The Maturational Processes and the Facilitating Environment*. London: Maresfield.

Winnicott, D. W. (1971). *Playing and Reality*. London: Routledge.

Yalom, I. (1975). *The Theory and Practice of Group Psychotherapy*. New York: Basic Books.

Yeats, W. B. (1983). *The Poems of W. B. Yeats*. New York: Macmillan.

Yontef, G. M. (1993). *Awareness, Dialogue and Process*. New York: Gestalt Journal Press.

Zinker, J. (1977). *Creative Process in Gestalt Therapy*. New York: Vintage.

BIBLIOGRAPHY

Assagioli, R. (1965). *Psychosynthesis*. London: Mandala.

Axline, V. M. (1964). *Dibs In Search of Self*. London: Penguin.

Balint, M. (1968). *The Basic Fault: Therapeutic Aspects of Regression*. London: Routledge.

Bass, E., & Davis, L. (1990). *The Courage to Heal*. London: Cedar.

Beck, A. T. (1999). *Prisoners of Hate: The Cognitive Basis of Anger, Hostility and Violence*. New York: HarperCollins.

Benjamin, L. S. (1996). *Interpersonal Diagnosis and Treatment of Personality Disorders*. New York: Guilford.

Berne, E. (1961). *Transactional Analysis in Psychotherapy*. New York: Grove.

Bion, W. R. (1959). *Experience in Groups*. New York: Basic Books

Bradshaw, J. (1990). *Homecoming: Reclaiming and Championing Your Inner Child*. London: Piatkus.

Bragan, K. (1996). *Self and Spirit in the Therapeutic Relationship*. London: Routledge.

Casement, P. (1985). *On Learning from the Patient*. London: Routledge.

De Board, R. (1998). *Counselling for Toads. A Psychological Adventure*. London: Routledge.

Deurzen-Smith, E. (1988). *Existential Counselling in Practice*. London: Sage.

Egan, G. (1994). *The Skilled Helper*. Pacific Grove, CA: Brooks Cole.

Erskine, R. (1991). Transference and transactions: critique from an intrapsychic and integrative perspective. *Transactional Analysis Journal*, 21(2): 63–76.

Erskine, R. (2003). *Beyond Empathy*. Philadelphia, PA: Brunner/Mazel.

Estes, C. P. (1992). *Women Who Run with the Wolves*. New York: Ballantyne.

Fairbairn, W. (1952). *Psychoanalytic Studies of the Personality*. London: Routledge.

Foulkes, S. H., & Anthony, E. J. (1957). *Group Psychotherapy: The Psychoanalytic Approach*. Harmondsworth: Penguin [reprinted London: Karnac, 1984].

Fromm, E. (1963). *The Dogma of Christ, Religion, Psychology & Culture*. London: Routledge & Kegan Paul.

Gomez, L. (1997). *An Introduction to Object Relations*. New York: New York University Press.

Green, H. (1964). *I Never Promised You a Rose Garden*. London: Pan.

Hammersley, D. (1995). *Counselling People on Prescribed Drugs*. London: Sage.

Holmes, J., & Lindley, R. (1989). *The Values of Psychotherapy*. Oxford: Oxford University Press.

Hycner, R., & Jacobs L. (1995). *The Healing Relationship in Gestalt Therapy: A Dialogic Self-psychology Approach*. New York: Gestalt Journal Press.

Johnson, R. A. (1994). *Owning Your Own Shadow: Understanding the Dark side of the Psyche*. San Francisco, CA: HarperCollins.

Kaufman, G. (1989). *The Psychology of Shame*. London: Routledge.

Kohut, H. (1971). *The Restoration of the Self*. New York: International Universities Press.

Kubler Ross, E. (1969). *On Death and Dying*. London: Tavistock.

Malan, D. (1979). *Individual Psychotherapy and the Science of Psychodynamics*. London: Butterworth.

Masson, J. (1988). *Against Therapy*. London: Fontana.

Miller, A. (1985). *Thou Shalt Not Be Aware: Society's Betrayal of the Child*. London: Faber and Faber.

Miller, A. (1995). *The Drama of Being a Child*. London: Virago.

Nathanson, D. L. (1987). *The Many Faces of Shame*. New York: Guilford.

Orbach, S. (1999). *The Impossibility of Sex*. London: Penguin

Peck, M. S. (1978). *The Road Less Travelled*. London: Rider.

Rogers, C. (1965). *Client Centred Therapy*. London: Constable.

Rosenfeld, R. A. (1965). *Psychotic States: A Psychoanalytic Approach*. London: Maresfield.

Ryle, A. (1995). *Cognitive Analytic Therapy: Developments in Theory and Practice*. London: Wiley.

Stepansky, P. E., & Goldberg, A. (1984). *Kohut's Legacy: Contributions to Self-psychology*. London: Analytic Press.

Stern, D. (1998). *The Motherhood Constellation*. London: Karnac.

Stolorow, R., Brandchaft, B., & Atwood, G. (1987). *Psychoanalytic Treatment: An Intersubjective Approach*. Hillsdale, NJ: Analytic Press.

Totton, N. (1998). *The Water in the Glass: Body and Mind in Psychoanalysis*. London: Rebus.

Yalom, I. (1983). *In-Patient Group Psychotherapy*. New York: Basic Books.

Yalom, I. (1992). *When Nietzsche Wept*. New York: Basic Books.

Yalom, I. (1996). *Lying on the Couch*. New York: Basic Books.

INDEX

abuse, 5, 29–30, 39, 45, 80, 88, 119,
    151, 207, 221, 223–225
    of power, 147, 203
    physical, 7, 40, 168, 213
    sexual, 7, 34, 38, 88, 90, 223
    substance, 66
    verbal, 3
acting out, 34, 42, 48, 54, 65–68, 71,
    79, 82, 84, 89, 118, 143, 145, 195,
    202, 209, 231
aggression, xii, 2, 12–14, 19–24,
    28–29, 36–37, 39–41, 44, 46, 48,
    54–55, 59, 63, 66, 71, 73–74,
    77–78, 80–81, 89–90, 127, 131,
    137, 142–143, 146–147, 172, 217,
    221–222
Ahmed, A., 205, 235
American Psychiatric Association
    (*DSM–IV*), 43, 61–62, 66, 70,
    152, 235
Angelou, M., 113, 193, 235
anger, 5, 8, 18, 28, 44, 46–47, 54, 56,
    65, 68, 73–77, 118, 145, 157, 160,
    175, 210, 221, 232–233 *see also*:
    rage
Anthony, E. J., 72–73, 236
anxiety, 2, 15, 38, 55, 57–58, 65–68,
    71, 101, 107, 125, 127, 135, 145,
    147, 167, 172, 186, 193, 196, 215,
    232
Apollo, 127–129, 131
archetype(s), 12, 14–15, 25–31, 33,
    36–37, 47, 63, 67, 76–77, 79, 81,
    127–128, 131, 135, 169, 231
    collective, 25, 34, 79
    dominance–submission, 29
    father, 25, 27–28, 76
    helper–helpless, 30
    mother, 14, 25–28, 76, 162
    shadow, 25, 28, 79
    trickster, 31, 36, 83–84
attachment, 22–24, 27, 30, 46–47, 71,
    94, 200, 203, 209

Bergman, A., 64, 68, 238
Berne, E., 45, 235